Death, Beauty, Struggle

CONTEMPORARY ETHNOGRAPHY

Kirin Narayan and Alma Gottlieb, Series Editors

A complete list of books in the series is available from the publisher.

DEATH, BEAUTY, STRUGGLE

Untouchable Women Create the World

Margaret Trawick

Foreword by Ann Grodzins Gold

PENN

UNIVERSITY OF PENNSYLVANIA PRESS

PHILADELPHIA

Published by
University of Pennsylvania Press
Philadelphia, Pennsylvania 19104-4112
www.upenn.edu/pennpress

Printed in the United States of America on acid-free paper
1 3 5 7 9 10 8 6 4 2

Library of Congress Cataloging-in-Publication Data

Names: Trawick, Margaret, author. | Gold, Ann Grodzins, writer of foreword.
Title: Death, beauty, struggle : untouchable women create the world / Margaret Trawick ; foreword by Ann Grodzins Gold.
Other titles: Contemporary ethnography.
Description: 1st edition. | Philadelphia : University of Pennsylvania Press, [2017] | Series: Contemporary ethnography | Includes bibliographical references and index.
Identifiers: LCCN 2016047654 | ISBN 978-0-8122-4905-7 (hardcover : alk. paper)
Subjects: LCSH: Dalit women—India—Tamil Nadu—Attitudes. | Dalit women—India—Tamil Nadu—Psychology. | Women and spiritualism—India—Tamil Nadu. | Women and religion—India—Tamil Nadu.
Classification: LCC HQ1744.T3 T73 2017 | DDC 305.5/688082095475—dc23
LC record available at https://lccn.loc.gov/2016047654

Contents

Foreword

ANN GRODZINS GOLD

Margaret Trawick's writings on Tamil women's songs and lives offer rare and intimate glimpses into kinship, myth, work, want, anger, reverence, and more. Revealing a subtle, never static, interplay between abjection and empowerment, this book testifies that human beings, low born and ill-treated within a punishing social system, neither acquiesce to fate nor simply rail against it, but may indeed radically create the world. And I stress that it is absolutely *the* world being created: not *their* world, but ours too.

Much that Tamil women shared with Trawick is rooted in the passionate attachments and acute wounds generated within families, but these women's voices resonate well beyond individually circumscribed lives. In their songs and life histories they critique social, political, economic, and domestic oppressions. They also incorporate visions of natural beauty and immanent divinity. Trawick presents Tamil women's words as relevant to universal human themes. She never hesitates to put high social theory in conversation with observations and assessments made by unschooled and often impoverished women, and thereby shows deftly how each body of thought may enlighten the other. Much of Trawick's work has at its center her gifted rendering of vernacular Tamil oral performances into an English that profoundly affects the heart.

Trawick's fieldwork in India and in Sri Lanka resulted in two monographs: *Notes on Love in a Tamil Family* (1990b) and *Enemy Lines: Warfare, Childhood, and Play in Batticaloa* (2007). Now she offers an ethnographically grounded book on women's expressive traditions. *Death, Beauty, Struggle* contains an original vision of gendered lives, poetry, devotion, and social hierarchy in Tamil Nadu. This book displays the full range of Trawick's ethnographic artistry: her acute attentiveness to feelings, to linguistic nuances, to fragile bonds, to fierce commitments, to the ways lyrical composition and storytelling articulate otherwise suppressed struggles.

If most of the fieldwork on which this book is based was conducted during the last two decades of the twentieth century, Trawick is reporting on conditions that have been slow to change, and her interventions are timely. Introducing a recent anthology of Tamil Dalit writings (all from literate authors, among whom approximately 20 percent are female), the coeditors write, "numerous bits of evidence show that even before the birth of the word 'Dalit', there was a recorded history of the 'untouchables'' fight against discrimination and literary expressions that spoke about it. A turn towards this recovered history of the region may help alter our vision of Dalit literature" (Ravikumar and Azhagarasan 2012, xv). While their volume contains a rich range of important and moving material, there is exactly nothing in it from oral traditions. Work such as Trawick's furthers the project of recovering regional history by bringing to the page eloquent voices from unwritten sources.

These chapters shed all kinds of light, providing a shifting radiance: sometimes flaming, sometimes flickering; sometimes glaring, sometimes soft. It is full-spectrum light. My foreword points to just four thematic elements in Trawick's book, considering each as a filament, each possessing a special glow, each at times delivering bright flashes. The light metaphor with which I am playing came to me unbidden, but I allowed it to proliferate, not merely for its versatility, but because the metaphor of "darkness" has been used by some authors—recently in Aravind Adiga's best-selling novel *The White Tiger*—to characterize, or in Adiga's case to caricature, rural India. Thus "The Darkness" with its erratic or nil electricity, its lagging literacy rates, its political impotence, its cherished livestock, is posed in stark contrast to the middle-class ideal of "India shining."[1]

If I may indulge in a bit more metaphoric play, let me say that these variegated lights in Trawick's chapters might also be likened to many alternative sources of light devised and employed in areas sporadically short on current as is much of rural South Asia. In our power-glutted world we fail to realize how many kinds of light can be tapped in times of need: candles, oil wicks, pressure lamps, torches both oil-soaked and battery powered, and lately the light from mobile phone screens. There is also moonlight, and even the fireworks that go "bang! boom!" (Chapter 4). Rural arts of improvisation, in lighting and many other areas, give the lie—as do Trawick's essays—to diminished views such as Adiga's of benighted country folk.[2]

Following the introduction, Trawick's six central chapters present to readers vocally powerful female beings whose identities may be goddess, priestess, singer, or ambiguously merged and shifting combinations of these. The four filaments I highlight crosscut chapters, although some are particularly evident in one or another. These are gender and social justice; intertwined emotions and ecologies; interpenetration of divine and mortal biographies, and an unrepentant anthropology.

Gender and Social Justice

> Then, as the song goes, Siṅgammā, having emerged from within the house, "rising up high, speaking with unsheathed energy, wearing pearls," addresses her lame older brother. . . . She leaves the house, she goes outside, they raise her up. (Chapter 6)

Gender and social justice, or injustice as is more often the case, painfully intertwine throughout almost every passage of Trawick's work but may be most vividly explicit in the tale of Siṅgammā's life as girl and goddess. Siṅgammā was an untouchable girl, raped and murdered. She emerges as a goddess from prison-like confinement as described in the above excerpt. That she is wearing pearls is meaningful. Of course it is a poetic convention to praise deities as decked in gorgeous and costly items. But in Siṅgammā's terrible and wonderful story, such celebration of a no longer vulnerable female beauty has extraordinary impact. Like the young woman renamed by the Indian press "Delhi Braveheart" in 2013, Siṅgammā bears painful testimony against gang rape, leaving behind not just a mutilated corpse but a transformative legacy of witness.[3]

Ghanshyam Shah and colleagues (2006) present a twenty-first-century investigation of "the extent and incidence of untouchability in different spheres of life in contemporary rural India." Their team covered 565 villages across eleven states including Tamil Nadu, where Trawick worked. They concluded: "Untouchability is a practice that profoundly affects the lives and psyches of millions of Indians. . . . Despite the abolition of untouchability by the Constitution of India, and despite the passage of numerous legislations classifying untouchability in any sphere as a cognizable criminal offence, . . . the practice lives on and even takes on new idioms" (2006, 164). The authors of this sobering study also note, unsurprisingly, "the particular double burden borne by Dalit women, for whom gender and caste combine to create greater vulnerability to social exploitation and oppression" (2006, 165).

Trawick makes her readers fully cognizant of women's double burden. She also teaches us that such burdened women have capabilities to escape their confines imaginatively, and that at times they emerge like Siṅgammā with unsheathed energy. Some of the women whose voices readers encounter in this book have charted truly alternative destinies whether as healer, teacher, or social activist. The majority live their daily lives compliant with a system that denies them value and power, maybe even humanity. But that system does not capture them, as their songs and stories available here show clearly.

In one unusual comical song critiquing European male authority, the singer's words are most explicitly fierce and rude. As Trawick puts it, "No punches are pulled" (Chapter 3). The singer describes a man sitting "idly on his porch," clueless because he "doesn't know any Tamil." She urges her companions: "Piss into his pot, girl. Pour it into his rosy red mouth." The foreigner's ignorance of Tamil surely makes him a safe object of derision in Tamil. It is more perilous to deride internal oppressors, whether male family members or high-caste predators. Toward such persons, women generally lodge aggressive complaints using more oblique language, and more elaborate poetic conceits.

Politicized, literate Dalit voices are loud and strong in the public arena, and no anthropologist is required to convince others of their active resistance and outrage.[4] The precious understanding that Trawick offers is an inner core of refusal to accept degradation among persons who are not activists, who are not mobilized, yet who vocally indict the socioreligious system that continues to hurt them. These voices speak and sing with shattering eloquence about injustice, about suffering, about pain. They also reveal embodied lives where moments of beauty, hope, and affection are cherished. Their identities are not defined solely by those who scorn, shun, abuse, exploit or even murder them. Justified anger is there, but so is delight—delight in something as simple as a bar of soap, something as deep as a quest for spiritual truth. This is true dominance without hegemony (Guha 1997). Trawick's particular genius is her ability to convince us of this and to inspire her readers by showing these women's courage, fortitude, integrity and ability to turn sorrows and trials into art.

Intertwined Emotions and Ecologies

> Today clusters and clusters of eggplants,
> O poor girls, though they fruit on the vine,
> With no one to hold and embrace us, no one to hold and embrace us,
> We rot with the vine, mother. (Chapter 2)

A vine laden with shiny purple eggplants is a welcome image of abundance, food, and fertility. To rot on the vine should not be its fate. In this crying song the verbal imagery of rotting annihilates a healthy source of nourishment, transforming it from plenty to waste. As Trawick explicates this and other verses, the song is about "ineffective containment, containment that offers no fulfillment, completion, or protection" (Chapter 2).

I marvel at this song's simultaneous evocation of lushness and deprivation. It is only one verse of a very sad song, and the song is not just about neglect. It is also about justice, in the family as well as in the community. It is only one song among many equally deep and compelling in their musical intervention in a world often deaf to the suffering of the lowborn and of women. The songs' organic imagery fluidly unites human and other forms of life.

Trawick's translations, of which the eggplant verse offers just a single glimpse, evoke an intertwined universe of plant life and human feelings as they permeate one another. This is a truly human ecology. Other scholars of classical South Indian literatures attest to similar resonance across species and landscapes. In Tamil poetics, as A. K. Ramanujan expressed it, there exists "a taxonomy of landscapes, flora and fauna, and of emotions—an ecosystem of which a man's activities and feelings are a part" (1990, 50). More recently, Martha Selby, a scholar and translator of Tamil literature, offers additional observations that complicate the poetic meshing of humans with environments. She writes that "in early Tamil poetry, it is not nature—that 'something out there'—that is the object of the human impulse to tame, rather human emotion and sexuality are the objects of capture and ordering; not nature, not the wild outside but the wild within, disciplined with networks of referents, symbols, and indices culled from the environment." Selby asks, "What does it mean to assign plant and animal natures to human beings?" (2011, 14). In Trawick's translations of the songs sung by day laborers, by rat catchers, by gypsy-like scavengers and hunters, there are similarly delicate, evocative, and complex visions of the "wild within."

Interpenetration of Divine and Mortal Biographies

> Sarasvati, through taped interviews as well as through conversations, showed me something I had never thought of before, which was that the woman and the spirit she worshipped had been through similar life experiences, in particular, problems with men. Māriamman was, then, a model of what Sarasvati experienced herself to be, and was struggling with Sarasvati, forcing her, to do what Māriamman in her life story had finally achieved. (Chapter 1)

In a compelling portrait of the priestess Sarasvati and the goddess Māriamman, Trawick shows us in Chapter 1 how closely intertwined the life stories of deity and devotee can be. Māriamman even grants Trawick, the young American anthropologist, an interview, speaking through the possessed body of her mortal medium. Māriamman literally rules Sarasvati's life in that she presents her with rules that must be followed. But she also endows her human vehicle with a financial and emotional stability that the priestess had not known in her life's struggles before her own being became so thoroughly intertwined with that of the mother goddess. In Sarasvati's case, however counterintuitive, to be possessed is to be, if not liberated, then at least relieved of some daunting hardships. It also enables her to help others deal with their own difficulties in life.

In Chapter 4, a woman with tuberculosis whose name is Kanyammā, which is also the name of a local goddess, sings songs about that goddess. She laments the goddess's decline, equated with environmental decline. Kanyammā the woman also sings of the attractive power of the virgin goddess in the form of a girl wearing flowers in her hair. Their fragrance is irresistible, a botanical source of divine as well as human allure (for Tamil women customarily wear fresh flowers in their hair). Trawick concludes about one of Kanyammā's songs that it suggests "a place where a woman is on top" (Chapter 4). That place is on the edge of the village settlement. In many rural South Indian communities, goddesses are regularly enshrined a bit beyond human habitations, a bit apart from the messy and imperfect human world. The exception of course is when they choose to enter someone's body as was the case with Māriamman, who possessed the priestess Sarasvati and intervened in hers and many others' everyday lives to alleviate their sufferings.[5]

Unrepentant Anthropology

> During one of my unpolluted spells I went to visit Chandra, and I found that she was now observing her time of impurity, so I went out back to where she was staying. we had been sitting alone together for some time when suddenly—defying the Brahminical rule which demands that during her menstrual period a woman shall touch no one—Chandra grabbed my hand, tightly, saying nothing.
>
> Our friendship intensified at that moment, and I realized that this too was a great source of śakti. (Trawick [Egnor] 1980, 28)

The words with which I epitomize my closing filament come not from this book but from Trawick's earliest publication (1980). They evoke for me the intimacy, the connection, the embodiedness at the heart of Trawick's anthropology and of *Death, Beauty, Struggle.*

Rather than a disembodied authorial voice, Trawick gives us presence—her own thoroughly embodied presence. Among observant high-caste South Indian Hindu families menstrual taboos would cause a woman literally to be "not in the house" monthly. Trawick as a good participant observer was trying to live by the same rules as her hosts.[6] But in an unexpected place she encountered transgression, and here she celebrates it. In a way, inspired by her Tamil friend, Trawick breaks disciplinary taboos, speaking of her own bodily processes and acknowledging in her friend's cross-cultural gesture that the presence of an anthropologist sometimes opens up a space for countercurrents in a cultural universe. In 1981, when I was just back from my doctoral fieldwork, it was genuinely momentous to encounter in Trawick's published anthropology such a strong human voice, true to her lived experience. For me fieldwork had never been about gathering and analyzing data but rather about forging relationships. Reading Trawick enabled me to acknowledge this in my own writing.[7]

Trawick's anthropology never apologizes for its humanity, its unabashed incorporation of anthropologist as person into the text, sometimes recursively as when Kanyammā sings about Trawick:

When they see you, desire takes hold.
When they see you, desire takes hold.
When one sees the West, it seems very far away.
It comes bearing thunder and lightning.
When one sees the West, it seems very far away.
It comes bearing thunder and lightning. (Chapter 4)

Commenting on these lines, Trawick writes, "Just as thunder and lightning coming from the faraway West must have been seen as fearsomely powerful, and capable of boding great good or great ill, so perhaps I was perceived. Although I just wanted to be a normal person there and melt into the everyday life of the village, that was not possible" (Chapter 4). Here she speaks for quite a few anthropologists perpetually chagrined by their proverbial sore thumb outsider status, by a desire for affirmed if ineffable belonging, by the burden of too many visibly attractive material belongings.

Trawick's anthropology demonstrates a conviction that persons without privilege—from the menstruating woman isolated in her hut, to the rape victim, to the gypsy peddler, to the landless laborer—possess both power and agency. Through verbal arts oppressed persons produce acute cultural critiques and also beauty. Trawick simply assumes these are persons worth hearing, that their words are worth the labor of a loving translation and that they have much to teach us. Such assumptions might be the purported stock in trade of our beloved, maligned anthropology, but they are rarely put into practice with such a delicate mix of humility and eloquence as that offered in Trawick's writings.

For the 2012 annual meeting of the American Anthropological Association I organized a panel honoring Trawick's contributions. Lawrence Cohen's paper used appropriately enigmatic poetic language to characterize Trawick's work, speaking of her "demonic rigor" and asserting that her writing is "*asli*" (Hindi, 'real'), in that she "crosses the line into a space marked by beauty but also hurt, chaos, and indeed death." One discussant, Anand Pandian, spoke of "the liquid appeal of that anthropological imagination that Trawick's work encourages us to exercise." He likens this "liquid appeal" to an attitude he learned from his grandfather, who would speak of his lack of fear under many trying circumstances including drinking water from dirty ditches: "What I learned, listening to my grandfather, is that there is health, as well as danger, in breaching the boundaries of the self" (Pandian 2012; see also Pandian and Mariappan 2014).[8]

Prompted by these appreciations, I slip, in conclusion, from a trope of light to one of liquid. I urge readers of this wonderful book to sip or gulp from the real, demonic, transgressive fount of Margaret Trawick's anthropology and the voices of South Indian women transmitted here. I hope readers will imbibe with these healthy draughts the energy to cross the lines and breach the boundaries, in modes that are not invasive but incorporative.

Preface

The fieldwork that resulted in this book was done intermittently from 1975 to 1991 while I was engaged in other projects in Tamil Nadu. The study for the book and the writing of it have been done continuously until now. Emergent from this work has been, among other things, a picture of how the government of India, and the British colonial government before it, tried to freeze groups of people in particular times, places, and occupations. Some are categorized as "Backward." Others categorize themselves as "Forward." Others are considered untouchable and categorized as "Scheduled Castes" or "Scheduled Tribes." All the castes are ranked against each other. This ranking developed in parts of India millennia ago through a long and slow process. But real time has disrupted such categories. What has changed quickly, what has changed slowly, how the life of one or another person or group has been broken by change, how one or another person or group has adapted to change, how valuable the work of memory is, and how damaging old moralities are—these are realities unsought but uncovered in this book.

Anthropology, my chosen discipline, the study of humanity, has a long history and has been through many changes, from ancient days until now. This book presents bits of that history in India, from poems and organized treatises created millennia ago, to accounts from the nineteenth century, to ethnography from the late twentieth century, to articles and books from the twenty-first. Some of these have been created by Tamil people who did not think in terms of anthropology or history but more in terms of poetry and song. Later works have been composed by journalists, authors, filmmakers, artists, poets.

Most of my life, whether in the field or reading and writing, I did not think much about caste or gender or systems of rank. All of those were boring to me. So was politics. But now I cannot avoid such topics. The focus of these chapters is not on caste and gender oppression, important as these issues are to Indian society, but on the verbal art of the oppressed. These were people I thought of as normal. This book is about human beings as they describe and express their own lives and the lives of others in narrative, song, and conversation. Although individuals are important, relationships are more so. Caste, gender, and familial relationships, though rarely mentioned in song or speech, constitute an important feature of each of these women's lived environments. In the larger view, caste, gender, familial, religious, and ethnic hierarchies in India cannot be ignored. This book shows clearly that nonliterate people living in the most abject circumstances, women of untouchable castes, may be the intellectual equals of great scholars far away from India. Caste is not overlooked, but it is seen in this book mostly through the eyes of Dalit women, or more precisely, through their voices.

Introduction

When you're looking for something you haven't yet seen, what you encounter may be entirely different from what you expect. Among my unsought experiences have been the people, the stories, and the songs appearing in this book. Franz Boas realized that the Inuit, then called Eskimo, knew more than geologists about the geology of the area that he studied and where they lived. This led him to the more powerful discovery that the Inuit language, though having no written literature, was as complex as any of the languages Boas already knew, and from there to the discovery that every human language is as complex, as intricately and precisely organized, as every other (Stocking 1974).[1] For others, it may be the breakthrough that some barely literate person knows better than you (who are highly educated) how your shared world is constituted. This discovery may or may not lead you to reconsider a whole category of people you previously hardly knew, and further to reconsider the premises on which human beings are categorized in the first place—the premises underlying divisions of religion, gender, race, family, class, and nation.

The world I inhabited in India could not be more different from the world in which I now live. True, there are many different worlds in India. Some are hellish, some are heavenly, and most are a mixture of both. The art, the food, the way coffee is poured, how everyday work is turned into dance, the music, the stories, the smiles, the laughter, the weeping, the jokes, the puns, the scents of jasmine and sandalwood are heavenly. But the poverty, the cruelties inflicted on the vulnerable, the needlessly dying children, the diseases floating through the water, lying in the soil, and wafting through the wind are hell.

Coming from America, traveling to India, and living there for eighteen months with my own baby changed me. I became addicted to *idlis* and *sambar*, with Indian coffee on the side. Total immersion in the Tamil language made me better at conversational Tamil, a skill more valuable than either

Tamils or Anglos could easily comprehend. Even some of those who have grown up multilingual do not perceive the value of this skill. I met babies who were taught two or three languages as they grew up. Those few with whom I have kept up have flourished.

The experience of living in India made me see, among other things, that people in India can and do live on less than I had been accustomed to. But beyond this I saw extreme poverty. I was waiting at a bus stop, with several other people, when a little boy came to us holding a limp, thin baby over his shoulder. The other people at the bus stop turned away. I had been taught not to give money to a beggar, even a beggar child, because the child would just take the money back to whatever adult was controlling him or her. I gave the boy some food I had just bought, and told him to share it with the baby. Later I witnessed other cases of children being used by adults in this callous way. It was clear that the baby at the bus stop would die if it did not get serious medical attention, and I thought to myself, what if that were my child? But if I took such a baby in my arms, how could I bring it back to life? Was there a doctor, an agency somewhere, that would do this?

Returning from India to America brought a series of new shocks. "Culture shock" it was called then, by returning Peace Corps volunteers. Over time we came to see that America and India have some things in common, bad things, in particular the fact that certain categories of people are subject to discrimination despite laws forbidding it. In both countries, such discrimination entails forced exclusion from some places, such as temples, where one might want to go, forced inclusion in other places, such as prisons, where one would not want to go, police violence, civilian violence, violence by men against women, violence by the highly ranked against those whose rank is low. And aside from violence is the sneering contempt for those one considers one's inferiors. Poverty of people marked from birth by skin color, by caste, and by sex is an inevitable consequence of such practices. Neglect and hatred of such people in both countries promotes terrible violence. Most people here have no clue of what is happening there, and vice versa. In America, the outcastes are African Americans. In India, they are Dalits. Both African Americans and Dalits have been known by other, uglier names. In this introduction, a disproportionate number of words are spent on caste, untouchability, and poverty. In subsequent chapters, other topics assume priority.

The three words in the main title—death, beauty, struggle—indicate what Dalits of both sexes mean to the Indian world, what untouchable women strive to be and to create, and what their lives are, relentlessly, to the end.

I chose to keep the word "untouchable" in the subtitle of this book because India has not modernized to the extent that is sometimes claimed. Untouchability was outlawed in India in 1948, but still it remains. To an American, a black or brown person who belongs to one caste or *jāti* looks the same as a black or brown person who belongs to another caste. But to a person born and raised in India, subtle clues are enough to give a lower-caste person away. The caste system, with all its prejudices, remains deeply entrenched in Indian society. The term "Dalit" means "ground down, broken, oppressed." This term indicates that it is not the fault of the oppressed people that they are oppressed; higher-caste people have caused them this harm. The use of the term "Dalit" is one of multiple efforts to change the caste system, based on old Hindu ideas of purity and pollution, and bit by bit, in some places, for some people, it has changed. But even for Dalits who make it into universities and colleges, the pain and the stigma remain.[2]

The word "women" in the subtitle is, on the surface, self-explanatory. I was not seeking out only women as informants, but it was easier for women to talk with me because I was also a woman. Women told me more than men did about their lives, and women are the main people in this book. The songs and stories relayed in this book are, with one exception, by women, and without exception about women. Numerous books and articles have been written by and about women in India. Few have been written about nonliterate Dalit women in India, real ones and not fictional ones. Perhaps even fewer of such women's songs and narratives have been considered to be verbal art. To my knowledge, few of their words, sung or narrated, have been published, although this situation is changing.

The most problematic part of my subtitle is the last phrase: "create the world." A widespread view holds that only the educated can understand what the world is about. Only the educated can philosophize and theorize. Only the educated can think. But that is not true.

The chapters in this book move over time, from oldest to most recent, as they also move over space from urban to rural to forest edge to placelessness, and back to urban again. Sarasvati/Māriamman lives in an accessible urban home and in a great temple. Siṅgammā comes from a nomadic tribe, and she herself is a wandering ghost, whose place of burial is inaccessible, whose name and story are obscure. It took this writer decades to get from the first to the last. There is an advantage to obscurity, to singing words with too many meanings, to being where one cannot be found. The disadvantages are both clear and abundant.

This book was made initially of memories—memories of personal experiences, of things read, of things said, of images created in my mind of realities that I never experienced. Reading gives me information, including memories, that I can come back to, or discover for the first time. Putting what I want to say into writing allows me to re-create all this and give it a kind of coherence. For people who cannot read or write, life is different.

Events of the Past That Have Contributed to the Formation of Present Conditions

The history of people now called "untouchable" is an intrinsic part of the history and prehistory of the South Asian subcontinent.[3] In present times, the presumed original people of India are called Adivasis and are considered by caste Hindus to be untouchable. The actual first human beings to settle in the subcontinent arrived fifty thousand years or more ago, with the first coastal migrations out of Africa (Pope and Terrell 2008; Wells 2002). Some may have followed the ocean coasts entirely. Some may have traveled up rivers like the Indus. But those who kept on, generation after generation, through centuries, went as far as they could go until they reached Australia, beyond which further travel eastward was not possible. As they traveled they left settlements along the way, including settlements in Sri Lanka, the Andaman Islands, and the southern part of the Indian subcontinent. Modes of living in the subcontinent moved from fishing and forest dwelling to small-scale farming and herding; to countless different ways of living, of speaking, of organizing families and communities; to walled towns, to warfare, temples and palaces, kingdoms and empires. People came and went throughout the subcontinent, and to and from distant lands. As time went on, in addition to solo travelers and small groups of travelers, there came large invasions, mass migrations, conquests, bigger wars. And as all of this was happening, all the other modes of living continued, albeit becoming increasingly marginalized.[4]

The Indus Valley Civilization was the first civilization in South Asia and the largest of the three great civilizations in the world at that time. It had no boundaries. People in that civilization practiced agriculture and horticulture, irrigation, trade with distant countries, metallurgy, and remarkable art. The cities had well-laid-out streets and well-engineered water management and sewage systems. There was writing but it has not yet been deciphered. The language spoken may have been Proto-Dravidian or Austroasiatic. No clear sign of royalty or religion has been found by archaeologists of the last century and a half, although some of the artwork could be interpreted as religious. Archaeological research remains ongoing. The civilization continued as such until around 1500 BCE. Possible causes for its decline and end are many, including immigration of new people, drought, and deforestation (Bryant 2001, 159–60; Lawler 2008, 1282–83; Knipe 1991).

Subsequently Vedic cultures came into their own. There were few or no horses in South Asia until around 1500 BCE, when horsemen came from Central Asia across the Himalayas, bringing not only horses (Doniger 2009, chapters 4–5) but their language and culture with them, including long poems that they had memorized. It is difficult to know when their technique of memorization began, as they had no writing system before they entered the subcontinent. The earliest written Sanskrit texts were called the Vedas ("what is known"). They were transmitted orally through generations of ritual specialists. Sanskrit, the language of the Vedas, an Indo-European language related to Latin and Greek, spread throughout the whole subcontinent, but mainly through northern India. The oldest and best known of the Vedas was the *Rig Veda*. It is said to have been composed in northwest India somewhere between 1700 and 1100 BCE. That would have made it nearly contemporaneous with the Indus Valley Civilization and geographically close to it.[5]

The *Rig Veda* contains some beautiful, evocative poems, beginning with one that says:

> There was neither existence nor non-existence then; there was neither the realm of space nor the sky which is beyond. What stirred? Where? In whose protection? Was there water, bottomlessly deep? There was neither death nor immortality then. There was no distinguishing sign of night nor of day. That one breathed, windless, by its own impulse. Other than that, there nothing beyond. Darkness was hidden by darkness, in the beginning. With no distinguishing sign, all this was water. The life force that was covered with emptiness, that one arose through the power of heat. . . . Who really knows? Who will here proclaim it? Whence was it produced? Whence is this creation? The gods came afterwards, with the creation of this universe. Who then knows whence it has arisen? Whence this creation has arisen—perhaps it formed itself, or perhaps it did not. (Doniger 1981, 25)

Doniger (2009, chapter 4) argues that a merger between Vedic cultures and Indus Valley cultures resulted in the Hindu cultures and religions that came after these two cultures met. But—again according to Doniger (2009, chapter 5)—whereas the Indus Valley cultures appear to have been benign (Doniger 2009, chapter 3), Vedic cultures were violent from the beginning. Distinguishing the beauty from the horror of the Vedic texts is not an easy job. An elderly Brahman who lived in southern Tamil Nadu told me that there were parts of the Vedas so cruel he had to wash himself after reading them. But the ideological construct of purity and pollution far predates my friend. Certain acts are polluting. Certain acts are cleansing. But no amount of fire or water can drive away certain memories. How could it have felt to sacrifice something as full of life, fine, and beautiful as a horse? The Purusha Sukta hymn in the *Rig Veda* describes the origin of humankind from the sacrifice of the Cosmic Self (Purusha). That self was divided into pieces, which became different kinds of human being. To whom could such a level of abstraction, with such a current of violence running beneath it, be satisfying?

A Vedic religion developed based on the *Rig Veda*. At first only wandering ascetics taught these ideas. But as time went on, Brahmanism grew as a religion. Brahmanism is a form of Hinduism, from which religion the idea of *varna*s arose. This idea was codified in a book called in Sanskrit *Manavadharmashastra*, or in English, the Laws of Manu. It was said to have been written about 200 BCE. The term *varna* meant "color" for adherents to Brahmanism and also meant a category of human being. There were four varnas: Brahmans, whose work was to be priests and teachers and whose color was white; Kshatriyas, whose profession was to be kings and warriors and whose whose color was red; Vaishyas, whose profession was to be merchants and traders and whose color was yellow; and Shudras, whose job was to be servants and workers and whose color was black. The top three groups were "twice-born" or *dvija*. The fourth group was not. Below the Shudras were people who were of mixed birth. The twice-born were inherently privileged. Brahmans were the most privileged of all. They were considered to be gods on earth. Their word was not to be gainsaid. Apologists for the varna system say that it has nothing to do with skin color. Others say that Brahmans were people who came from the north, and that is the reason they are white. The current love of white skin in India is said to be an aesthetic preference only. But the social damage done to dark-skinned people in India, most of all dark-skinned women, is enormous.

Before the varna system was established, there were kingdoms as well as many endogamous groups of people throughout India, and probably also exogamous ones. These groups were not necessarily ranked against each other. One may trace concepts of ranked castes and untouchability back to the ideological development in the subcontinent that started with the Vedas. This ideology moved on and took hold and still is powerful in India. The subjugation of women and of working classes was and remains part of this ideology. According to the Laws of Manu, women are carnal creatures and should never be trusted, while molten lead should be poured in the ears of a low-caste person who hears the Vedas.

Any hierarchical social system can be maintained only by violence. Vedic society was hierarchical and violent from the beginning. The situation of people categorized by social rank, prescribed types of work, color, and sex in India extends to the first implementation of Vedic ideology. The text by Manu is still considered sacred by many Hindus. Not all Hindus follow it, though. Some Brahmans abhor the level of cruelty preached in the Vedic texts. The Tamil text *Thirukkuṟaḷ*, said to have been composed during the fifth or sixth century CE, teaches kindness, love, and generosity toward all, including wife and children. It is a much read, much adored book among Tamil people. Manu, who wrote the Laws of Manu, is believed to have been a Brahman. Thiruvaḷḷuvar, who wrote the *Thirukkuṟaḷ*, is said to have been a Jain, a Paṟaiyar, a weaver—definitively the first, but conceivably all three. In Tamil Sangam poetry, written about two thousand years ago, Kuṟavars, now classified as untouchable, were described admiringly.

Alternatives to Vedic Hinduism were always there, and they too developed and drew followers. Buddhism and Jainism were strong movements. Christian communities became established in India from the coming of Thomas the Apostle in the third century CE. Muslim traders lived in India from shortly after Islam was founded in the seventh century CE. In southern India, around the sixth century CE, an intensely emotional form of self-sacrifice developed. The saints were worshippers of Siva or Vishnu, two Hindu gods. Caste differences were not acknowledged. Personal devotion was everything. This form of religion continues in southern India. It is called *bhakti*. Christianity and Islam continue in India as minority religions. Buddhism flourished for centuries then moved to other parts of Asia.

Muslim rule in northern India started in the thirteenth century. Until the sixteenth century, Persianate Muslims (with Persian language and culture) ruled most of northeast India. They were supplanted by the militarily superior Mughals (Mongols), who claimed descent from Genghis Khan. A hybrid Muslim empire developed in India, where they remained as warriors, conquering almost all of India except the very far south. Though militarily mighty, they are said to have been good rulers and good administrators. They also introduced fine Muslim art, literature, textiles, architecture, and maritime and administrative skills. These rulers were not in principle opposed to Hindus or any particular caste. Islam teaches the equality of all men. Therefore caste differences were not officially recognized by Mughal rulers, but status and rank remained in the form of zamindars, whose positions were sometimes hereditary; they owned vast tracts of land and taxed the peasants who worked on that land. The zamindars maintained military organizations, took royal titles, lived in lavish splendor, and acted as sovereign kings. When the British proceeded to gain control of India by military means, zamindars fought the British who challenged them. Area by area, the British won. Muslims did not recognize women as the equals of men. Neither, for that matter, did the British, some strong and valiant queens notwithstanding. In Pukkatturai, the small town where I lived for a year, there was an old broken temple that had been destroyed by the Muslims, I was told. The family deity of the Hindu household was a grandmother who killed her grandchildren to save them from Muslim depredations. There is no way to ascertain whether this actually happened. But there are still antagonisms, sometimes murderous riots, between Muslims and Hindus in India. Partition between India and Pakistan, implemented at the end of British rule, contributed to this antagonistic division of people and religions.

Subcontinental thought changed with the British Raj, which brought in its own ideas about people in India and how they should be organized, classified, and characterized. Every tribe and every caste was considered to be what it always was and what it always would be. Absolute determinism was law. Nobody could change caste and nobody could take on an occupation different from that of his or her parents. All forest-dwelling tribes and all itinerant tribes were judged by the British Raj to be criminal because they were able to live outside the organizations established by the Raj. They were outlaws in a sense, therefore outcastes, but they were not necessarily killers or thieves. Laborers who worked for landowners were slaves, bonded to the land on which they worked. The caste system was solidified under the British then pronounced illegal by the early postindependence government. This law could not be enforced. Subsequent laws prohibiting untouchability and discrimination against lower caste individuals were passed with little effect. Cross-caste marriage was encouraged by the chief minister of Tamil Nadu, C. N. Annadurai, in 1967, and a number of marriages between Brahman women and men of scheduled castes have happened after that and have been successful.[6] But in 2007, the Supreme Court of India ruled that social organization based on caste is inherited and cannot be changed.[7]

Events of the past remain also in the form of stone carvings and written materials. Experiences of the past are inscribed in bodies of the present. Hunger is passed down through generations. If a woman cannot eat well, her baby will be smaller. If her baby grows up and has a baby, that baby will be smaller still. And so on. Events of the past held only in memory are free to change. Bodies may take generations to recover from trauma. Written materials, whether old or new, can be read and discussed today, and they may change people's lives today. But written materials are fixed. These are inaccessible to the nonliterate. Literary information comes to them from a variety of sources, all of them human, most of them having their own agendas. To a nonliterate Dalit they may say, from a distance, "Your job is to do such-and-such and not so-and-so," and some Dalits may accede to this command. Others may not.

Memory is selective. The British Raj did much to rigidify caste boundaries.[8] When the Mughals ruled, they ruled over a hierarchical civilization which they themselves helped create. Hindu kingdoms before them managed varna hierarchies. The histories of peasants have been mostly forgotten, as have been the histories of forest-dwelling peoples. Victorian mores together with the necessity of caste and the oppression of women have been accepted as primordial by many people in India who call themselves Hindu. But none of the people now classified as scheduled castes or scheduled tribes were always untouchables. A few centuries ago, some histories say, they were respected and honored. It is safe to say that ten millennia ago, when people were as human as they are now, there were no hierarchical orders in South Asia at all. To have a hierarchy you need material surplus. Before the Neolithic age, people had no such surplus. Descendants of those who lived in South Asia then still live in South Asia now. This concept may be hard to grasp for Americans whose ancestors came to this continent just a few centuries ago or more recently still. Native Americans are as marginalized here as Adivasis are in India today.

Poverty and Disease

As early as the Sangam period in Tamil Nadu, drought for lack of rain was named in the texts as a danger. Rain is praised lavishly in ten early verses of the *Thirukkuṟaḷ*. During British rule, famines in India took countless lives. Millions of Dalits in the Madras Presidency, now Tamil Nadu, died from the famine of 1876–78 (Kolappan 2013). During famines in the British period, grain was hoarded by landholders. British in India took what was grown as food and sold it overseas. The workers were the ones that died. These events have been remembered by survivors. Food is carefully looked after. Food is the most important thing. No hungry person must see another eating. The necessity of feeding another before one feeds oneself is an unwritten rule, closely followed. But in a hierarchical social system, which direction the food goes in is of utmost concern, and the direction is down. The lowest eat the leftovers. Those who own the crops own the world. Hunger is always just around the corner and has been that way for millennia in southern India. Memories are passed on through generations. Seeds are cherished, planted, and reaped. The memory of a past better than the present remains. In the struggles of the present, little space remains in the mind to consider the long-term future. And honestly, how much can anyone predict? Memories of mythic heroes and heroines played out in street and temple dramas, Bible stories, stories of gods, stories of sacrifice, battle, triumph, and slaughter all enter into the lives of people who watch them as street or temple theater. Such stories from long ago are reenacted in household and family dramas, in village dramas, and in song. In such dramas, a man may beat or kill his wife or sister if he deems her faithless. A landlord may beat or kill a worker if he catches the worker stealing. Epic battles of higher versus lower castes are carried out. People of lower castes may be deemed monkeys. But children are to be loved, cherished, enjoyed, dressed up.[9]

Disease does not affect only the poor. Communicable disease spreads to everyone. Immunities can protect a person but not completely. Bacteria and viruses change every year so that an immunity from last year will not necessarily help this year. And there are many different diseases caused by many different kinds of organism. All diseases caused by microorganisms spread. Some can be prevented and some can be treated; others one just has to live through. Most preventions and treatments fail to reach everybody. Those who are not reached can only pray, recover by themselves, or die. In India, countless millions are not reached.

The people who must clean up raw human excrement and untreated sewage in India are people of the lowest castes. Manual scavenging of underground sewers by men, and of above-ground excrement by women, continues throughout India to this day. Disease and death from this work are not uncommon (*Times of India* 2015; Campbell 2014). This is a special problem in the cities and in tropical areas.

Poverty causes hunger, which weakens a person and makes them more vulnerable to disease, which in turn can kill the afflicted. Babies and little children are the most vulnerable. They get into contaminated water, get diarrhea, and die of dehydration. Antibiotics and careful rehydration combined with nourishing food can save a child in danger of dying. Cholera is a big killer of children as well as of adults, but again, skilled treatment can save the sufferer from death. If there is no therapy available, the person, whether adult or child, dies. In India, for the very poor, no prevention is available, and likewise no therapy can be had. Wherever people, including children, defecate in the open, other children are likely to get sick. Some will recover and some will die. There are simply not enough doctors in India willing and able to treat so many sick and dying children. I once saw a doctor turn away such a dying baby, washing his hands and telling me, "That baby is dead."

What poverty does to people, most of all to people categorized as untouchable, is painful to contemplate. Poverty can mean humiliation. Poverty can mean starvation. It can mean not having enough. It can mean having to decide which children to feed how much. Poverty can lead to malnutrition, which can cause vulnerability to disease and ultimately to death. The prospects of poverty, starvation, and death are terrifying to anyone who must face them. Dalits are most likely to face poverty, because they are considered dispensable by landowners and indeed by anyone of a higher caste. If they can make themselves indispensable by any means, then they can eat. But they will not necessarily eat well. This topic is addressed most poignantly in Chapters 1 and 5 of this book.

Pregnancy and childbirth are dangers afflicting only women. These dangers are well known. Healthy young women with good midwives and/or doctors available, and modern technology to assist, are in less danger of suffering and dying. Such care was not always available even for the wealthy. Now it is. But the poor in India, above all untouchables, have little or no access to such easy amenities. Doctors are often not kind and not fair. Fair treatment means treating all patients with the same degree of competence and concern.

Breast-feeding a baby for as long as three years or more is, among the poor in India, one of the best ways to keep a child healthy. Babies are passed around. In some societies, women will share the breast-feeding of babies. I don't know if this happens in India, but I have seen a grandmother nursing a grandchild of hers in a village of Tamil Nadu. Such practices are considered backward by modern Indians. In other contexts, they make perfect sense.

In India, people who live in cities stand a better chance of making a living than people who live in the countryside. But life for the poor in an Indian city is no easier than in the countryside. The poorest in the countryside flock to the cities, where giant slums have grown and continue to grow. Raw sewage runs in the streets, iridescent black or green and toxic. People sleep wherever they can. If they have a work space, they sleep in the work space. The hardest working, most ingenious people in the world live in Indian slums. While information technology and other computer technologies have become a source of employment for educated Indian youth, the slums are where recycling of plastic and other useless waste is done, not by machines but by human hands. Dharavi in Mumbai is the largest, most renowned slum. But there are slums in every city. Infectious disease is the biggest killer. Starvation, mostly of children, continues. Tiny, skeletal, barely alive bodies may be seen with their mothers in railway stations. A starving girl child may still be dressed in pretty clothes.

Contempt of the poor is undisguised. Most Dalits are poor. Although India is, in name, a democracy, democratic sentiments are scarce in that country. The continued reality of caste discrimination is both cause and result of the long-standing malice against the poor and people of the lowest castes. Maltreatment accompanies malice. Neglect fosters poverty and death. The feeling expressed again and again is that the poor deserve their fate, just as low-caste people deserve theirs. Poverty in India is severe, with rural Dalit women and children faring worst of all. Meanwhile some Dalits, in efforts to raise their status, are encouraged to join right-wing political parties which promise that everyone who joins their party may "become a Hindu"—as though Hinduism were a club. The reports go on and on.

Polarization of wealth is now more serious than ever in India, as it is in America. Political corruption, use of political office to enrich oneself and one's friends, and use of wealth to obtain political office have reached new heights in recent decades. New opportunities for individuals and corporations to amass enormous wealth have increased with globalization, and cheap labor is easily found in India. The tremendously wealthy benefit directly at the expense of the very poor. This is happening in the United States, too, but the poorest are not as poor as the very poor in India.

Most of the people I have written about in this book lived in poor villages. Even the children of landlords about whom I have written previously were malnourished. They lived in crumbling old houses. Brahmans, and those who sought to be like Brahmans by adopting a Brahman diet, were badly disadvantaged unless they owned many cows and could provide their children with ample milk and milk-based products. But owning and maintaining even one milk cow was out of the range of some landlords. A buffalo would have been more practical. Goats and chickens would have been more practical still. But all of these animals require space, water, and feed.

Those who lived and worked in the fields and forests were sometimes better able to handle poverty than people whose lives were more rule-restricted even than untouchables. People of the lower castes were sometimes better nourished than Brahmans and those who aspired to be like Brahmans, because lower-caste rural people had a more diverse diet than poor Brahmans. Lower-caste people ate wild food, including field crabs and snails and wild greens, all of which the higher-caste people abjured. People of lower castes ate meat when they could get it, including beef and pork, and raised chickens and ducks when they had the means. But as the forests are destroyed and farmland is depleted, options for living are reduced.

Young people of every caste often aimed to get out of the village and into the city, where they had chances of getting better jobs. Decent nourishment in the hinterlands, when available, was not in itself enough to provide for a decent job. Good education could only be gotten in the cities. Some children moved up in this milieu. The children who moved up and out of poverty were those whose families valued education, who accepted this value, and got university degrees and good work in the cities. These children were both boys and girls. But they had to be allowed into school before they could be educated, and for most Dalits, school was a distant dream.

Those who came from families where literacy and learning were not part of the tradition had to work harder to learn and get ahead. Moreover, Dalit children were often excluded from village schools where caste children studied. Therefore they had little choice but to continue as physical laborers.

Unless one is a landowner, trying to make a living in rural Tamil Nadu is difficult if not impossible in most of the state because of droughts and desertification. Educated people born in villages head to the city for work. So do some uneducated people. But it is dangerous for a woman or girl to travel to a big city. She is in danger also if she stays in the rural village where she was born or into which she married. Thus being born a rural Dalit female is a multiple curse.

The Situation of Dalits in Southern India Now

One event affecting everyone in India, including Dalits, is the rise of the Internet. The accessibility of the Internet has greatly increased the quantity of available information about Dalits, much of it coming from Dalits themselves.[10] But most Dalits, in particular the ones I write of here, have no access to the Internet, and so, no matter how insightful and useful what they say may be, they are effectively silenced. No newspaper story, no matter how accurate the content, no matter how riveting the account, can tell what nonliterate Dalit women may be thinking and saying as you sit, stand, or walk with them.

The word "Dalit" comes from the Maratha language and means "ground," "suppressed," "crushed," or "broken." These are people who until very recently were called "untouchable" in different languages throughout India. In Tamil, "untouchable" is *tīṇḍā*. People of higher castes have not automatically complied with the recent change of nomenclature. Untouchability was outlawed in India at independence. But most people have ignored this law. Nobody told the untouchable people that they were no longer untouchable.

People tagged as untouchable are not to be touched because their caste-assigned work is to clean away human feces, prepare human corpses for burial or cremation, skin dead animals and tan the skins, consume the meat of cattle who have met their end, and catch and eat other animals, including field rats, termites, and disease-bearing bandicoots (*peruccāḷi* in Tamil; translated word for word as "big rat"). A person born to a tīṇḍā caste is herself tīṇḍā. Regardless of what such a person eats or does not eat, touches or does not touch, does or does not do, she is considered poisonous, inferior both in body and in mind, inherently diseased and infectious. Even high-caste people who know that the system is wrong are disgusted at the thought of eating food prepared by a person of a much lower caste, no matter how clean in body and habits the person actually is. The word *tīṇḍā* indicates that a person so designated is inherently poisonous. That property is within her and she cannot change it, any more than a venomous snake can change the fact that its bite can kill.

The term Dalit implies that the oppression, the breaking, the grinding to pieces of Dalits was performed by someone other than the Dalits themselves, by foreigners and by higher-caste Indian people. A high-caste man said to me of the Dalits who worked for him in his village, "They call themselves 'people who have been put down [*tāṟttappaḍḍavarkaḷ*].' Did anyone order them to live as they do?" Even children of higher castes cannot play with children of the lowest castes, because then the higher-caste children would become "like them" (Trawick 1990, chapter 3, section 2).[11] The very proximity of a tīṇḍā person could change you, who were innocent, into tīṇḍā. The concept of venom, of poison, is joined with the concepts of danger, of beauty, and of womanhood. These concepts are shown in Chapters 5 and 6 of this book.

In principle, possession of such a dangerous characteristic could confer a certain power on the person who was tīṇḍā, and in some villages such people did have an indispensable place in the ritual order. In some villages, certain deities with certain powers are controlled by the Dalits of that village, who benefit from this control. If they withdrew their services, the village could lose protection from malevolent spirits (Mines 2005). But as the status of a deity grows, the deity's Dalit association may change. The politics surrounding ritual power and privilege is complex and involves all castes, from the highest Brahmans to the lowest untouchables. Extracting oneself, partly or entirely, from the bonds of Hindu ritual is a difficult task. Today the great inequalities imposed on those classified as tīṇḍā eclipse any ritual privileges they may have.

The poorest of the poor include the tīṇḍā. They are poor largely because they are tīṇḍā. When you are born into poverty, when you are turned away at every turn, when your children are not allowed in the village schools and you can't afford schooling for them anyway, when you are forbidden to enter holy places and subject to scorn and discrimination in countless other ways, it is not so easy for you as an individual to raise your status higher. Members of lower castes have been working collectively to raise their status for generations.[12] They try to raise the status of their caste as a whole—to behave as well-regarded people behave, to get education for their children, to secure reserved seats in governments and in universities, to make money. Housing and ownership of land can make the difference between prosperity and poverty, between food to eat and starvation. Those who seek to raise their living standards commonly think in terms of raising their caste status and think less of individual breakaways from tradition. Such breakaways happen, but they can carry high costs. Few people renounce the caste into which they were born. Although cross-caste marriage has been encouraged and rewarded by members of the Periyar movement and by M. G. Ramachandran of the DMK party in Tamil Nadu, such marriage is risky for the families involved. If one family member behaves in a forbidden manner, or even if a woman is shamed through no fault of her own, the whole family may be brought down. Hence "honor killings" continue to happen and continue to be honored even when relegated to the past.

The question of what it means to be Dalit brings in values of rank and caste, matters affecting, whether positively or negatively, Dalit social mobility and the role of language in Dalit social mobility.

It has been said that Dalits in modern South India accept the caste system as a whole; they just do not accept their place in it (Moffatt 1979). There is a ranked caste system among Dalits in some parts of Tamil Nadu. Those who are low in the overall system find people still lower than themselves. The overall caste system has been replicated on a smaller scale among Dalits in some places. Reports have recently (December 2014) appeared on the Internet of Paṟaiyars beating, raping, and killing members of the lowest castes. These reports come from members of the lowest castes, called Chakkilis or Arunthathiyars. Such reports indicate that solidarity among different Dalit castes is minimal. The power of the caste system appears ironclad on all levels. A highly educated Tamil friend of mine, who lives in Canada now, has suggested that the caste system is so widespread and entrenched because it is "sexy." I disagreed with him when he said that, but maybe he had a point. Caste and sex in India go together hand in glove for more than a few men.[13]

Like people in India, people of all classes in the Anglophone nations are concerned with the minutiae of social rank. Likenesses between caste in India and race in America have been drawn by some scholars.[14] The likenesses do not overshadow the differences, but the likenesses are indisputable. African Americans in the United States are regarded by some with fear and contempt just as untouchables in India are.

Nowadays the untouchable status of Paṟaiyars is linked to the ritual jobs that only they are allowed to do, jobs that are considered by caste Hindus to be severely polluting. The concept of pollution among caste Hindus is as entrenched as the caste system itself. In the American south, slaves could be cooks, and still today, black people cook in the homes of wealthy southern whites. They also clean the house and mind the children. Proper southern ladies do not do such work. In the days of slavery, a slave woman might nurse the baby of her white owner while the slave's own baby would be left alone in the fields. Songs about this practice are sung even now. No antipathy toward the owners, no anger comes through.

Dalits in India are considered too polluting to cook for non-Dalits. Only Brahmans are allowed to cook in Brahman homes, at weddings, and at vegetarian restaurants. Just as untouchables are considered inherently impure, Brahmans are considered inherently pure. I knew one Brahman man in Madurai who sent others out to kill a snake in his backyard. It was considered wrong to kill a snake, so this Brahman sent his servants to do it for him. This Brahman's morality and mine were strangers to each other. In some areas of Tamil Nadu, Dalits treat ritual jobs as a niche market reserved for them and guard that privilege because it is also one of their main sources of income. Others disdain all such work.

The most numerous Dalits in Tamil Nadu are Paṟaiyars, whose numbers give them power. Close in status are those who by tradition are nomadic forest dwellers, but there are not so many of them. These are so-called tribal people, those outside the caste system, who once lived as hunters and gatherers and now have nothing to hunt or gather. Some have homes and land, but others move from place to place, gaining subsistence by a range of means that will be detailed in Chapter 4. Some of those who have been given homes and land cannot use them because they have no water there, and they have no income and no jobs.

By far the worst off are truly homeless people in India who have been lost to or rejected by everybody, including their own families, and have neither a home where they belong nor a group who will take them in. The bodies of such people are picked up in the morning by members of scavenging castes and discarded in places not named in news stories.

Members of named scavenging castes are those who pick up all the discarded filth on the streets, by the railroad tracks, and in the sewers. This filth includes not only human feces but also human bodies, body parts, animal feces, and dead animals. Formerly members of these castes were called "sweepers." They are subject to humiliation and early death.

One notch up in the ritual status hierarchy are agricultural workers. They are not itinerant, but they are still untouchable. Living as an agricultural laborer, or any kind of day laborer, is almost always a losing proposition. Most of the wealth is concentrated in the cities. People who live as small farmers or agricultural laborers suffer. Agricultural laborers have been the pariahs, the outcastes of former times, and to a great extent they still are.

Some remain bonded, at the mercy of their owners. But some do escape that life and find employment in the cities.

Middle and higher castes do not generally see themselves as oppressed but feel severely threatened when lower castes gain power. Those considered to be members of "other backward castes," as well as those who employ Dalits as agricultural laborers, fight harder than anyone else to keep the Dalits down (Narula 1999; Scuto 2008; Human Rights Watch 1999, 2008; Mayell 2003).[15] Intercaste marriage is an especially contentious issue (Shaji, Kumaran, and Karthick 2012; Subramanian 2012; Jagannath 2013). While a well-placed higher-caste man may marry a Dalit woman for progressive ideological reasons, if a higher-caste girl marries a lower-caste man, the whole family may be shamed and the girl may be in danger and despised. Even if a low-caste girl marries a man of higher caste, she and her family are likely to be subject to shame, as are the boy and his family. Only the most progressive families can make such a marriage work. Again, these are notable exceptions to the general rule. Other backward castes, sometimes identified as Shudras, are said by some Dalits to be the main killers of Dalits. But "other backward classes" (OBCs) still struggle for dignity, which they can find only in a caste-less society, by joining the Buddhist religion in the hundreds of thousands (Suryawanshi 2015). And the Hindu right is recruiting Dalits to become Hindus, from which category Dalits were previously excluded. Religions thus become political parties. For how long, in which countries, and by which religions has religion been used or not used for political purposes?

Before Dalits were invited to become Hindus, there was a movement in India called Hindutva, which still exists and professes to follow the social texts of ancient Brahmanism, equated by members of the Hindutva movement with pure original Hinduism. This movement controls the government of India now. From a different perspective, one may reasonably say that Hindutva represents a narrow understanding of what it purports to represent—that there was no original Hinduism, there were just assorted groups of people in what is now India, engaging in assorted practices, worshipping assorted gods and goddesses. As valuation of the Sanskrit language grew and as literacy also grew, Brahmanism took hold. In this view, a clear hierarchy of human beings existed, in which Brahmans owned and controlled the sacred texts. Brahmans in India became powerful because of their exclusive access to certain forms of knowledge. But Brahmans as a caste are not the chief oppressors of Dalits today. Some Brahmans, most notably Arundhati Roy, are supporters of the Dalit cause. By nature, one is not born a Brahman any more than one is born a Dalit. One must learn how to be what one is said by others to be. From this writer's point of view, Brahmans are not the problem. OBCs are not the problem. The whole caste system is the problem.

While Hindutva continues, a movement exists among modern Dalits in Tamil Nadu against Tamil nationalism of any kind, because these Dalits consider that Tamil nationalists have used rhetoric in support of caste abolishment to advance their own cause while paying scant attention to the plight of real Dalits, who are sometimes themselves considered to be foreigners from the north, with a language of their own, and therefore not really Tamil (Omvedt 2015). Kuṟavars, technically a scheduled tribe, are romanticized and at the same time excluded from advancement because of their supposed otherness. Modern Dalits consider that such romanticization is harmful to them, just as Gandhi's calling them Harijans and thereby romanticizing them actually demeaned them and did them no good. Some modern Dalits therefore may despise the image of Gandhi while elevating Ambedkar to first place in their movement.

As cosmopolitanism advances among Dalits, local knowledge and local dialects, most of all nonliterate dialects, fall by the wayside. But as long as violent oppression continues, a prime motivator of the old folk songs remains. Anger in traditional Paṟaiyar songs is directed toward the god of death (Yama), the blue sky, and the singer's own departed kin. Low-caste singers dared not express direct anger toward higher castes in traditional laments because of possible reprisal. This was earlier. Now some are singing of their oppressors by name, and what they sing of is not pretty.

Understandably, modern, educated Dalits reject the traditions in which they have been trapped for generations. They have been wrapped in a cloak of death, filth, and slavery that has constituted their very identity, and they want nothing of that now. Some of them work at office jobs in the cities, they are educated, and they do not want to be associated with this old, horrible, village life, still less with the monstrosities that lie behind the rituals. It is an act of bravery for them to come to the villages in which they were born, speak to a foreigner collecting village songs and stories, and remind her that something else is going on, an effort to free Dalits from all this.

Traditional songs of untouchables and modern literature of Dalits are bound by the fact that both address the oppression and violence to which these lower castes are subject. As violence against Dalits continues, Dalits, both women and men, become more bold.[16] Their boldness in turn provokes more violence against them. We have seen this before. The inseparability of caste oppression and gender oppression is clearly laid out in the songs of untouchable women, as in the song of Siṅgammā performed by Sevi. Violence against Dalit women is widely documented in modern Indian literature as well as in scholarly articles and media reports (Irudayam, Mangubhai, and Lee 2006; *The Hindu* 2013, 2014; Hopkins 2008; Office of the High Commissioner of Human Rights 2013; International Dalit Solidarity Network, n.d.; Evidence Team, n.d.; Gaikwad 2012; Krishnan 2014; Soundararajan 2014; Fontanella-Khan 2014; Tamil Nadu Women's Forum 2007). Domestic violence against women in India is carefully hidden within higher castes, in part because the better off have houses in which they can conceal what goes on within the family; but it is less easy for Dalits to hide. But what actually constitutes a "house," *vīḍu* in Tamil, is not necessarily what Westerners think of as a house. This matter is addressed extensively in the chapters on Sevi and Siṅgammā. I have asked a Tamil friend living in New Zealand what is the Tamil word for "privacy," and after some thought she declared that there was none. I looked it up in a Tamil dictionary, and the closest words I could find denoted "secrecy," something quite different from privacy.

Learning, education, language, and literacy are combined topics addressed in this chapter and others. Barring of untouchable children from school hurts them not only educationally but socially. A young adult has no way to hide his caste identity if he is a member of a Dalit group who is admitted to a university where reservations are held for members of such groups, as the student must carry a card stating that he is a certified member of a scheduled caste (SC) or scheduled tribe (ST)—in other words, an untouchable—in order to prove his status as a student. Reservations were meant to level the playing field, but they have not made education easier for those admitted under the SC/ST rubric. Known untouchables are treated badly in school and university settings. Girls and women born to untouchable castes are easy prey.

Sociolinguistics includes the study of dialect variation marking place, gender, and rank. This discipline enables one to see, among other things, that the dialects of the unschooled are not inherently inferior to the dialects of the schooled, that they tell about life as it is lived, remembered, and dreamed by outcaste speakers and singers, and by those with long memories. In modern India, literacy is necessary for advancement. One must know how to read and write the language that one speaks. But knowledge of one's own language is not enough. Knowledge of English is necessary. Such linguistic obstacles hurt Dalits. And oral literature by Dalit women, beautiful and telling though it may be, is ignored.

For Dalits, as well as for higher-caste people, linguistic cosmopolitanism is a key to success. Additionally for Dalits, success may mean abandoning, or "forgetting," their village dialects, because Dalit dialects are in themselves stigmatizing. Thus for a Dalit, success means ceasing to be what one was before, abandoning ways of life and ways of speaking that are identifiably low caste. In America, it is not necessarily uncool to speak or sing with a working class dialect. In India, it is.

In this respect, the situation of Dalits is in some ways the opposite of the situation of African Americans, some of whom deliberately choose to maintain and develop African American ways of speaking. If they can speak both like an educated white person and like an African American, as the situation warrants, their road to success may be smoothed somewhat as they can be comfortable in both worlds. William Labov has noted that in inner-city New York, blacks change their dialects so that they will not be understood by whites.[17] As soon as whites catch on to the meaning of a word such as "foxy" (this was decades ago) and start to use that word, inner-city blacks change their usage so as once again to be beyond the understanding of whites. Everything depends on the image of African Americans as having something extra, a style, a fillip, a kind of soul that whites can never achieve. Young whites want to talk like them, to listen to their songs and learn them, even if the words may be hard for whites to follow.

In India, the opposite prevails. There, educated Brahmans and others with multilingual knowledge practice creative code-switching between English, Tamil, Hindi, and other languages, so that people who do not know all of the languages mixed cannot follow them and can only look on in dumb admiration.[18] In displays of linguistic and intellectual virtuosity in South India, it is important that a person not show knowledge of low-class, low-caste, or nonliterate dialects, just as a high-caste person should not know how to do physical labor. Just as the clothing one wears has political significance, so does the work one performs and the language and dialect one speaks. This does not mean that all cosmopolitan and multilingual people are of high caste, however. Indira Peterson notes that in early eighteenth-century Tamil plays known as Kuṟavañci, the casteless Kuṟatti fortune-teller is sometimes adept in multiple languages, including English. The itinerant Kuṟavars I met in Tirurunelveli and Saidapet were also multilingual. For such a fortune-teller, multilingualism would have been both a practical and a magical advantage. The Kuṟavars were likewise cosmopolitan in the sense of having traveled to distant places, and some traditional Kuṟavars of modern days still make this claim of themselves. But Kuṟavars are not admired by Dalits of the present day. Conversely, despite differences in geography, history, and culture, modern Dalits have found inspiration in African American movements. The Dalit Panthers were thus named after the Black Panthers of the United States.

An obstruction to mobility, in addition to the other obstructions Dalit women face, lies in the obscurity, to outsiders, of present-day rural Dalit women's verbal art. In some forms of oral literature, the obscurity may be intentional. But it is also a consequence of the details of locale, of the language and its use in some social situations, and of local dialect variations, which are not to be found in dictionaries—what is sometimes called "local knowledge."[19] Therefore, in order for one to know what is being said, one must know the place where the singer or writer lives, one must know the people who live there, one must know how they live, and one must know the language in which they speak, chant, or sing. Whereas there are universally knowable aspects of old and new Tamil literature, oral and written, when local realities are not understood, the flesh can fall away from the bones. This is true of popular English literature of the present age, which is meant to appeal to a wide audience, as it was true of literature, both oral and written, when few people could read or write, and rural people steeped in local knowledge could not be well understood except by others who spoke the same language/dialect. In the current millennium, cosmopolitan intellectuals may lose all knowledge that cannot be conveyed in a universalist medium. The modern Tamil Dalit poetry that I have seen so far is not in song form but in written free verse form and printed. The oppressors in the poems are often Brahmans, although in Tamil Nadu, the oppressors are not so much Brahmans as high-caste landlords who practice a form of Brahmanism involving notions of caste-based purity and pollution. In the Dalit journal *Murasu* an explicit aim is to universalize Dalit voices. The prominent young Dalit poet Meena Kandasamy writes mainly in English and has won national and international prizes for her poems. Some may say that she has moved too far from her Dalit "roots." But who would want to go back there?

The unschooled are told that they cannot speak or write adequately. But the well-schooled, the powerful, the technicians, the managers, the professors, and some who wish to improve the lot of the very poor will not listen to and cannot hear what the unschooled have to say. Some of the privileged among those without privilege will learn the language of privilege. They are motivated to do so, after all. Few among the privileged will learn to speak, or think, like an old laboring woman from some village somewhere. Still less will they find the time to learn a "tribal" language. This is not just a matter of negligence and laziness, it is a matter of difficulty. The inability on the part of the highly schooled to learn the languages of the unschooled is a diminution of mental power for humanity. It is an intellectual loss for us all.

Claude Lévi-Strauss wrote that every human mind is equal to every other. It is the reflection of one mind in another that is the real thing, the real mind, free from external restrictions, just playing for the sake of playing, thinking wild thoughts. All human minds are equal on that playing field. Lévi-Strauss valued the great diversity of human cultures and the essentiality of communication among them. He pointed out that the people once called "primitive" are in fact people without reading and writing. Such people are more aware than the highly literate of realities that the literate do not see. A sacrifice is involved in the transition to literacy, but without that transition the accomplishments of the literate, communication among them, cannot be achieved. It is a trade-off, then.[20]

I cannot agree with everything that Lévi-Strauss says—in particular the nature/culture divide, which among anthropologists today is rapidly dissolving, and his omission of women and children, to say nothing of animals, as people of interest—but I do agree with the general idea that without a connection of one mind with another, without a reflection of each in the eyes and the mind of the other, without a great number of minds all connected and all reflecting and refracting each other's lights, there is no reality at all. For Lévi-Strauss, the story told, the myth, was more real than the minds that reflected and refracted it, like mirrors, among each other, without any awareness on the part of an individual mind that it was a vessel for the transmission of that myth. Likewise, for me, the act of communication, the fact of connection, is more real than anything to be found in a purportedly isolated mind.

A repeating theme of this book is the congruence between the verbal art produced by laborers in the fields of India and theories of the highly literate who come from far away. Is this congruence, this harmony, a sign that the theory works, or is it a sign that laborers in the fields of India have minds able to play in the fields inhabited by famous theoreticians? Lévi-Strauss's dictum that the meeting of minds is what is important, whether they are studying me or whether I am studying them, and the discovery that something in the distant theoretician's mind meshes with something in the proximal laborer's mind, shows that these minds, on the profoundest levels, know each other.

How does this happen? Life is less a matter of binary oppositions than it is a matter of mutual perception, less a matter of inheritance than a matter of development, less a matter of growing up than a matter of reaching out, less a matter of not touching than a matter of touching.[21]

The abandonment of traditional ways, and the learning of the English language, is stressed not only by South Indian Dalits but also by North Indian ones, who see it as the only way for them to escape the oppressive caste system under which they are compelled to live.

The spirit world is not exactly the same thing as religion. Religions have rules. Spirits have only habits, which they may change. Spirits in India, including gods, have no fixed image, no fixed stories attached to them. They have personalities, but these personalities grow in multiplicity as time wears on. A spirit is not independent of mortals. If nobody sees it or believes in it, a spirit cannot exist. A spirit can turn into a god only if some people decide to make it so. A spirit is not a thing floating through the air. It is not a thing at all. A spirit is a memory, a feeling, a desire. A spirit may occupy a living person, or a statue or a temple or a rock. A spirit who is a god is a movement, with fans and followers, who give money to keep it going, or in some circumstances offer their own suffering to the spirit, even sacrifice their own lives, to achieve a certain desired goal. Protect my son who has gone into combat. Protect my father who has lost his ability to work. Protect my sister from danger. Protect my children from hunger and disease. Protect the world. A spirit can give protection or cause harm, just as a living human being or animal may do. A spirit may instigate a war or fight on one side or the other. A person may believe or disbelieve in a particular spirit, or in a category of spirit. For instance, a man may say that Māriamman does not exist but that ghosts definitely do. A ghost (*pēy*) is the spirit of someone who has died. It is scary, and a person may die of fright from seeing it. But a pēy may be turned into something else.

This happened with Siṅgammā. The spirit of a woman who has died in childbirth is both honored and feared. A memorial stone is created for her, to soften her anger. An ancestor who has performed some horrible valorous deed, such as killing her grandchildren to save them from Muslim raiders, may become a family deity. Some live human beings are treated like gods. If a person gets high enough in politics, he can be a god if he wants to. Narendra Modi, the current prime minister of India, had a temple built to himself. Spirits like nice homes that belong only to them. Māriamman told me to build a temple for her to spread her fame. Siṅgammā demanded that a home be built for her, and so it was. If she grows in popularity, her home may grow into a regular temple. But such a growth is unlikely, as her people have turned to a more secular life. There is no structure to the spirit world. It is not in itself an organization. A spirit, great or small, may slip through anyone's fingers, in or out of a person's mind, or of many people's minds simultaneously. A great spirit such as Draupadi (Chapter 6, note 4) has done that.

Sarasvati (Chapter 1) had skills and experience that, in America, might have brought her higher education and a career. In Chennai and environs, she went to all the temples and participated in their rituals, but she considered that people who appeared to enter a state of trance were fake. She laughed at them and mocked them. I agree with her that some are surely fake, but you never know. At the temple, she slipped into the spirit world, or it slipped into her, when a Māriamman temple was being consecrated and she found herself desiring proof that, although the people she mocked were fake, the spirit world itself was real. The consecration ceremony was a conjunction between ritual and the spirit world. Sarasvati prayed to the god of the temple, Māriamman, that the god come for real into somebody, anybody. Then Māriamman came into Sarasvati herself. "She came into my person [*en peyarle*] only." At that point Sarasvati knew that she was special. From then onward, she and Māriamman were one.

The Pa̱raiyar singers did not show any sign that they thought themselves specially blessed. In their situation, how could they imagine such a thing? They did not mention any god but Yama, the god of death, and that mention was only in passing. Although they did not think themselves special, when they sang they became different people. Anyone who sings may feel this. The singers whose songs I recorded had no text, but they remembered, and somehow the song, fully formed, came out from them and the tears flowed. When you sing, something comes upon you or into you that carries you beyond yourself.

Kanyammā was by inheritance an Iruḷar, a person of the darkness, of the forest, and the forest was a spirit world in itself, a world that Kanyammā could bring forth only with difficulty. And Kanyammā was a woman who had lost her home, the forest itself, the whole boundless forest that was scary to some but mother and father to others, animated by many beings with many voices. Now, from the point of view of those above, she was little more than a ghost, or worse still, a useless half-dead body. But still she could sing. She sang of life in the forest.

By the time I learned of her, Siṅgammā had been dead for decades, her body buried in pieces behind a mill that had later been built after she died. The area behind the mill was surrounded by barbed wire, and I was not allowed to go there. In her life, Siṅgammā may well have sung, as singing was part of her work of selling birds in the marketplace. Sevi, the woman who sang the story of Siṅgammā, was not one of Siṅgammā's people. Sevi was of a caste considered higher than the one Siṅgammā belonged to. In her song, Sevi cast doubt on Siṅgammā's virtue. But the song was so beautifully performed that perhaps Sevi silently cared about Siṅgammā, regretted what had happened to her, and on a certain level saw the similarities between herself and the girl who had died.

Veḷḷaiccāmi performed a narrative/chant/song to and about Siṅgammā. In this performance there is no question that Siṅgammā, having died as a girl, lived on as a possessing spirit, attacking young, recently married girls of the area and ultimately becoming a deity of beauty, generosity, and power. Whether she will continue as a deity or will cease to exist is questionable.

At the end of this introduction are two questions: How does it feel, how must it feel, to be an untouchable woman? And how do creativity and insight arise from situations of abjection?

It must be said, first, that every woman who sang or spoke to me or for me was different from every other. Any generalization about Dalit women must be approached with care. Shared environments, shared memories, shared experiences, shared longings are some of the things that bind them to each other. In Chapter 1 of this book, Māriamman told me, "For Tamil women only, I will do much good." Tamil is a language different from any other. It is an old language. It is a world embracing emotions, pain, and oneness of self with other. Every language creates and is created by some world, some cultural ontology. The concept of Tamil womanhood both precedes and transcends caste. Caste is something that Tamil women have fought but have not been able to break. Instead, many of them are broken by caste. Such brokenness comes through in every chapter of this book.

Creativity, insight, and abjection are at the heart of the book I am writing now. It is not that you have to be suffering to make beautiful songs. Many fine singers/songwriters can attest to that fact. The question is why and how people living in deep misery are able to create things of beauty nonetheless. One is reminded of Maya Angelou's book *I Know Why the Caged Bird Sings.*

Here the similarity between the situation of African American women and the situation of Indian untouchable women makes itself known. Given all the great horrors that both groups had to endure, it may seem trivial to point out that both African Americans and Indian pariahs were denied education. But certainly both cultures were affected by this deprivation. Their songs may have given them the strength to carry on.

The similarity between African Americans and untouchables in India has been discussed by Gerald Berreman (1960) and more recently by Gyanendra Pandey (2013). A defining feature of African American memories and history is that they were slaves for hundreds of years and still are treated as inferiors and worse by some white Americans. Before independence, untouchables in India were slaves. Those then called pariahs included farm laborers, who could be used at will by their owners (Viswanath 2014).[22] Some, such as Kanyammā in Chapter 4 of this book, are virtual slaves now because they cannot run and have no place to run to. In other parts of the world there are child slaves and prostitute slaves. Does slavery in itself bring song from the slaves? It can, if the slaves do not mention the cruelty of their masters. If they do, they must be very brave. Kanyammā was very brave.

All of these topics are intertwined and inseparable from each other. Throughout the whole book, some named topics appear as parts of others. So does writing of my own experiences to the extent that they bear upon the topic at hand.

The people I knew in India were all good people. The ones I have written about in this book were brilliant and original narrators and singers who struggled with the handicap called womanhood, who were poor, had no schooling, were despised by the people they worked for, and were subject to domestic violence, as well as to the violence of men outside their families and castes. They never spoke or sang to me about such violence directly, except for Sevi, who spoke of the terrible violence against her sister, whom she never named, and against a Kuṟavar girl who died before Sevi was born.

I have been tempted to suggest that the very fact of suffering gives rise to beautiful creations. After all, what were these beautiful songs but laments? What were they but displays of pain? However, in the midst of terrible suffering you may scream out, but you do not sing. Afterward you sing laments, songs of sadness, songs of feeling blue. But while it happens, you lack the ability to speak. And about shameful and painful things that happen to you, you never speak or sing a word, ever. Generations later, your story may be told.

Chapter 1

Māriamman

One is not born, but rather becomes, a woman.
—Simone de Beauvoir

First Meeting

My first encounter with Sarasvati was in 1975, while I was doing research for my doctoral dissertation. She did not fit into that dissertation, but what she showed me was more enduring, if less elegant, than what I was able to write about then. The dissertation was about Tamil views of the living body. The people who taught me their views on this topic were a scholar who lectured about *Tirumantiram* and other difficult Tamil texts, an octogenarian Brahman Ayurvedic doctor who described his work as *nāḍḍu vaidyam*, "country medicine," and the women who worked in the fields owned by the doctor. The people who taught me were very different from each other, but their views were remarkably congruent, and so I wrote a well-put-together dissertation.

Sarasvati's view was completely different from that of my other teachers. She lived with a spirit with whom she struggled, a combative alter ego who told Sarasvati to do things she did not want to do, and not to do things she wanted to do. When Sarasvati rebelled, the spirit punished her. Both Sarasvati and the spirit were female, but they were not the soft interior female that my other teachers spoke about. This spirit was hard as rock. Sarasvati was tough, and torn between living the life of a good married woman and the life of someone else, a life like that chosen by the spirit Māriamman.

The story of Māriamman (aka Rēṇukā Paramēswari) is centuries old, as,

I learned later, was attested in a Sanskrit text. She was a woman betrayed by both husband and son, a Brahman woman merged with a woman of untouchable caste via the bloody murders of both. She came back to life as a goddess with the head of a Brahman and the body of an untouchable. She was angry and she controlled bloody diseases, most notably smallpox.

Some say that Māriamman was a much older goddess, pre-Sanskritic, therefore thousands of years old. She was and remains a spirit in control of the rain. But the disease of smallpox may have emerged earlier than Sanskrit, in the Neolithic, when the first cities appeared. A disease like smallpox needs large, close populations to continue, as everyone who contracts this terrible and terrifying disease either dies or is rendered immune. When a small isolated place with a small number of people in it is hit for the first time by smallpox, there remains nobody left to infect. To fight it, there was nothing for people to do but resort to whatever spirit they believed controlled it. Maybe there was a time in human prehistory when the spirits were kinder and gentler. Or maybe there was a time when there were no spirits at all.

The Māriamman that Sarasvati knew had renounced her family and children. But Sarasvati manifestly loved her children and grandchildren, both male and female. She was in addition an attractive woman and she liked to be that way. But Māriamman commanded her not to cook for her family and not to comb her hair or wear ornaments. Sarasvati obeyed the commands of Māriamman.

Some art, not all, as well as some theory, is autobiographical, in the sense that the idea for it comes from experience, from life as lived by the artist or theoretician. Einstein believed in unity and simplicity, in his own life as well as in the universe, and lived his life and developed his theory according to that belief (Holton 1988). Mikhail Bakhtin developed his literary theory as a model of the society in which he desired to live, a nontotalitarian society in which the ideals of Martin Buber held sway, and as a model of the kind of person he wanted to be. He could not describe this social and personal ideal as such, because he lived under the totalitarian regime of Stalin. So he encrypted it in his literary theory (Bakhtin 1978, 1981, 1984; see also Chapter 3 of this volume). Claude Lévi-Strauss (1978) found that the way his mind worked resembled that of the Amazonian people whose myths he described and analyzed.

Similarly, some gods, not all, are models of what their worshippers are, or aspire to be. The original Buddha was a model of what his followers aspired to be, as was Jesus, as was Mohammed. Māriamman is a model of what her worshippers experience themselves to be or aspire to be, as are some other Hindu gods, such as Ganapathi or Murugan.

Like all deities with name and form, Māriamman is a creation of human beings. Why did they create her in this form? Her worshippers say she has many names, many forms, and lives in many places. She is made by and of many people then. Her story, her forms, and her actions were created by many people, out of their own experiences and their own discoveries, and out of themselves. As Māriamman is unambiguously female, it is reasonable to conclude that she is made of and by many women. But it is said by some Western theoreticians that the mother goddess (including Māriamman) is a projection by men of what men imagine a woman, most of all a mother, to be.

Sarasvati, through taped interviews as well as through conversations, showed me something I had never thought of before, which was that the woman and the spirit she worshipped had been through similar life experiences, in particular, problems with men. Māriamman was, then, a model of what Sarasvati experienced herself to be, and Māriamman was struggling with Sarasvati, forcing her, to do what Māriamman in her life story had finally achieved. Māriamman had attained freedom by renouncing the ideal of perfect Tamil womanhood. Māriamman's is a centuries-old Indian story, but it resonates with what some American women experience today: that you can't have it all, that you have to choose. In one trance session, Māriamman (through Sarasvati, whose body she possessed on and off) engaged in a conversation with a young woman who had come with her mother. Māriamman aggressively asked the young woman, "Do you want life (*vāṛkkai*) or do you want work (*vēlai*)?" The young woman replied that she wanted work (vēlai), and she did not want vāṛkkai, which meant not only life but in particular married life. In Tamil, "life" or vāṛkkai is family life. Life outside of family goes by other names.

This young woman was now saying to Māriamman that she wanted to work and did not want to marry. The young woman's mother evidently wanted her daughter to marry and had brought her to Māriamman in hopes that Māriamman would bring the girl to her senses. Who, when, and indeed whether to marry are not uncommon disputes between parents and children in Tamil Nadu, but usually the parents win. I don't know who won in this case.

Sarasvati was intelligent and successful at her work. Unusually for a woman of untouchable caste, Sarasvati grew up in the Mylapore neighborhood of Chennai, had a retired businessman as a father, and spoke a Brahman dialect.

Her first name was a common first name for Brahman women. Parvati owns power, Lakshmi owns wealth, Sarasvati owns knowledge. When I played the tape of Sarasvati's narrative to a Tamil linguist, he asked in surprise if she was a Brahman. Brahmans in South India pride themselves on their mode of speech, which, among other things, differentiates them from lower-caste people. She was not, then, a rural Dalit woman. She was fully urban. But although she could "pass" as Brahman, she still, by birth, belonged to one of the lowest castes and had chosen their side when she might, with difficulty, have gone the other way. The path she chose was hard enough.

I learned from a famous Ayurvedic doctor who lived in the city that some people of untouchable castes learned to speak, act, eat, and appear exactly like Brahmans. That is, they could "pass" as Brahmans. The most famous singer of classical South Indian music, adored by Brahmans, M. S. Subbulakshmi, was said to have been born into an untouchable caste.

Sarasvati was, apparently, one of those of untouchable caste who could be mistaken for a Brahman, or could have been so mistaken had she not assumed the matted hair and unadorned appearance demanded of her by Māriamman. Sarasvati supported her family by working as a medium for Māriamman. Over the years, her clientele grew in size while she tended to her work, which entailed intuiting the problems of others and helping them overcome those problems. Some of her clients were Brahman women. Her sessions with clients were sometimes agonistic. Possessed by Māriamman, she would demand of her clients to say what they wanted, and would make them say it loudly. Through her tutelage, if one can call it that, some of her clients became mediums like herself.

Sarasvati did not speak of passing this work on to her daughters, however. She was more interested in passing it on to me. She spoke of the intelligence of her daughters, and how well they were doing in school. She saw that Tamil women were oppressed, and she worked in her own way to liberate them from the oppressors whose beliefs they had internalized, the men of their own families.

When I first met Sarasvati, in 1975, she was thirty-eight years old and I was twenty-eight. I was living with my husband and baby in Shastri Nagar, near Adayar, in what was then Madras. We were in the second floor of a bungalow on one side of a road. On the other side of that same road was what people called the slum—a settlement of mud huts. I was starting my research on concepts of the body in Tamil culture, casting about for people with whom

I could study and from whom I could learn. A young American woman living in the same neighborhood told me I should go and meet a priestess who lived nearby. So I walked over to the hut in which Sarasvati lived, carrying my baby, who was about six months old.

After that first meeting, I visited her regularly, and got to know some members of her family. I called her grandson *puli kuḍḍi* ("tiger baby") and my son *yānai kuḍḍi* ("elephant baby"). This was because my son, normal sized for an American baby, was so much bigger than her grandson, who was the same age as my son. I worried about the health of little Puli Kuḍḍi. I took Puli Kuḍḍi with his mother, Sarasvati's oldest daughter and first child, to see a doctor because he had scabies all over his legs. The doctor sighed and said, "I can give him medicine, but the scabies will just return. These people live in filth. There is no help for them."

At our first meeting, Sarasvati asked me questions, and I tried to answer them. I asked her if I could do a tape-recorded interview with her, and she assented, right then and there, but told me to come back a few days later. I think she wanted to assemble her thoughts.

We did the first interview, then the second, and Sarasvati sent her daughter Vasanti to help me transcribe. Slowly, word by word, we went over the tape. It took days; my knowledge of Tamil was sketchy, and Vasanti was manifestly bored. But I wanted to know exactly what Sarasvati had said. At a certain point, while we were transcribing, I looked up at Vasanti and said to her in my broken Tamil, "Your mother has an amazing mind!" Vasanti smiled.

I visited, with my baby, a number of times after that, watching the trance sessions that Sarasvati conducted, taking notes. But Sarasvati would not allow me to be just an observer and recorder. She wanted me to be part of what she did, to take a stand. I was shy and embarrassed, had no desire to commit myself to goddess worship, and did not know what to say. Māriamman was bold and insistent, however, and would not take my confused mumbles for an answer. She stated that I had come to her because I had "troubles with my husband." But I said that was not the reason. I had come for research.

When I first met Sarasvati, I was married with one child, and was also embarking on a career. I was not a feminist and was not thinking much about gender issues at all. Both my husband and my infant son came with me to this difficult place. I did not understand, then, that ultimately I, too, a Western woman with many roads ahead of me, would have to choose between life and work—or at the minimum, would have to chop off vital parts of both my life and my work if both of them were to survive and somehow thrive.

Although I was not a feminist, Sarasvati was, and so were many other Tamil women I met, whether or not they had heard the word "feminism," whether or not they could read. The knowledge that it is a misfortune to be born female was part of the air that all Tamil women breathed.[1] The knowledge that the gender system was unfair was obvious to them. We Western women had not come to that point yet, or some of us hadn't. Simone de Beauvoir tried to convince us, but still we refused to believe. We believed we could wriggle out of our misfortune, that biology was not destiny, that we could reach the top of the professional world and also enjoy a fulfilling family life, with all parts of both intact.

Māriamman exemplified escape of a woman from slavery through sacrifice. In her life story, she went through a kind of domestic slavery and decided to renounce it. Ultimately, Māriamman confessed through Sarasvati, "for Tamil women only I will do much good." I wondered then what Māriamman meant. I guess I was assuming that Māriamman, as a great spirit, had to be a universalist. In fact, she was enshrouded in the specificities of place, time, history, and culture. Most of all, a belief in the power of self-sacrifice is a significant part of the Tamil world. In this sense, Māriamman was and is very Tamil. However, Māriamman was also, in Simone de Beauvoir's terms, both immanent and transcendent. She had attained, in her own word, freedom (*moḍcam*).[2]

When I returned in 1990 to visit Sarasvati, Puli Kuḍḍi was in his midteens, handsome and sleek. By then, the LTTE (Liberation Tigers of Tamil Eelam, a powerful Tamil militant group fighting against the government of Sri Lanka for freedom from discrimination) was at the front and center of Tamil thinking. I had not yet started research on them, and only thought it was crazy for the LTTE (if it was them) to set off a bomb in the Madras airport, killing many civilians, leaving shreds of bloody flesh all over the walls and ceiling. I imagined that Sarasvati, basically a peaceful woman, would be opposed to the Tigers. And maybe she was. But when I asked her what she thought of the LTTE, Māriamman, speaking through Sarasvati, said, "I wear different colors. Sometimes I am peaceful, and wear sandal-colored clothing. But sometimes it is necessary that I wear red." I took this statement as a symbolic declaration on the part of Māriamman that she was in support of the LTTE and their violence.

That year was the last time I saw Sarasvati. Though she and most of her family were flourishing, a horrible thing had happened. Vasanti, Sarasvati's eldest daughter, had died. She had complained of back pain, and then she died. The causes of her pain and her death were unknown. When this happened, Sarasvati told me she fought again with Māriamman, saying, "You were our protector. Is this the way you protect my daughter? By killing her?" To this question, Māriamman replied, "Who is more important? Your daughter or me?"

There is more. At the beginning, I was afraid to ask Sarasvati her caste, because it was impolite. But one day I asked. She answered, "Chakkili." To me that meant "sandal maker," and I thought no more of it. Later I learned that Chakkili was not only a caste name but a deeply derogatory term. In some parts of India the main job of Chakkiliyars was removal of human excrement, and some of them still perform that work. The history of antagonism between Pa̱raiyars and Chakkiliyars is long-standing.[3]

During my research on the war in Sri Lanka, I learned that Chakkili is also a derogatory Sinhala term for Tamil. The implication is that all Tamils are as low and foul as excrement. The term Chakkili was most commonly used by Sinhalese for members of the LTTE, the Tamil Tigers, who renounced caste divisions altogether.

Another name for people of the Chakkili caste is Arunthathiyar, named after the unmoving polestar, Arundhati. The activists among them protest the fact that they must remove the contents of sewers, raw excrement, by hand, carrying it in pots or baskets on their heads. A person doing this work can pass out from the toxic fumes of the sewer and fall and die in the sewage. It is terrible work.

Arunthathiyar activists promote literacy and English-language learning for Dalits. They consider that, in India, learning English is essential for success. They search for and publicize white-collar jobs and university scholarships for which Arunthathiyars are eligible. They also publicize violence done against any Arunthathiyar. They protest the fact that Arunthathiyars are too often beaten, murdered, and dismembered with impunity.

In 2011, an Arunthathiyar woman, elected Panchayat president in a village of Tamil Nadu, was beaten by men who did not want to take orders from a Dalit woman. Four reporters, at least one of them himself of Arunthathiyar caste, visited the place of the beating, took notes, and wrote a report. They plan a documentary about this incident. The full report is too long to repeat here, but it includes these words.

> On the street next to her house, at the turning past Karuppansamy temple, they attacked her. Opposite the library she had built, upon

> the road she had laid, they stopped the auto. The auto driver leapt out and fled. They clamped her mouth and eyes shut. They had already broken the streetlight on the road to ensure perfect darkness. They pulled her head back by her braid. They cut off the braid. They cut off an ear. They hacked at her, all over her body.
>
> In photographs, she stands bold, straight and beautiful, radiating confidence and strength. . . . In every picture, she stands straight, shoulders square, her courage writ large upon her posture.
>
> In hospital, she lies on a stretcher, both her arms and legs, her body covered in bandages. Her head shaved, the scar of the lost ear turning a sickly yellow, a blood stain on the bandage on the left hand, her sister holding up the bandaged right hand because it hurts too much to put it down. "I am afraid now," she says. Krishnaveni, the brave. Krishnaveni, the strong. Panchayat president Krishnaveni, the woman who was given the title of Vīra Peṇmaṇi (Heroic Woman) by the women of her village. Panchayat president Krishnaveni, first woman panchayat president in the state to be attacked with such cold-blooded brutality. (Jayanth 2011)

A message one may draw from this article is that powerful women of the lowest castes live in danger in Tamil Nadu. In fact, all women of the lowest castes are in danger, whether they speak out or not. The protection of a powerful deity may or may not mitigate this danger.

The Narrative

The narrative comprising the bulk of this chapter is a translation from Tamil of my tape-recorded interviews of Sarasvati/Māriamman.[4] Although the interviews were conducted in 1975, Sarasvati may be in the same neighborhood, doing the same work still. She is, or would be, in her later seventies today. What is certain is that mediums for Māriamman practice now in Chennai, as Māriamman is a popular god, and spirit possession continues to thrive in urban as well as rural areas of Tamil Nadu. What I write below remains in the present tense.

The central portion of Sarasvati's mud house is a shrine for this deity. It contains an image of Māriamman—a triangular black stone with an angry face skillfully carved on it, with gleaming metal eyes and long fangs. Weekly the priestess adorns the image, first rubbing oil on its face, then painting it black with ink, red with *kumkum*, or yellow with turmeric, carefully outlining the eyes, then wreathing it with flower garlands, putting on its jewelry, and laying a clean petticoat in front of it. She performs this ceremony with all the absorption of a young person before a mirror.

She calls her mud house a temple, and neighbors and visitors also regard it as such. At the time that I met her, she lived there with her husband, ten children, three sons-in-law, four grandchildren, and several buffaloes, goats, and chickens. Although, through her skill as a priestess and healer, she had acquired some material wealth in the form of saris, stainless steel kitchenware, and livestock, she said that she could not move out of the mud hut because of the tradition that mediums of Māriamman live in poverty. That was then. Later she built a larger house in the same spot.

On Tuesdays, Fridays, and Saturdays, or whenever someone arrives with a special request, she calls Māriamman to come upon her. At these times, and especially on the full moon and other auspicious days, her house will be crowded with supplicants. Several hundred people may come to her in a single day.

When she is ready to call Māriamman, she leaves the house, bathes, and returns, and sits cross-legged in front of Māriamman's image. She closes her eyes and breathes the smoke from the camphor burning in a plate of ash before her. She yawns and is silent. In a few moments suddenly she shudders and lets out a roar. This is Māriamman. She caresses and scratches her body and tousles her matted hair. If someone has brought butter she smears it all over herself, eating some and giving the rest to visitors. She may stuff neem leaves in her mouth and wash them down with turmeric water. She laughs loudly, and begins to speak in a sign language to one of her sons-in-law or daughters sitting nearby, who interprets her gestures to the visitors. The gestures state who has come with what problem, and what the outcome will be. After this she whips her head around and around as in a bolero, scattering drops of water from her wet hair all over the room. Then she begins to speak, stating each visitor's problem and calling the visitor up to her. There is a tightness in her voice as though she is in pain. She speaks with each visitor, ascertaining his problem and promising to cure it. At the end she emerges from the trance by opening her eyes.

People come to her for mental and physical illness, for demon possession, or for family problems, or because they cannot find work, or they are not doing well at school, or they cannot find a husband for their daughters, or for other difficulties. Māriamman will give them ashes or lemons (both cooling) as medicine, will touch the afflicted with her hair (which conveys her power) or will blow ashes upon them or brush them with neem leaves (sacred to Māriamman and used for all skin afflictions), or she may perform more elaborate ceremonies for them, or she may simply promise that she will make everything well. When she is out of trance also, the priestess may perform similar acts of healing. On festival days, she organizes celebrations for Māriamman. She also performs *pūcei* (puja) or worship ceremonies on behalf of individual patrons who wish to secure Māriamman's blessing.

Although this priestess is particularly popular, there are many like her in Madras, men as well as women, though the majority are women. Similarly, the majority of the devotees of Māriamman in this city are women, who follow their own volition in coming to her temples. This priestess' strongest supporters are well-to-do, middle-class, high-caste women, who give the priestess gifts of clothing, jewelry, and money and seem to value her friendship highly, though the priestess is of an untouchable caste and lives in what the wealthier people of the neighborhood call "the slum." During trance sessions, the possessed priestess may sometimes be seen teaching one of her followers to enter a trance, coaching her in growling and spinning her head, and exhorting her, in the voice of Māriamman, not to be afraid. At least one of the priestess' middle-class Brahman followers has now herself become a priestess to Māriamman and a successful trance healer, in opposition to the wishes of her husband, transforming the structure of her family to serve the needs of her new profession.[5]

Māriamman is often pictured as a beautiful woman seated on a throne made of a many-headed serpent, and at her feet, a disembodied woman's head, Māriamman's own head, which acts as an oracle, like the stone in our priestess' temple. Therefore, when Māriamman speaks through the priestess, she sometimes refers to herself as one who has two heads.

Even as smallpox has died out, the popularity of Māriamman of smallpox has grown in recent years, as is evidenced by this priestess's success, and on a larger scale, by the newly flourishing condition of a large temple to Māriamman near Madras, the Karumāriamman temple at Tiruvērkāḍu. *Karu* means black, because Māriamman herself is black. The temple at Tiruvērkāḍu has become one of the wealthiest temples in the Madras area. Since the early 1970s (about the time of the eradication of smallpox in Madras) the whole temple has been rebuilt, together with beautiful ornate temple cars and stone sculptures created by top artisans from out of state, a large tank, and a new monastery. On Tuesdays, Fridays, and Sundays, buses to the temple at Tiruvērkāḍu are packed with people, as is the temple itself, so that it is almost impossible for all but the most aggressive to get in.

The worship of Māriamman in modern Madras is a blend of Brahmanical and lower-caste, non-Brahmanical components. The Tiruvērkāḍu temple has Brahman priests, who perform Sanskritic ceremonies for Māriamman. But associated with this temple, living separately from it, is a medium like our priestess. Our priestess also lives near a small, Brahman-operated temple to Māriamman, and such associations are the norm. South Indian Brahmans are strict vegetarians, but the mediums perform animal sacrifices to their own temples.

Our priestess is of an untouchable caste, but like some other Madras untouchables she knows the Brahman lifestyle perfectly and is able to imitate it down to the smallest detail. Unlike most untouchables, as herself she is a vegetarian. She was raised close to a Brahman neighborhood and her first name is a Brahman woman's name. Her speech contains many Sanskrit words and borrowings from Brahman dialects. She is proud to have Brahmans among her followers. But in the state of possession, her speech and comportment alter radically. She belches, yawns, scratches her body, rolls in the dirt, and kills chickens by biting through their necks and drinking their fresh blood.

Māriamman is said to be born of earth. The small hillock that she was born of is enshrined at Tiruvērkāḍu. Women have a saying, it is better to be born as mud than to be born as a woman. Earth is the strongest and humblest of elements; it bears everything, accepting excrement, yielding fruit. People also say that Māriamman has a form of wind, that is, she has no solid body of her own and must take the body given by people, either by possessing them or by entering the stone or earthen images that they make for her. Wind is the embodiment of motion and restlessness and is associated in popular thought with free-wandering spirits and unsatisfied demons, and contrasted with the peaceful higher deities. Wind is also the form of breath and of the soul. It is invisible, and so its color is black.

The name of the smallpox deity, Māriamman, has different meanings. *Amman* means "mother" or "woman." *Māri* means "rain." The rain is cool, and Māriamman likes cool things, foods that are supposed to cool the body, such as milk, coconut water, buttermilk, turmeric, lemons, neem leaves. It has been suggested that she is named after rain because the pockmarks she leaves look like the craters left by raindrops in the dust. But smallpox is a disease of heat; it used to strike during the hot months, and people believe that it is caused by excess heat in the body or by the heat of Māriamman's anger. The month sacred to Māriamman, when a large festival is held for her, is Āḍi, July–August. This is an inauspicious month, when nothing is supposed to be started, so no new houses are built, and young couples live separately during this month to avoid conception. The smallpox deity is said to hate the sight of a married couple. She is said also to hate the sight of a pregnant woman.[6] According to the report of a Madras physician who studied the epidemiology of smallpox in that city, pregnant women who contracted smallpox invariably contracted the most lethal form of the disease (Rao 1972).

A homonym of the word *māri* is *māṟi*, "changed," so that Māriamman becomes "the changed mother." This is the interpretation of her name that our priestess chooses.

The origin story of Māriamman is an old and well-known one, with numerous variants told throughout Tamil Nadu. In one famous version of the story she begins as a Brahman woman, whose name is Rēṇukā Paramēswari, as noted above. She is married to a famous ascetic named Jatharagni. She is a perfect wife, possessing perfect chastity, as a consequence of which she has certain magical powers. She is able to hang her wet sari to dry in the air without a line. When she goes to fetch water, she is able to carry it without the aid of a pot, by forming it into a ball and rolling it back home.

One day when she goes to the river, she sees in the water the reflection of a beautiful male deity flying overhead (some say this deity is a divine musician or *gandharva*, some say it is the sun, some say it is an airplane pilot). She remarks to herself in her mind that he is beautiful. Then she tries to roll her water into a ball and return home. She finds that she is unable to roll it up any more. Because of her trivial and momentary mental lapse, she has lost her perfect wifeliness and with it her magical powers.

She returns home and her husband sees what has happened. In a rage, he orders her son to kill her. The son pursues her with his axe, while she flees, taking refuge in the hut of an untouchable woman. She embraces the woman in fear, and the son enters the hut and beheads both of them with a single stroke of his axe. He returns to his father with news that the deed has been done. The father in turn grants him a boon. The son asks that the mother be restored to life. The father acquiesces and the son returns to the decapitated bodies and revives them by putting the heads back on. But he switches the heads, attaching each to the wrong body. Rēṇukā Paramēswari awakes to find that she has her own head but the body of the untouchable woman. She returns to her husband, who sends her away because she has an untouchable body. Thereafter she dwells in the forest alone, but in dual form. In this form she has been worshipped by Tamils for many centuries as Māriamman of smallpox.

Not only the smallpox deity but other deities as well receive massive support in Madras. One of these is the Catholic Veḷḷāṅkanni ("the White Virgin" or "Virgin of the Tide"), who is famed for her healing and other boon-granting powers. Near the Veḷḷāṅkanni temple, a Vaishnava temple has been built to Lakshmi. Visitors to one temple may also stop at the other; there is evidently no rivalry between them.

Each of these large temples seems geared to urban, middle-class tastes. Māriamman is portrayed in posters sold at the Tiruvērkāḍu temple as a smiling, doll-faced, pink-skinned lady, despite the lion she rides on and the adjective *karu*, "black," prefixed to her name. In the smaller temples and in the villages, however, the angry demeanor of Māriamman remains unhidden.

The blackness of Māriamman represents not only her anger but also her fertility. Often in pictures she is colored green. Her greenness is complementary to the redness of her male partner, the great deity Siva, whose name in Tamil means red, beautiful, and auspicious. Among Tamils, who are mostly dark brown, a light-skinned person is described as red. By the same token, the greenness of Māriamman represents her darkness. Green and black, the colors of vegetation, are the colors of Māriamman. Red and white, the colors of animal life, are the colors of Siva. Paradoxically, animal sacrifices are offered only to Māriamman, never to Siva. Siva's whiteness also symbolizes his purity, the purity of fire; Māriamman's darkness symbolizes the fruitfulness of water.

One of the most important attributes of Māriamman in India is her possession of many forms and many names. Thus the temple at Tiruvērkāḍu is decked with dozens of large paintings portraying the multiple forms of Māriamman, and the newly built Vaishnava temple is called the Ashtalakshmi temple, the temple of eight Lakshmis, each of which is given an equal place in the temple, like the many paintings of Māriamman in the Tiruvērkāḍu temple, and unlike the hierarchical arrangement of deities associated with the temples to the male gods. The multiplicity of Māriamman suggests not only that she embodies the changing nature of all life but also that she is found in all women, and that all women are equal.

Interview I: How She Became a Priestess

I was born in Mylapore.[7] My age is thirty-eight. At sixteen I was married. I have two younger brothers, one younger sister, and I am one. I am the oldest.[8] The oldest in the family is me. My name is Sarasvati.[9]

My father had a big business, a store. You know toddy? Liquor. That trade.[10] That is gone. Afterward, the *Hindu* [newspaper] office, he worked in the *Hindu* office. He is retired.[11] He retired in sixty-seven.[12] Now he is just in the house. Two years have passed since Mother died. Two years have passed. Now there is only father.

From a small age, from the age of eight, I had devotion to the gods. Often I would eat only once a day. In the person of the mother I had much desire. In the person of the mother only. Murugan and the mother I liked very much.[13] Often in the house I would fast. Friday and Tuesday I would go to the temple without fail. In Mylapore, the Kaṯpakambāḷ temple, the Muṇḍakkanniyamman temple, the Kaṯpakavalli temple, I would go there. After marriage, in Maṇḍaveḷi the Piḷḷaiyār temple. Every Friday I would put oil there, circle the temple and return. I did nothing else. In my sixteenth year. From the tenth year, some difficulty came to us. Then Kumāri Kamalā, the cinema actress—have you seen Kumāri Kamalā? She dances Bharat Natyam. In her house, our husband worked for her, as a driver.[14] He was working as a driver, and my father had no work; it was very difficult. After that, the two of us, we followed our desire and got married. In my sixteenth year, as soon as I came of age, in my sixteenth year, the marriage took place.[15] That happened, and in fifty-three Rukmaṇi was born. In fifty-three, May twenty-sixth. After she was born, the next one in fifty-six, this one, Vasanti, was born.

I had much devotion, I had very much devotion to the gods. Nevertheless, I thought that the mother was only in the temple. If she came into someone's person (possessed someone) I had no belief in that. If some shaman beat a drum and danced and all that, I did not like that, I had no belief in that at all. I would come up to them and tell them. If someone becomes possessed by a god, they are pretending, it is not a real god.[16] If I heard the sound of a drum and saw them dancing like this, I would wave my head and make fun of them.

In sixty-four, nine years ago, eleven years ago, we went to my father-in-law's house to shave the heads of all the children.[17] Thinking that we should go to that place and worship Māriamman, make an offering to Māriamman and worship Māriamman, he took us to that town. When we went, then too I was fasting. But I did not think that the god would come into my person. Then the priest of that town decorated the image of the mother and called her, trying to make her come into someone's person.[18] She did not come. She did not come upon anyone's person. I thought, "O Mother, who are you? Are you a god? If you are a real god, you have to come into anybody's, somebody's person." So saying, we prayed. When we prayed, in my family she came upon my person only. When she came, no one believed. Everyone said it was a demon that was in my person. Not a god. Everyone said there was a demon in my person, there was no god in my person, they said.[19] Then the mother said, "If you want to know whether I am a demon or a god, put fire in my hand and see. If I am a god, I will carry that fire."

Thus speaking, I held that fire, and put it on my head.[20] Then they said it was a god. Everyone believed. From then on, for this many years, if anyone had a demon, or if there was a sickness in the body, or if they were without children, for everybody she would cure it.

After that, ten children were born to me. Six girls, four boys were born. After Māriamman came, five children were born. When Māriamman came into my person, she said, "For five more years only you will have a married life. You may be with your husband. For this long, children will be born. If you have more than five [more] children, I will have no more connection with you. In the family, without a single desire or attachment to your husband or children, I myself will come to your house, I myself will suddenly come. To you I will give in this way my tangled hair and my appearance and all."

That is what that mother said. I must not cook in the family. I must not serve meals to a group of people. I must not go to a wedding. If anyone dies, I must not go to that. My whole body will catch fire and burn. After that, however we want to be, that way we will be. I do not put on wet [ritually pure] clothes, I have no Sanskrit Veda, I have no learning.[21] I do not know what that mother's history is. I do not know. But she, for everybody, whatever history they want her to tell, whatever cure or atonement they want her to give, whoever has whatever disease of the body, for all of that she will make a way.

[Interviewer asks if she remembers afterward what occurs during the state of possession.]

There is no recollection. If that mother comes, and after an hour says, "Will you ask anything?"—that I know. But when words are said, they come to me only in the form of feeling. I know that we say these words, but afterward, how we say them, how it happens, that I do not know. The feeling of it comes.[22] The feeling comes, when she ways, "I will protect you," that feeling comes to me.[23] Then the thought comes to me, "We spoke this way—will it be true?" But it will be true.

In dreams she will come directly. She has come countless times. Just the day before yesterday she came. That temple must be built. It is this kind of very small place. Everyone brought stones and cement. I was thinking, "By means of whom will this be carried out for me?" The place you are in now, can it be like this, without convenience for the people who come and go? Then she came, wearing a white sari, making a lap like this she was seated, holding a pot.

She said, "This pot will only fill halfway. No one in the world can fill this pot to the brim. If you pour gold, if you pour silver, if you pour rice, it will only fill this much. It will not fill completely.[24] Don't you worry. I am having a person make preparations. They will come and build this temple. Don't you feel sad. I am going to do good for everybody. Therefore I will make a group of people come, I will build and give you a temple." Thus that mother spoke.

[Where will the new temple be?]

This same one! This here! This here! It looks like we are building something of stone, doesn't it? Everyone bought cement and gave it. A few people, five, then, a hundred, two hundred, everybody put some. We are keeping it all in one place. But how to build a temple? Can I build it? I am living with eight children. Only one person is earning. I give them food, I buy clothes and things for the children, I have given three daughters in marriage, I have to see to that. How can I alone build a house? My husband gets a hundred, two hundred rupees salary. Can we eat on two hundred rupees? A group of people I have made better and done good for. For that, if everything is built and given, okay. If there is power [*śakti*], anything will happen. If there is power, it will happen by itself.

[What is power?]

She asks what is power. An illness comes . . . Now what have you come here for? You have come for research. If you go thinking of that mother, you will complete all your research perfectly. "O Mother, you must make everything happen. When I go, whatever you want me to do I will do." If you pray like this, whatever you need, she will do and give. Then you, following your wish, give me a gift. If I make everything better for you, you give what makes you happy. Then how, that gift, that is that mother's power.[25] It is the power given by that mother. I could do nothing. I have Māriamman herself. Karumāriamman. All power is one female only. Mothers have many names. For every town, a deity. For every deity, a name. For every name, a power. Some deities will not speak when they come into someone's person. They will not open their mouths and speak. When they come into the person of other people they will speak. When Māriamman comes into someone else's person, they will bite and eat a chicken. They will take camphor and put it in their mouth. She will not do all that in my person. That is a different power. But in my person, the power of that mother, whoever has a need, whatever is on your mind, she will say exactly. She will bring it about. There are different powers, but as long as she has been in my place, what has happened to me is just this.

[You said once before that you don't eat meat?]

Yes, I must not eat it. The reason . . . I have suffered much trouble. In the year seventy, marrying off the eldest daughter, we suffered much difficulty.[26] There was no food, there was no clothing, there was no comfort in the house, there was nothing. When I was suffering much difficulty, crying and crying and crying and crying, and I had to protect eight children, in this town there was no one of my heart.[27] I was in a separate house. He had his religion; I had a separate religion. And so many children, three girls had come of age, the whole group of children had to eat, all were school children, I had to buy books for school, I had to educate them, didn't I?[28] Then, with all those children, how to survive? At that time, from your country, from Germany, that woman came. Through her help, Vasanti was educated. But that woman went back to Germany.[29] After that, only Vasanti was educated. She came to the front in her studies. But she only studied to the ninth grade. We did not have the means to educate her further. Thus having all these troubles, I was crying. We married off the eldest daughter and stayed in her husband's house. He earned a salary, and for the sake of the children, eating only one meal a day, somehow we remained. Then my relatives all saw me and would not speak to me at all. "She has no money" [they said]. And with all these children, I was filthy; no relatives would come to my house. They would not even ask how I was doing. So much trouble I have suffered. I was alone with the children. Then Vasanti, Mallikā, Selvi [three of her daughters], and I went to work as construction laborers.[30]

Even before that, the mother was in my person. If someone's body is unable, she will come and protect them, everyone. If someone has a trouble, she will make it better. One Friday I wept, "If you are like this, why are you sending me to such labor?" I bought some poison. I was going to give it to all the children and we would die. I would give it. We could not stay in that town. There was no one to help us. No one came forward to protect us. So instead of this slavery, we all must die, I thought. So I bought bedbug poison and was going to mix it in their coffee. Thus one day I carefully bought it, and put it away, and lay down to sleep. All three or four children, without even coffee, silently lay down to sleep. Then weeping I lay down.

Then a snake came by way of the rafter. There was a stick there—now we have a bigger house, then we had a small house—it came by way of the stick, it went to the place where that mother was, and circled her picture. Māriamman herself. First it was seen as a snake coming, then that disappeared, then like a little child, wearing a sari and a jacket, she came running pitter patter like a little child, wearing a necklace, with her hair all braided, and flowers, saying, "Don't you cry. Tomorrow I will protect you, don't you cry. Tomorrow a woman will come to you, she will give you a hundred rupees. You cook and eat well and fill your stomach. That woman's husband has suffered much and has separated and gone away. I will give him protection, from then on I will keep you well."

Thus that child came and spoke. "Don't you cry, don't you cry." Wiping my eyes. "Don't you cry, I will come and protect you."

"Who are you?" I asked.

"Don't you know who I am? Look at me well," was all she said.

When I looked again, a woman of your height. In her hand a spear, a red sari, a red jacket, in her hand a fire trident.[31] Wearing a red sari with a yellow border, running to me she said, "Don't you cry, I will protect you, I have come, you will be happy. All those people who don't come to your house, who don't speak well of you, who don't give you comfort, they will all come to your house seeking you. I will keep you well; I will give you your own house; I will find good husbands for your three children; I will give you much money; I will give you cattle. Whatever you want, you believe in me, I will bring it about." Thus speaking, that mother disappeared.

From that day on—on Friday I had lain down crying, that night I saw the dream—the next Sunday a woman came, her husband had left her sixteen years before. In Alwarpet. Then that woman had gone everywhere to the temples, her husband had not come back to her house.

I knew the servant girl who worked in her house. She told her, "If you go to this place, that mother will tell you what happened to your husband, and will make him come home. But she has many children. Māriamman comes only in that woman's person. In the house there is no god [statue] at all. That woman has been there for three years. Before that there was no god or anything."

That woman came. She brought good money, much money. As soon as she came, I asked. She said, "I want to ask Māriamman. That mother Māriamman must give me some answer."

So I said okay, and bathed and returned and asked Māriamman. She answered, "In three days I will make your husband return. A prostitute has got your husband. A girl, a Malayāḷi girl has got him, has performed sorcery on you, and has separated him even from your language. I will heal that sorcery, and will bring your husband and join him with you." Thus that mother spoke.

As soon as she said this, that woman became very happy. She took out a hundred rupees and put it in my hand. As soon as she gave the hundred rupees, Māriamman was gone. After that I went and cooked meals for the children for two or three days, and it was that way. On the third day, her husband came. That woman's husband returned.

As soon as he returned, one of their children, a big boy, went crazy. His intelligence was not well. He would not brush his teeth. If he went to defecate, he would not clean himself. A boy who had finished high school. It was as though a madness had seized him. Then this mother healed him. The doctors said it was a brain disorder.

But when they said that, this mother said, "That is all untrue. That is all untrue. That Malayāḷi Brahman, that Malayāḷi girl, she went and did some magic. I will give protection."

So saying, she brought that boy here, said a spell over a fruit, rubbed it on his head, poured the juice on his head and made him well.

Because of that they became very happy, and they gave me six hundred rupees. They brought six hundred rupees and gave it to me, and said before everyone, "You make an offering."

As soon as that woman's husband returned, this mother said, "From the time that I protect you, only I can end all your troubles. No one at all will protect you. No one will heal you. Only I will protect you."

After the family was all well, this mother said, "For your sake, I have brought your husband back to you. You buy me a yellow sari, buy me a *māṅgalayam*[32] and put it on me. Only then will your husband stay with you until the end, without parting."

Thus she asked. After that, they brought the māṅgalayam and put it on her. After that, she cured many troubles for them.

I had many debts, having borrowed a little from everybody, and I was afraid that someone was going to come and ask to be repaid. Then, at that time, that mother brought various people to me and I healed them, and through them she made me well off. Today, I am a woman of her well-being.

[What kinds of people have come to you?]

Many. It is impossible to say who. Thousands of people have come. Last night there was a girl seized by a demon. They put her in a taxi and brought her here from Mylapore. When they took her to a doctor, he said that someone had poisoned her. They said, "No, a demon has taken her; that mother will say it is true." So saying, they carried her and put her down here. Examining her, we found that it was a demon. As soon as that mother gave her a lemon, that girl was healed. "From now on, nothing else will happen; take her and go," she said. The girl got up nice and healthy and went. Then they put ten rupees in my lap and said, "We came without telling the doctor. You did well." So saying, they went.

If there is asthma [using the English word] she will cure it. That sugar disease [diabetes]. Cancer in the belly, that disease.[33] If the ears don't hear, if the eyes don't see, she will cure all that. If you say it, she will do it. If you say that she can, she will do it. If you say that she can't she won't. If something won't heal, use a doctor to care for it. "By means of him, I will cure it," she will say.[34] "If you cannot do it that way, then I myself will heal it," she will say, and she will undertake it.

In an ordinary day, she will come three times. If we think of her and offer camphor, she will come as many times as we want. However many times people come to us, that many times I must bathe and be clean. I must not eat meat or anything like that. I must drink only plain milk. If I want rice or something, I will eat it. I must eat only what is prepared in the house. I eat only what is in the house. I must not go out and eat. I must not go out and eat in anyone's house.[35] If I do eat, it will not stay with me. I will vomit immediately. My eyes will burn, a great dizziness will come. Therefore I must not eat. Afterward, when she comes, she will be angry. "Why do you eat in all the houses?" she will say.

[In the picture on the wall, your hair is neatly braided. Now you wear it matted . . .]

My hair was neatly braided. Five years ago, she said, "You must not wear flowers; you must not braid your hair; you must not put oil and all on it." Now if I go to relatives' house, or if I go to anyone's house, ugly like this, they will laugh at me, won't they? But it is a true deity.

People were continually saying, "So this is the way it is with you. You say you won't comb your hair. You say you won't wear a *poḍḍu*."[36] They were continually talking like that. So when I went out I would comb my hair. Otherwise, those who saw me would think me ugly. I was continually doing that, saying, "I have my hair."[37]

And she was continually saying, "If you come in my person, you must not braid your hair, you must not wear a poḍḍu, you must not wear earrings, you must not wear nose ornaments."

If I wore earrings, blood would come in my ears, my ears would swell. If I wore a nose ornament, much blood would come, my nose would swell up, I would get a great headache, my whole head would throb. If I wore kumkum, my forehead would swell until it was round. If I took it off right away, it would get well. It was just like this. And she would say, "I tell you that you must not braid your hair, you must not comb it, and you keep doing the same things."

So saying, one night she came in a dream, she came in her own form, and she said, "If you adorn your face, my power cannot come to you. If bad men look at you with desire, my power will not seek that place.[38] If you do as I say, I will protect you."

And so she made me promise that from then on I would wear no ornaments or adorn myself. But one day I did. And she came in a dream and said, "Now, instead of wearing my appearance, you adorn yourself. You watch. I tell you and tell you, and you keep putting a comb in your hair and braiding it. I wear my form that has no comb. I wear matted hair."

So saying, she went. The next day when I looked, my hair was all matted. That mother has made me wear many appearances.

[You said that you must not speak with your husband?]

I must not speak with him. Before, we spoke all the time. Now five years have passed. You know that boy [her smallest child]? From the time that that boy was born, there has been no spoken word between us. Even if we did talk, there was no other enjoyment of the body. Even though we were like that, this mother came, and said, "Call your husband." And he came and offered her a mango, and she peeled off the skin and gave it back to him.[39]

Then, three years ago she tore off my marriage emblem and put it in his hand,[40] saying, "From now on, you must not touch her. You must not look at her or call her. From now on, between her and you there will be no relation of any kind. If anyone scolds her, if anyone does anything to her, I myself will punish you. Therefore, no one must touch her." Thus she spoke.

[How does she punish people?]

Suppose someone scolds me, and I can't take it and am crying. That person's body will become unable. She will give them some kind of difficulty. However we speak of her, she will punish us in that way. She will do nothing else.

I eat only what is in the house. I do not eat anywhere outside. If I do eat outside, I eat in a Brahman hotel, but I must not eat on a plate. I must eat on a leaf.[41] But now for a year I have felt no hunger. I have no desire to eat anything. Now it has been more than a year. To adorn her, to have that mother come into my person and to be continually doing good for all who come, that has become my only thought. If the children become sick, I won't take them to a doctor; I won't ask what they have. If anyone is in the house, if anyone speaks a little angrily, at first, from pride, I feel like I want to answer them with a beating.

[How does it feel when Māriamman comes to you?]

When that mother comes, our arms and legs tremble and shake. The nerves inside all tremble, and we cannot open our eyes. At the time when that mother comes, we must sit down and think only on that mother. "O Mother, you alone must do good for everybody." So saying, first we must think of her. How must we think of her? "Ōm nama sivāya. Ōm parāśakti. Kāñci Kāmāḍci. Madurai Mīnāḍci. Kāci Vicālāḍci.[42] Power with so many names who is one power, you must come in my person, and do good for everyone. To everyone without failing you must speak the truth." Thus we must pray to her.

When we pray to that mother, the eyes will be closed, it will be dark to us. Who and what there is, none of that we will know. Then in our body a feeling will arise. Like a trembling, all the nerves will convulse. Only after that will we be aware that our whole body is trembling. If we try to stand up, we will not know how. It seems that it is flying of its own accord. Then our feet dance by themselves, circling round. She is creating a dance in our bodies. It is she who comes and dances, her power it is. When she comes and dances, then in whoever's family is whatever evil, whoever has whatever trouble, whatever illness, whatever they want to take place, then in the person of that feeling, she will come and tell it. We cannot tell it. In that time, her wisdom is in our place. She will speak with our voice. Her voice cannot speak, can it? Our voice cannot speak at all. With her voice she comes and speaks to us. For three and three-quarters *nāṛi*[43] only she will be in our place. As long as she is there, that feeling is in our body. When she is gone, that feeling will subside. Then we will have our feeling. What happens after that, what has to happen now, we do not know. That is her power.

[What happens when a ghost possesses somebody?]

Ordinarily, if someone is seized by a ghost, a dead person, someone who has died leaving many children, that spirit will circle around in that family. It will not go out. Then, whoever it likes very much, in whomever's person it has much desire, that spirit will seize that person. The way the feeling of the mother seizes one, in the same way the feeling of the dead person will seize someone. When it seizes, it is wind. It has no form at all. But in that child's person day by day pain in the arms and legs, pain in the body, dizziness, it will not take food, it will take no responsibility in the family, it will dislike everybody, it will have no affection. It has so many characteristics. However she died, that feeling will dance in her person. Then her name, her address, how she died, how she lived, what she died of, how many days her sickness lasted, she will come in her own form and give word of all that. Then the feeling of this mother will come in my person, and will ask that dead spirit for a detailed explanation.

Now if in my person the mother comes, and in your person that spirit is attacking, as soon as the mother comes, that spirit of its own accord will come into your person. In the same way it will dance. When, in the same way, that feeling dances, the mother will ask you, "Who are you? How did you die? Of what did you die? Why have you come into this child's person?"

When she asks like that, you will answer, "I had this same kind of desire. When she came to a certain place, I, my spirit attacked her." So speaking, that which is in your person will give an answer to the mother.

Then the mother will say, "What is the matter with you? You have been here for so long. For you to go, what food do you want? Whatever you like, take it and eat it. You come with me."

Thus that mother will invite it away. It will take it. That is the power of that mother. It is true that ghosts exist. It is wrong to say that they do not. The disease in the body that the doctor cannot cure, the mother has the power to cure. The doctor is second to Māriamman.

In this religion . . . for all religions there is a deity. Ordinarily for you, you are Christians, that is that Jesus's thing, isn't it? In the same way, Christians have three kinds, seven kinds. Those people who say hallelujah, who don't wear jewels or anything, they too have belief in our deity. In your religion or in the Christian religion, however many mistakes you make, there is a husband. You follow your desires and make love with him and marry him. For ten years or five years they lie with him. If they write that they don't want him, they can take on the next husband. You must know that well. They can take another on, can't they? Then to your god you say, everything I have done is wrong. Creator, you forgive me. You take on all that sin. If you say that, your deity will take it on. Our god too takes it on.

At a small age, a child was married. Her husband failed and died. That child must be just like that to the very end. She must not wear kumkum again, she must not wear flowers, she must not wear beautiful clothes and jewels. The custom of that time. She must be just like that. Now even that widow can marry. One who is a small child can go to the next man's place, her life must not be ruined, an ugly name should not come to her, for her too they make a life. Whatever deity made that wrong, it is wrong. If there is a husband, to follow one's desire and want another husband, and be like that, is wrong. Our god does not like that.

For our god, we must make a prayer. For our god, if a child is sick, for that sickness to become well, for Māriamman I take a child's skirt and place it [before her idol], and place kumkum, and I put a garland there, and I pray. That child will get better. After it becomes well, we must go and do as we said in that prayer. If we do not, the same kind of thing will happen again. Our god has that power. For our god you must light a candle, mustn't you? A candle and roses. Just that, flowers and a candle for your god. For our god, we can do whatever we want. Every god has its way. For Māriamman, *cuṇḍal* [a kind of bean dish], sugar *poṅgal* [rice cooked in milk], they sacrifice a goat, they kill a chicken, they do all that. For your god there is none of that. For your god, killing a chicken and all, and coming as feeling into someone's person, does not exist. Does it? Your Jesus does not come into anybody's person. Only in that Bible, his birth in truth, in truth his coming and disappearing in light, because of that you put a cross [before his image] and pray.

This mother is not like that. In a town, when they put up an image of a mother, and perform a great ceremony, and make oblations, and perform worship for a god, the power of that mother will come into that place. That is a great temple.

[What people will Māriamman enter into?]

That mother will not come and celebrate in everybody's person. She has a desire. The heart must be clean. Lies, thievery, a lack of charity toward people, if you have these qualities, she will not come. There must be charity. If there is hunger, for that mother you must do good. Mustn't you? In a family, you must not cause any harm. Into the place of that kind of heart only, that mother will come and she will stay. If Māriamman comes, if that mother has come bringing pearls [pox], we must not call a doctor. We must not use a needle, we must not give medicine, we must not take pills. We must think of that mother, grind turmeric and neem leaves and apply them, and give good, cool substances. Coconut water, milk, buttermilk, varieties of fruit, we must give all this. We must not give hot spices. We should not give meat and all. Like that, for the mother. That mother makes pearls [causes pox]. In the person of a child, or in the person of an adult, following her desire she comes, because she feels attracted to someone she comes. She will not enter everyone's person. Ordinarily, the kind of person she likes most is someone of an untouchable group. In such a person she has much desire. Into them she will come very often. She will come in a Muslim's person. Christians—she recognizes no caste or religion. She will come in every kind of caste. But, only in your religion she will not come. Will she come in your religion?

Has the mother come to you? In your religion she will not come at all. In all the other religions she will come. In your one religion only she will not come. Because . . . desire. We have a belief that in your heart is a god. Nevertheless, you will not use it. You will not use her power.

Now you are doing research to see what she is. Does she have a form? Does she have a power? What all can that power accomplish? This whole world, that is her power, isn't it? The creation of man is her power. She has a power to create. The saying that the harvest of her life is peace, that is a power. Everything is her power only. Therefore, we are unable to accomplish anything. By our own efforts we can do nothing.

Those who do not have the devotion of Māriamman, they do not know belief in her at all. They do not know what she is or what her belief is. To those who have her belief, "If we make even a small mistake, it is just because we made this mistake that we must be like this?" So saying we must pray to that mother. Mustn't we? When much trouble comes, when there is a torment that we cannot change, that will not go away, "O mother, you will end my sorrow." But she will not come directly and give us money. Her way is this: for our living, for our earning, the way of clearing our debts, is that by means of her power, somehow or another she will show us something. If we go to this place, something good will happen. Her work will bring about good for us. If she seeks and gives us work, from that work we will be able to move forward. Because of that work, praise will come to us. Because of that, we will be able to clear all our debt and lead a good and happy life. Thus a word of feeling she will come and say. That word will be true. That is her belief.

She has a name, she has power, she has substance, everything is in her hands. We cannot stand opposite her and ask her who she is. According to the wish of her mind, whatever she wants she will accomplish. If someone says, "This is wrong. You are no deity. Where is Māriamman?" In that place, very close to them, she will not show her power. Patiently waiting, afterward she will show it. People will say there is no deity, they will not be good. The foods they eat will not be good, their family life will not be peaceful, they will have no learning, they will have no good customs.

[Even if someone has no learning, can't he be a good person?]

A man who has no learning is poor, but he will have that mother's devotion. If someone wants to do research in the world, they can do nothing. But the man with devotion, no one can deceive him. In any life, in any labor, he will have all wisdom. The reason is that he has that mother's grace. Because he has belief, even if ten people come to get him, he can say, "Go away. My mother is here to protect me."

Those ten people will think he is lying. One of them will say, "Let your mother come and speak in person. I'm listening." Thus he will ask.

But what word is that? A word without action, a word of disbelief. But because the man who has no learning has belief, he will say, "My mother somehow will protect me."

And what will the educated man say? "I have education, I have money, I have everything. What do I need a god for? I have more charity than a god. Do you have the luxuries I have?" Thus he will ask.

But how is this? Do you understand? The educated man will suffer disease, he will suffer torment, in his family a lawsuit will arise. He will not have wisdom at all. He will have money and luxury. But he will not have the stomach to eat till his stomach is full. She will cause a disease to arise in his body.

But the man who does not know how to read, look at him, if any disease comes into his body, he will say, "Only you, O mother." Gathering up sacred ash, he will put it in his mouth and say, "Only you can protect me." And in the morning he will be well. He has belief. Everything will happen to the man without belief, but she will never make it better. That is her power. We cannot ask, unbelieving, "Do you exist or not?" Even if we ask, we will get no answer. Thinking that what is made to happen will happen, and being at peace, is belief.

But suppose that, in some kind of place, nobody keeps her alive, no one performs a consecration ceremony for her, there is no temple, therefore there is nothing. She must cause it to occur, with someone assuming leadership for the temple. Then, in what way do you keep that mother? She comes by means of me. Using me, everyone will come and see her. Everyone will hear her.

In the same way, if a big temple must be built, there will be in that town someone with a good charitable heart. Whoever is honest, and true to the truth, she will come to him in a dream, and tell him, "Build me a temple in this place. You alone must make the effort to build it. I desire to come and live in this town."

When she speaks to him thus in a dream, immediately he will make the effort, gather the people of ten towns, make gateways and build a temple. There he will place that mother's statue, and then, just as Māriamman comes in my person, in the same way that mother will come into someone's person, and say, "This is my name. To this form, give this name." Thus speaking, he will say that mother's name.

Besides that, the people of that town will perform the consecration, they will make offerings to her, they will light lamps, they will plant a neem tree. All of this is by her power only.

Ordinarily, we will not be able to eat neem leaves. But when that mother comes into my person, she will take many neem leaves and eat them. And she will drink much water. Can we consume all that? When that mother comes, if she comes in the month of Āḍi (July–August), at the very first you must give her neem leaves. She will chew them well and fill her belly with them. In my person she will eat them. Māriamman will come and eat them. Then if you mix much turmeric water and give it to her, she will drink much. Whoever gives coconut water, she will drink it. Whoever gives milk, she will drink it. But we have a belly of only a handspan. Ordinarily, if we drink one cup of coffee, we will be unable to drink another cup. Even if this is the way we eat, when that mother comes, we will be able to eat continually. Through us she eats. Through me she eats all that. If a drop of blood comes on our body, we can't bear to touch it with our hand. But she will take a whole chicken, take it in her mouth and bite it, and skin its belly. The chicken will die. She will put it down. She does that by means of me. Thus for one form, there are many powers, there are many substances. That which is a deity is one deity. Some people come and say, the mother is this or that. What they say is all wrong.

Interview II: An Evil Sorcerer

I was very sick. At that time this girl had been born and was seven months in the arms. At night a fever came to me. As soon as the fever came, from my belly to my chest there was a great burning. I could not eat hot spices; I could not bathe in warm water; sleep would not come; hunger would not come; if I cried "hhah," a bunch of blood would come. From my mouth I would bring up bloody, bloody vomit. Then for that child, we went to see a doctor. The doctor said, "This is a disease called TB, therefore, you must be very careful. This is a very dangerous disease. In your heart, there is no power at all. It is all burned up. Therefore, you must not wear silk, you must not eat hot spices, you must drink milk with ice in it. We must take X-rays of you." So he said. Then I said, "I have children, and an unable body. When the neighbors see the disease that we have, they will be afraid. They will say, 'She has some kind of dangerous disease. If we go and have spoken words with her, it may come to us or something.' And they will be frightened. At such a time, one cannot even bring a relative and keep them in that place. And I have to clean the children. I have to see to their food. And I have to see to my body. How can I do this? There is not even a man in the house."

At that time my father was not in Chennai. My husband was a driver. The owner of the car had taken him and gone on a two-month tour.

So from the doctor's office I called the owner and said, "My body is very unable, it is serious, you must send the man of our house [my husband] right away." Then he said, "What is the matter with your body?" Then I said, "I have a great bloody vomiting; the doctor said it is very serious; he is going to take me to Royapettah Hospital for X-rays, and then send me to Tambaram Hospital and commence treatment there."

As soon as I said that, what did this man do but make a long-distance phone call. From the office to the house he made a long-distance call. "There is much danger in your house," he said. "You must start home at this time. You must send your driver."

By the time he came home, my health was completely gone. It was very serious. When I lay down, at one time my whole body would be like ice, and at another time it would be boiling. I was vomiting and vomiting, and there were pearls and pearls of sweat, my whole face had darkened, my whole body had become black. I could not speak at all. If I tried to speak, there would be pain in my chest. I could only show things with my hands. That much power had been lost. Immediately, they took me to Royapettah Hospital to show me to the doctor. At that time, that mother had been in my person for only a year. We were not accustomed to being thus without the use of this body. She was in my person. But no one came to me to ask anything of her. If there had been older people, they might have done it. But there were no older people there. How could I do it myself?

It had been a year since she had come. Before the next year was over, this was a test of me. She created this disease in me to make me believe, as a way of saying, "I am here."

Out of all the doctors in Chennai, one lady doctor saw me. She was called Kaṇaka Valli Nilāvati. That doctor too said that this was TB. After taking the X-rays, this TB disease has to be treated in Tambaram. The doctor wrote a recommendation, a letter, and gave it to us. We took it and went straight to see the doctor. She tested my whole body and said, "Only if you come into a dark room and let us take X-rays can we make a decision."

It was she who reminded me, the doctor who reminded me. She said, "If your god is a good god, you say that you have six children, that god will protect you. You should pray that you should not have this disease." As she was taking the X-rays, she said those words to me. After she said this; she said, "It would be very difficult for you to be admitted again. There are twenty injections for this. You must take these twenty injections. You must take four of these pills a day. And you must take eight of these pills a day. After that, if it is healed through that medicine, you will not need to be admitted. You must rest. You must not speak. You must not cook for anyone over fire. You rest. Otherwise, go to a peaceful temple and sit down. Or else, go to a beach and sit down by yourself. That beach wind should blow upon your person."

That day I had come wearing a silk sari. She said, "Mother, you must not wear this sari. Wear an ordinary voile sari; silk is too hot. Therefore, don't you wear this." Thus she said.

After hearing all this, we came from there. As soon as we entered the house, it got worse for me. She prescribed an injection. We were wondering which doctor to go to to get the injection. Then my uncle telephoned my husband at work, and he came. As soon as he came, he said I was going to go, I was going to die. My husband wrote letters to all my relatives, telling them to come. The house was full of people waiting. They put me on a cot, and they turned on the fan, and kept guard. They did not have the heart to carry me away. They thought if they took me to the hospital, I would die. Besides, if we went to another hospital, how could so many people stay there and keep watch? They were expecting all of these things. Then my uncle came directly. My husband's employer gave his car and said, "If you want to take her to a doctor's house, take this car and use it. First take care of her body, she has six children; that child is a good-hearted girl, you protect her however you can." So saying, he himself, our employer, gave us five hundred rupees, and said, "You must take her first to a doctor; I will recommend you to a good doctor. Whatever doctor you go and see, you telephone that doctor's address to me, I will recommend you." So that employer spoke.

After that, each day we were suffering a great agony continually. My uncle came and took me to the doctor at Lodhra Hospital. He was a good Murugan devotee, with sacred ash on his forehead. They took me in a taxi and made me lie down in a room. The man in Lodhra Hospital looked at me and said, "What does she have?" They answered, "This bloody vomiting will not stop, sir."

We saw doctors in all different places, and he took me to Royapettah Hospital and gave me an injection in a vein. As soon as they gave it, it was lost. Half the needle stuck in my vein, and half the needle was broken. It stopped at the vein. It would not go in. Immediately they came there and tied ropes and things, and gave me intoxication [anesthetized me], and pushed and pulled this and that, and cut the needle and got it out.

From then on, I did not go. If they gave me an injection, it would not go into the vein. If any doctor put medicine in the needle, the medicine would not go inside. The medicine would come out. They were baffled by this. They were frightened and said that my circulation had stopped, therefore the injection would not go in. Thus they said.

With that, we left. They took me to Lodhra and made me lie down and did tests on me. He came and looked. My husband began to cry, "I have this many children, it has become this serious; you must protect her, you must protect her." So saying, he wept.

Then the doctor who had comforted me said, "This is nothing dangerous; whatever disease this is, I will give something for it; give her that medicine, the tonic and the pills; put a little ice cream in milk, and give it to her ice cold. If you give her that, it will be a little restful for her. Even though I haven't given her a pill to sleep, I am worried. There is much weakness in her body. You must not put any shocking news in her ear. Even if she gets better, for many days she will not have the power to bear shocks. Therefore, the god must protect her." This doctor thus spoke in the same way. Then he prescribed injections and pills and said, "You must take an injection every other day. Take this pill continuously," he said.

I said, "Okay." Then he said, "Bring the medicine for the injection and come, not today but tomorrow." He prescribed only the injection. But when I went that day, he said, "We have no injection medicine; we are out of stock; come tomorrow and take this, just take this pill," he said and gave it to me.

We came from there. When we reached the house at seven fifteen that night, they carried me to a cot and laid me down on it, and everybody, my mother and father and brothers and all had come and were sitting down crying. The children were all on one side, everybody on one side. Because of being brought in the car and the bus, I had become very tired. I was in a swoon and not aware of anything. My health was completely gone. Then laying me on that cot, everybody wept. So many people were on the doorstep wailing, "O Sarasu, you good heart, you are gone, *ayō*, little girl, you have left all your children." In the middle of the road they were standing, really wailing and crying. I was not aware of anything.

After that, after the crying and so forth was finished, it must have been about ten thirty, at that time a mother, well decked out, wearing a yellow sari and a yellow jacket, wearing sacred ash and kumkum, in her hand a lemon, carrying sacred ash, carrying neem leaves in one hand, an aged woman, her hair all gone white, of a ripe old age, with a bag under her arm, a bag that looked like a bag of medicine under her arm, taking that lemon and the neem leaves and sacred ash, told everyone to stand out of the way.

Except for what this old lady did, which it seemed that I saw directly and well, the weeping and all did not reach my ears.

"Why, why do you cry," she said. "Get out of the way. Look at this, I am going to make her well. Why do you care for her with a doctor and with medicine?" Thus that mother asked.

Then from my head to my chest, that mother rubbed sacred ash and neem leaves, and said, "Do you expect her life to be destroyed? This life will not be destroyed now. Only at the age of sixty-two will this life, this soul, come to peace. To make the world believe, I caused this disease to arise in this body. Even she has no belief. Therefore, to make her believe, I have caused this disease to arise. Only we can make it well. Medicine, pills, injections, you must give none of these." So speaking, she took from her bag a piece of turmeric and a green leaf. She crushed it well, and put it in a conch shell, squeezed the lemon and put the ash there, and said, "You must eat only this medicine. By tomorrow, I will make a way for you to eat good food. Do you know who I am? My name is Rēnukā Paramēswari." Thus that mother said. "My name is Rēnukā Paramēswari. Tomorrow I myself will come and bring about anything that you wish to happen. From this day, you must not use a doctor or take medicine." So saying, that mother disappeared.

That was all. After that, after one hour, in my health, in my body, I let out a deep breath. When I let out the breath, sweat poured from my body. I had died, they thought, and they wept. My breath had come, and without my knowing, water had come on my body. After that, I blinked my eyes, and opened them, and looked around. It was after eleven o'clock when I opened my eyes. Then everybody stopped their crying and said, "There is nothing wrong with Sarasu, Sarasu has survived, she has survived, there is nothing at all wrong with her, she has nothing at all, nothing at all."

When it was still very dangerous, that mother came into my

person and said, "Hey, why do you have to plant a needle in her body? All the needles that you give will break. Just watch. It has been exactly a year since I have come, and you have not worshipped me. Don't come to me and ask, 'Why didn't you protect her?' To make her believe, I have caused this disease to arise. From now on, blood and so forth, nothing like that will come. She will have no disease at all. Tomorrow, go take her and show her to people."

That was all. From that day to this, so far we have not given even ten rupees to a doctor. That disease does not exist in me. Otherwise, when this hot season came, this bloody vomit would always come to me. When I was pregnant I would vomit like that. Ordinarily, when the heat was excessive, it would come like this. After that mother came, she made that disease cease to exist, for eight years.

After the disease left, in the end this girl was born, and she told me in a dream. This is the seventh child, and she was born in the eighth month.

[That mother said,] "That seventh daughter of yours has been born. She will be in my form. You must give her my name. Call her Rēnukā Paramēswari." So she came and said.

In that way, I have called her Rēnukā Paramēswari. We had given her the name, "Love." She didn't cry, she didn't drink milk, it was as though she were dead.

That mother said, "Call her by my name; I will make her cry. I will give her all powers."

After we called her Rēnukā Paramēswari, she drank milk. Today she is well. In her studies, in everything she gets the first mark. Since she was born, many astonishing things have happened in my house . . . .

After that, so many people driven by demons have come, people whose bodies were unable, people whose families were not well, people whose lives were not well, to all of them, if she said something, all went well. But that image was not in my house. That mother's object was not there.

At that time I lived in a rented house, and for so many days suffered hardship. We had to pay fifty rupees a month rent. What he earned was a hundred and twenty rupees. How could I eat on seventy rupees, and feed seven children? We would eat one meal and skip the next. When my relatives saw me they wouldn't look at me a second time. They would not even come to my house. They would not ask me how I was. They said, "She has borne nothing but girls. How is she going to marry off all those girls?" They said all of that then.

After she healed my body, I would not forget this mother. She had saved my life. Other people did not believe that she was the protector of life and family.

I would say to her, "Those who abuse me because you are here, you must protect me against them."

Afterward, in sixty-seven, that mother showed me this place. In sixty-seven, I came here. As soon as we came here, she said, "I myself am going to come and settle in your house. But no matter who you have, no matter how many kinsmen are yours, no matter what money they give you, your poverty will not cease. I myself will come and sit in this place and protect many families, and heal many people's ills. I will keep them in a good way and happy." Thus she spoke, and those words even today continue to happen for me, without fail.

Three years have passed. The fourth year has been born. But whatever person, whether son, or son-in-law of this house, or someone from outside, says a word to me keeping in his mind some wrong, as soon as I hear it, for some reason a rage[44] comes to me. I cannot stand to hear such words. Then my rage becomes four times greater than theirs and the power to question them comes to me. Later, in my mind, a kind of shock comes, and we wonder, "Why did we question like this?" Then we know we have done wrong and we ask, "Why did we speak like this?" But for that, too, "To make peace, this too is all right." It is as though someone comes and says this in my ear.[45]

Since that mother came, no disease has come to me. But this year, on the thirtieth of January, thinking to himself, "Does she have such power?" from Saidapet, all spruced up, he came. On Tuesday night, when *kuṟi*[46] was taking place here.

"The whole world could catch fire and burn. Whoever performs sorcery and causes trouble for a family, if you go to this place it will end. If studies are not going well, that will change.

Whatever trouble is in the family, she will heal it." So speaking, everyone in Saidapet was praising us.

He was listening to all of this, and he set out on the thirtieth, so as to arrive here on the first. When he got here, he sat down in a chair outside. He did not come in. He was sitting outside.

The mother came. As soon as she came, she said, "Hey, you make money out of my power, you are a destroyer of people's families, a destroyer of chastity, a destroyer of families, a spoiler of lives, a creator of many kinds of trouble. You take me, and in my place, you torture me. This is why you have come. You have come to destroy this lady. You could not destroy her before." So saying, she called him.

As soon as she called him, he was afraid to come inside. He came to this place out of jealousy, thinking, "She has shown us up." When he was seated outside, they say she called him, saying, "Come here. I have come to do only good for you."

When he came in, she said, "Do not give me room for destructive power only. Do not call me. I am not a destroyer. In this place, I am a creator. You have come with a power to destroy. If you can, destroy. Only beyond sixteen feet from me can you destroy. In this place you cannot destroy. In truth, I am in her person. I am made of earth. Because of my greatness, I am in that lady's person. She does not know sorcery, she does not know Sanskrit, she does not know *slokas*. She knows nothing of my history. She does not even know how to read and write. I have come into such a woman's person. Therefore, you cannot destroy her." Thus she spoke.

After that, thinking, "She has exposed me," he went sixteen feet away, took mud from my left foot and went, and called a hard place to come [on my foot]. For sixteen days I was bedridden. He made my foot unable to walk well. Afterward that mother came, rolling a lemon, and she said, "You must not go to a doctor or use medicine. For fifteen nights, this will be painful. For fifteen days, you will have torment. On the fifteenth day, I myself will come and make it well. Thus speaking, she gave me a neem leaf and turmeric, and told me to use them. I used them, and on the fifteenth day, the carbuncle broke by itself. After it broke, it became well.

But to destroy me, how many sorcerers come to this place.

> This whole town thinks of me with enmity. But I do evil to no one. Everyone should be well.
>
> I pray, "O Mother, if anyone comes believing in you, you must speak truthfully to her. Everything must happen truthfully. If you ask them to make an offering, and they make an offering for you, you must show them twice that share of wealth. Whatever boon they ask of you, for that boon you must give a suitable answer, and in that place you must always stay as protection."
>
> In the same way, still. Whatever sights there are, whoever sees them, that is her power. There is nothing that we are able to do. I have no desire to build a fine house and lie in it. To build a house of several stories, to be good and Sanskritic, all of that I don't want. Except to be without poverty, to be without disease, peacefully in the family, creating one heart for all, to be happy, other than that I have no thoughts of how I want to live. At least, there should not be disease, there should not be quarrels in the family. These two boons only I ask of her. I have nothing else.

Thus Māriamman tested Sarasvati, using not smallpox but tuberculosis to do so. Despite the change in disease, however, many of the key symbolic properties of smallpox remained, in new guise. For instance, one of the outstanding characteristics of smallpox, as interpreted by South Asian culture, is that it was a disease involving extremes of hot and cold. Here, Sarasvati interprets tuberculosis, which does cause chills and fever, in the same way. She said that she had a great fever, all the "power in [her] heart" (itself a significant image) was "burned up," and the doctors therefore advised her to keep her body cool and to eat milk with ice and ice cream. Instead of "pearls" of pox covering her body, there were "pearls" of sweat, and beneath the pearls, a darkened (flushed) body, such as appears with smallpox also. Bloody vomiting, too, is a symptom of smallpox.

More important, for Sarasvati this illness experience was associated with pregnancy and childbirth. At the time the illness climaxed, she had one seven-month-old baby in arms and was pregnant with another. The child that was subsequently born nearly died but was saved, like Sarasvati, by the intervention of Māriamman. This baby was the seventh child and the sixth daughter. Six daughters were a great burden for Sarasvati, because of the necessity of marrying them all off, with dowries and expensive festivities. But

Māriamman transformed this last daughter into a blessing, investing her with great intellectual and magical powers.

Interview III: Māriamman Speaks Through the Priestesses

What have you come to ask, girl?[47] What is your history? What town were you born in? How many names do you have? What different towns do you live in? How were you born? What kind of woman are you? You can do good; can you also do evil? What are your characteristics? You have come to ask that, haven't you?

What I was born in was mud, girl. Do you know the town I was born in? In Pāḷayam I govern and was born. My story begins in Periyapāḷayam. Why girl I am a married woman. I have a husband, too.

[Who is that?]

Do you have to ask about my husband? You cannot see him at all. That woman nearby has said his name [Jatharagni]. That holy man is my husband. My son's name is Parasurāman.

Why girl, one day I went to the Ganges to see the sun and do homage to it. When I took a pot to that place and was getting water, the great one went over my head. I raised my head to look at him. My husband considered that to be wrong. The story I am telling, this is my history. Do you understand?

My husband said that my gift of austerity had changed [her chastity was lost] and he sent my son to take revenge. "Why, girl," my husband said, "You are not a fit woman for me. Desire for the gift of your chastity has occurred, girl. Therefore I am not ready to accept you," he said, and he sent my son to kill me.

Why girl, my son chased me and chased me and chased me through forest and jungle, he beat me, and I was afraid, and hid in an untouchable, low-caste house. Then seeing that I was without a place to stay and was frightened, those low people stopped me from running, and gave me protection. At that time my son violently chased the lady who gave me protection, too, and cut off her head. And he cut off my head in the same way.

After that, my son came with nothing but blood and gore, and showed them to my muni.

In a fury [*āvēcam*], he said, "Have you really cut off your mother's head, boy? For this there is no atonement." He said this and wept.

At that moment wisdom was born to my husband. "Somehow you must save your mother," he said, and gave me freedom again.

My son ran up and said, "I beg you to give me life," and in that very place he rolled close to my side and lay there.

That woman was a shoemaker by caste. That is a caste of untouchable form. Taking her body and my head he gave me freedom [Ta. *moḍcam* < Skt. *moksha*]. Do you understand, girl? Many powers, many forms, many names, for many towns I have an incarnation. But I have one word, *māṟi*. Because the body was changed [māṟi] and joined to the head.

How did he renounce me? Up until this time, I have had my power. This is the substance of my own form. Why, girl, no one can touch my body. This is another woman's body. This is not my body.[48]

There is a *tāṛam* plant in that place called Tāṛanūr, in Periyapāḷayam itself.[49]

I said to my son, "I will not go to your father's place again. You have changed my body, and I have changed my form, boy. In Tiruvērkāḍu, I have taken the name of Karumāri. In Pāḷayam I have taken the name of Periyapāḷayattā. Since I am settled here [at Tiruvērkāḍu], take me and lower me into the earth again," I entreated my son. In that very place, my son worshipped me, girl. In my form I am always *māṟi* only as far as my neck.

I have one thousand and eight incarnations. Māriamman named Bavāni, Māriamman named Bāmini, Māriamman named Lakshmi, Māriamman named Rājā Rājēswari and Māriamman named Mīnākshi, and Māriamman named Kāmākshi, and Māriamman named Vicālākshi, I am all of these. In the world you have taken many names and many forms, woman. But I am the sign of belief. If many people unite and make me an image out of earth, or out of gold, or out of anything, and confer a name, and make a power of mine come down there, and build a temple in that place, and hold many ceremonies and consecrations for me, and perform many kinds of worship for me, calling the form of my power only Ōm, that is my form. My son, too, has that Ōm. My Sivan too has that Ōm. For all of us, our magic is in that Ōm. The form of power is for us Ōm only. In the same way, in a great wise person also one may see that power.

If, in the person of a poor lady like this one, there is a place for the power of knowledge, there we will make a home, and that will have all grace, that will be the distributor of grace.

Two thousand three hundred years ago this world was born. To us, power was born. To your country, too, I will come. You yourself can make me in this way. Buying an image of gold, buying my image made of the five metals mixed, keeping a separate room like this, in that place do worship daily. What need have you?

[Knowledge.]

For that knowledge there is a power. That is my power.

Why, girl, that which is called knowledge you can't buy for a price, can you? And you can't learn it from someone else. And you can't read it. Even if another person sits in front of you and daily feeds you that knowledge as experience or wisdom, you must understand it, mustn't you? There is something that power can bear for you.

The testimony of the mind must be one testimony. There must be no changing of it. To the power of courage, to the power of knowledge, to these two powers you must give a place.

If, when you leave this place, they stop you, saying, "A woman in a hut like this, she will deceive you, she will ask for money and everything. Why do you go to that place?" If they ask like this, what must your power of knowledge say?

[I don't know.]

Why, you have knowledge, girl! Why don't you know? If you say, "I want to gain the thing I came believing in. What if it is a hut? What if it is a tower? With belief only, I have come here." A heart strong with belief, someone else will spoil, saying, "Why are you going to that hut?" Some woman, for the sake of her belly's survival, has made something out of mud and does worship. Can such people learn honesty? She is stopping you and changing your heart.

If they say all this, they are wrong, aren't they? They are wrong. You must not change your heart. I have truly come here out of earth. But for Tamil women only I am one who will do much good.[50] Those who come here believing me, do not reject me even for a blink. Why, girl, my foot[51] and my marriage emblem are like a married lady's. This suffering too is mine. Suffering attacks that lady. Therefore, I will always be in a dark room. I will not be in the light. Because of this, all women are able to praise me and sing of me, calling me, "O brilliant light!" If I am made of earth, I have glory. If I am made of gold, I have glory. If there is any lady making strong the form of belief, for her I will do good.

Within this lady, is a deceitless, splinterless heart. That heart I understand. I reside in that heart. To end many people's troubles, there is a possession [āvēcam] like this for a while. If it becomes more than three and three-fourths nāṛi, I will change. In this child's body, her own feeling will arise. Until then, in the person of this child, coming as wind, I speak like this.[52]

Chapter 2

Sorrow and Protest

In the dark times
Will there also be singing?
Yes, there will also be singing.
About the dark times.
—Bertolt Brecht

One day when I was standing near the rice mill by the road, a woman dressed in a Catholic Sister's habit came walking by from where the bus had stopped.[1] She saw me, smiled, and beckoned me to her. We spoke, and she told me she lived in a village just down the road, where women would come at night and sing traditional folk songs. She invited me to join them. When I arrived, bringing my tape recorder, a group of maybe twelve older women was sitting around a fire, and one by one, they sang and I recorded.

I brought the songs back to my host's house and played some of them, and Aṇṇi, my host's wife's sister, said, "We didn't know you were interested in these songs. Our Muttammāḷ can sing those." And Muttammāḷ, a Paṟaiyar woman of about twenty-five, did sing, and some of her songs are in this and the next chapter of this volume. Also other women came to sing for me, in the house near the rice mill belonging to the family who hosted me. In all, I recorded dozens of songs sung by these women. Of those songs, I was able to transcribe and translate only a few.

I had been looking for what I thought of as real folk singers, not singers of movie songs, but wherever I looked, I could not find what I was looking for and was beginning to doubt whether "real" Tamil folk songs existed at all anymore. My problem was partly because I came for other work, which I did, but also because nobody I knew was interested in those kinds of songs. Once the people I lived with knew my interest in such songs, the rest was easy. Paṟaiyar women came, singly or in twos or threes, to the house where I was staying, near the rice mill. The women sang for me, to me, songs about their own experiences, but never directly. The words of their songs, though not the music of them, were hidden from public ears by the singers themselves. Thus the meanings were doubly concealed. I was tape recording their songs as they sang, and the singers knew that the tape recordings would be heard by other people beside me. For them to allow me to record their singing was perhaps a more courageous step on the part of the singers than I knew at the time. I remain grateful for the trust and respect they showed me.

Afterward my host helped me transcribe the songs. Until then, nobody that I knew thought those songs were important, although my host found them interesting because he had never heard them before. But what I found were not just artifacts of no import. They were songs of a genre performed in many countries but not always easy to find. The meanings of the words of the songs could be understood cognitively, but the meanings of the songs themselves, the feelings involved, were not expressible in words alone. A language is a whole worldview, and every worldview is different from every other. A. K. Ramanujan taught me the words "Traduttore, traditore," which means "The translator is a traitor." But music can be neither translated nor betrayed. It is what it is. In the case of lament, the music and the words go together. One is not complete without the other. The music of the Paṟaiyar women embodied unjust suffering and loss, expressed through the tears and through the voices of the singers, who called them "crying songs" (*ayiṟa pāḍḍu*, shortened from *aṟukiṟa pāḍḍu*). More formally in English they would be called laments.[2]

Paṟaiyars constitute a large Dalit caste whose main job is farm labor and whose ritual job is management of death. Paṟaiyar women's laments were intrinsic to that management. In the eyes of higher-caste people, anyone whose work was to deal with death was untouchable, even though the job had to be done. Proximity to death was considered deeply polluting. A woman was inherently polluted because of the bodily aspects of being a woman. She had more orifices than a man, so that she was more permeable, and fluids came out as well as going in. During her menstrual period, she had to be kept secluded. She was not allowed to prepare food or to touch any kitchen utensils. The concepts of purity and pollution are intrinsic to Hindu culture. High-caste male Hindus must keep themselves "pure," and women and low-caste people must carry the pollution. The untouchable women with whom I met were oppressed by higher-caste people because of their caste and by men because of their gender. This was not a difficult thing for them to see, but it was dangerous to say. Laments may be embarrassing to others if the singer of the lament blames some other for her suffering or for the death of another. Laments may be met with violent retaliation for this reason. Outsiders, such as scholars, can then claim that the singers, who send their message obliquely and are "clouded" by emotion as well, are unable to see their situation clearly. And higher-caste people of the same village can say that the oppression of which the singers sing does not exist.

Because of A. K. Ramanujan (1967, 1991), a man who inspired many people, including me, to study Tamil, I was interested in Tamil folk songs, but although they were abundantly sung, I had never been able to find them. In retrospect, I guess I asked the wrong questions, went to the wrong places. Now, here, by accident, engaged in a research project having nothing to do with songs sung by Paṟaiyar women, I came upon them, and they were remarkable and beautiful songs. In this chapter, I write about the structure of some of these songs. The songs I have chosen to write about in this chapter are laments. They are longer than other songs, and I recorded more of them than could be included in this book.

Previously, I had learned about a genre of Tamil song called *oppāri*, which means "comparison" and laments the death of a person, comparing the happy time before death and separation with the unhappy time after. It is not considered to be of political import.

At the time that I did this bout of research, in 1980, nobody seemed to have heard of "crying songs," though educated people knew of it. The word *oppāri* means comparison, in these songs, between the past and the present. Brahman women sing *oppāri*s, or used to, about people in their families who had died. What the Paṟaiyar women sang were not *oppāri*s, as described above. The crying songs were heavily veiled and at the same time highly structured. They compared the past with the present, but they did not mention "the person who had died." The singer sang instead, metaphorically, of her own plight, or of and to her own mother or father, who may or may not have been living at the time she sang. She did not sing about the death of some higher-caste person for whom rituals, including these songs sung by Paṟaiyar women, were being performed.

The women who sang directly to and for me, at my request, with my tape recorder going, were more audible than they would be in the regular ritual context where the songs were performed. Normally in that region, Paṟaiyar women sit to the side at a higher-caste person's funeral in Tamil Nadu, bear no relation to the dead, and sing their crying songs but are scarcely heard.

The fact that these songs were, in their normal context, scarcely heard, made them, to me, more important. The women could sing of their own plights as rural untouchable women and feel moderately safe that nobody would bother them. They sang of caste issues without ever mentioning caste, and of gender issues, such as child marriage, as though it were a personal matter. But caste and gender are not just personal matters.

In 1980, the Paṟaiyar singers, all women, were emboldened to sing for a Westerner's tape recorder, perhaps by the changing times. By then, male Paṟaiyars had become strong in the Dalit movement. I saw the men arguing loudly, face to face, with their own landlords. The female singers may have also been emboldened by my gender and my obvious interest in their songs. Word may have gotten around.

The Paṟaiyar women of Pukkatturai near Chingleput wept as they sang. Tears rolled down their faces and they sobbed. The weeping was part of the singing. The rhythm of weeping formed the rhythm of the song.

Paṟaiyar lament differed from lament in other parts of the world, in that the lamenters were inextricably tied, in the minds of higher-caste people, to death. They were thus the most appropriate people to lament the deaths of others.

Formal and structured though they were, the laments remained spontaneous in their content. The Paṟaiyar laments were formulaic, like the Homeric epics (Lord 1969, 1990) or like epics recorded in Tamil Nadu itself (Beck 1982; Blackburn 1988). Because they were formulaic, with highly structured meter and rhyme, they could be spontaneous even as they were formal. Neither the performers of epic nor the singers of laments worked from any set texts.[3]

The Paṟaiyar women's songs are undeniably protest songs. Many laments sung throughout the world are protests against injustice. Laments may be embarrassing to others if the singer of the lament blames some other for her suffering or the death of one of her loved ones. Laments may be met with retaliation for this reason. Though the Paṟaiyar women's weeping songs take a traditional form, there can be no doubt that Paṟaiyar women in Tamil towns of 1980 had already been exposed to Dalit protests that were taking place at that time. The changing cultural winds had not left these women unchanged. Songs that at one time may have been laments for the dead became complaints about the singer's own plight and complaints about the cruelty of more powerful people, higher-caste people. These are the kind that I came across. Lament is the song of the powerless, and everybody is powerless in the face of death. But people are not always powerless in the face of human injustice, nor in the face of changing times. The household in which I lived was already beleaguered by other landlords and other castes, and Dalit men were not afraid to argue directly with their landlords. Ultimately, that whole family moved to the city and did not return. As long as there were paddy fields to work, Paṟaiyars would be there to work them. But paddy was becoming more and more difficult to grow. Some of the people who were not landlords but owned smaller plots of land grew millet instead. It was hardier, more nutritious, and much easier to grow than rice. Even high-status families in the region said that one or two generations ago, rice was saved for special occasions, but now it was eaten every day. Millet didn't taste as good as rice, was harder to digest, and remained a low-status food.

Paṟaiyar laborers, like other low castes and tribes, lived close to the wild, to spirits of the wild, and close to domestic animals, mainly cattle. An educated young Paṟaiyar man, Kuppusāmy told of his experience of cattle as protectors against night spirits of the wild. But cattle could be dangerous and could kill with their horns. So a young Paṟaiyar woman told me of a friend of hers who was gored and killed by a cow. Paṟaiyar women are close to cultivated plants, mainly rice, which these women tend. In Darisanamcope, a village in the far southern area of Tamil Nadu where I worked in 1975–76, the women who worked in the rice fields spoke of rice plants as though they were children (Trawick 1978).

At the time I listened to the Paṟaiyar crying songs, recorded them, and wrote them down, I did not know that laments were an important topic among scholars worldwide. But they were and are. Steven Feld (1982), Greg Urban (1988), Charles Briggs (1992, 1993), Nadia Seremetakis (1991), Aida Vidan (2003), Elizabeth Wickett (2010), and James Wilce (2009), among others, have documented in detail laments performed in Highland Papua New Guinea, the Amazon jungle, ancient and modern Greece, the Balkan countries north of Greece, ancient and modern Egypt, and India, among other places. The Paṟaiyar singers were therefore hardly alone.[4]

The songs of the Paṟaiyar women of Pukkatturai include references to other human beings, as well as to assorted plants, animals, and birds. Sometimes, the singer likens herself to one or another of them. In particular, these singers liken themselves to plants, or crucial parts of plants, as though they know how it feels to be such a plant. Other times they join themselves to animals or birds whose thoughts and feelings they seem to know. And they liken themselves to substances that have been stolen or ruined. These likenings are more than "just" metaphors. They are metaphors that, as George Lakoff said, "we live by" (Lakoff and Johnson 2008). We construct our world with icons and indices. The symbolic is incidental. Thus, in these songs, the singers show the world in which they live, the environment they make and that in turn makes them, the beings they perceive themselves to be, by means of the metaphors they live by and the music that they make.[5] The Paṟaiyar women did not use similes to describe themselves. They could have said "I was like a lotus" (*nān tāmarai pōl iruntēn*). But they did not say that. They did not place that kind of distance between the plants, animals, and substances of which they sang. They were of the environment that they made, and that made them. Here is a summation of what the Paṟaiyar women sang.

> I was a lotus. Knowing the sun would burn us, you threw us into the sun. O mother who bore me; what you grew us was a full body, a beautiful crop. Now, having grown, we blacken. I am a measure of grain. Today my measure, mother, has become chaff. We poor girls are the kinds of paddy drying in the sun. Mother, we are jasmine that has blossomed on your vine. We took root in your belly, O mother who bore me; if we had taken root in a forest, we would be colorful trees. O mother who bore me, we would be flowers for the doorstep. We fruited on a vine, O mother who bore me; if we had fruited in a tank we would be *koṉṟai* trees. O mother who bore me, after you left, we would be flowers for the temple. Since I have no children, the female crow, mother, will not touch the food I cooked. I was born in a conch shell. I was born in milk. I am a lily. I am red gram, mother; I am unbending gold. He bent me and took me away; he took the flesh of my shoulders. I am white gram, mother, I am unmelting gold. He crushed me and took me away. He took the flesh of my legs. For us poor girls, clusters of eggplants fruit on the vine. With no one to hold and embrace us,

we rot with the vine, mother. Mine is the sorrow of the elephant. Mine is the sorrow of the horse.

Songs

First Song

For you, a young girl's garment of *makuḍam* flowers,
O mother who bore me, a folded skirt for you.
The fold has not parted for me.
O mother who bore me, and I do not know the hidden place to
 which you have gone.

For me, a young girl's garment of *tāṛam* flowers,
O mother who bore me, a skirt stitched for me.
The stitching has not yet parted for me,
O mother who bore me, since the day of our searching.

For you, a plantain tree grew in the river,
O mother who bore me. With a thread from the base,
A garland was made and placed around me at five,
O mother who bore me, a garland without love.

For me, a plantain tree grew in the pond;
O mother who bore me, vine-jasmine blossomed for me.
But the garlands placed round me in childhood,
When I was a lotus, still so young, were not good garlands, mother.

Knowing the sun would burn me,
O mother who bore me, in your fingers you held an umbrella.
But now you have parted your fingers;
On the day you left, you threw us into the sun.

Knowing the heat would burn me,
O mother who bore me, father, you held an umbrella in your hand.
Now, the umbrella has parted from your hand.
On the day you left, you threw us into the wasteland.

For me, every month, an axe,
O mother who bore me, splits my heart.
For me, don't think there is medicine.
Since the day you left, for me, poor girl, the hurt has remained.

For me, every day, an axe,
O mother who bore me, splits my heart.
For me, don't think that there is any moon.
Since the day you left, for the girl you bore,
In her heart, the hurt has remained.

I had a white goat on the doorstep,
O mother who bore me, and a colored parrot who would watch for me.
To come and listen to my troubles,
And to see me on my way, now there is no one.

In the south, mother, the rain would fall for me;
O mother who bore me, father, on the south wall the clouds would come
Today, to search for things to tie in the fold of my sari,
O mother who bore me, and to see me down the road, I have no mother.

In the north, the rain would fall for me,
O mother who bore me, on the north wall the clouds would come.
There, curved bangles were sold.
O mother who bore me, for me different good things were sold.
To buy them and tie them in the fold of my sari, for me,
O mother who bore me, father, and to send me on my way, there is no mother.

I had an unfading lamp,
O mother who bore me, father; if dust fell on it you wept.
Now I am a poor wasted girl.
Now, when I suffer here, mother, why don't you see?

I had metal from ten miles away;
O mother who bore me, if our shaded lamp
Was blown by the wind, you would weep.
Now, when I am a wasted girl, and am troubled, mother, why don't
 you see?

This song was sung by Pushpam, a woman in her mid-twenties with three young children. Both of her parents are dead. Pushpam, like all the singers whose songs are discussed here, is an agricultural laborer belonging to the Paṟaiyar caste, which comprises nearly 40 percent of the population of the village in which these songs were collected.

The central topic of Pushpam's song is separation, and interwoven with this major theme is a subtheme—the oneness of mother and daughter. The mother is the source and spirit of the daughter, and cut off from her, the daughter senses her own death. Each stanza of the song is in metaphorical relation to all the others, because each stanza contains one or more images embodying the central themes. In the first stanza, the unparted cloth, still folded and sewn, contrasts with the parted mother and daughter—the mother in a "hidden place," the daughter searching for her. In the second stanza, the wedding garland, a conventional image of the bond of love, becomes an image of love's severance. The heat of the sun and the wasteland, sung of in the third stanza, are conventional images of separation, hatred, and death, contrasting with water, which is a symbol in Tamil thought for love, unity, and flourishing life. Where water appears in this song, it is seen as a thing of the past. In the fourth stanza, the protecting hand is parted into useless fingers; in the fifth stanza, the month into painful days. The singer feels that her heart itself has split. In the sixth stanza, she has no companions and no one to send gifts of love with her when she departs from home. In the final stanza, the darkness of death hides mother and daughter from each other's sight.

By itself, a particular stanza may point to a dozen themes; many stanzas have no clear focus. But when they are in juxtaposition, whatever meaning or meanings the different stanzas share come to the forefront. In some cases, a meaning may be imparted to an image, or extracted from it, by neighboring images. Thus the images which more obviously or conventionally denote the central theme act as metaphors for those which less obviously denote it. In this way the signhood of each stanza, the fact that this particular image or cluster of images has this particular meaning, is brought to light through the internal parallelism of the song.

Much of the significance of a crying song lies not in its open declarations but in its allusions. A single word, for those who share the singer's world, opens onto complex realities with multiform meanings; but for those who do not share the singer's world, her words are closed and opaque. This density of word-pictures greatly deepens the song—deepens it, first, because much of the song's meaning is not immediately accessible but takes intimacy with the singer's subculture, and time, to sink in. To the extent that the meanings expressed by the song are encoded in the culture, they may be unconscious or only partly conscious, perhaps even for the singer herself. The song is deepened, secondly, because this dense imagery touches upon dimensions of human relations that no words express directly. The more profound the relationship itself, the more is this true.

Most profound, perhaps of all for South Indians is the bond between mother and daughter—a bond which is felt to be part of all growth, of all continuance and creation. The bringing to birth of one like oneself, who in turn will bear another, is an image engraved everywhere in Tamil culture. Hence a singer need not seek far to find metaphors for mother-daughter continuity, and often a single word will go a long way in this regard.

As an illustration of how much meaning is contained in a few words, consider two lines in this song in the first and second stanzas:

> For you, a young girl's garment of *makuḍam* flowers . . .
> For me, a young girl's garment of *tāṛam* flowers . . .

A young girl's garment (*cittāḍai*) is the top piece draped over the shoulder, worn by girls come of age but not married. The same garment is tied on statues of female deities, because a deity is always young and always a virgin. The *cittāḍai* is also offered to certain women on their death anniversaries, because after their death they are deities. In many households in the village, a deity named *pūvōḍakkāri* ("she with flowers") is worshipped in this way, as the principal household deity. *Pūvōḍakkāri* represents all the women of that household who died still unwidowed or still unmarried—still wearing flowers—for flowers are forbidden to widows. Thus the mother who died in her youth, and the young daughter she left behind, have in common the garment and flowers and the untorn perfection they represent.

But the particular flowers allotted to mother and daughter are different.

The *makuḍam* (*makiṛam*) flower is a small, very fragrant flower growing in clusters on a large tree. The *tāṛam* flower is a large, strongly scented single flower growing by the sea on a spiky bush frequented by snakes. The *tāṛam* is never permitted at weddings and is rarely used in worship, an exception being the Varalakshmi ceremony, a household ceremony performed by women honoring the goddess Lakshmi.

On the contrast between these two flowers, a high-caste man hearing the song recited to me a poem which he attributed to the poetess Auvaiyār:

maḍal peritu tā̲lai, maki̲l initu kantam
kaṭal peritu maṇṇīrum aka ataṉaruku
cittūṟal uṇṇīrum ākiviṭum
The *tāṛam* has great breadth,
The *makiṛam* has sweet scent;
The sea is great, its water muddy;
Near it in the small spring,
Is water to drink.

In other words, what is small and fine is more powerful in certain ways than what is great.

Though Pushpam, who cannot read, would not know the poem by Auvaiyār, she shares with the ancient poetess a knowledge of the two flowers, their properties and their uses, and the sentiments associated with each. In her song, the contrast between the small and desirable *makiṛam* flower and the large and aggressive *tāṛam* flower parallels the contrast between "you" (the spirit of the mother, the small subtle body with great power of the dead) and "me" (the lonely and tangible living singer).

In the second stanza, the plantain tree becomes the basis of comparison and the symbol of the bond between mother and daughter. The plantain tree is of utmost importance in Tamil ritual and poetry, and to understand its meaning there and in this song we must know some of its characteristics: An immature plantain tree is called a *vāṛai kaṉṟu*, "plantain calf," because the plantain tree is like a cow—no part is useless; it gives many things to eat and to use for other purposes. The plantain tree grows from the base, not from the tip like most green plants. When the tree dies, new trees are started from the roots. Until the tree fruits, new trees are not allowed to grow from its base, as they will divert nourishment from the fruit. The fruit, because of its shape, has a male/phallic significance. After one fruiting, the tree dies. After the tree fruits, new trees are allowed to grow. They must be transplanted to grow well and bear fruit of their own. All of these characteristics of the plantain tree's growth contribute to its metaphoric nature, especially as a metaphor of mother-daughter separation through death and marriage.

Single words in these songs, then, can harbor great allusive significance. It is not only the presence of such key words, however, but their place in the sound structure of the song that gives them impact. Earlier in this essay, it was noted that the two halves of a stanza usually duplicate each other except for a few variant words, which form contrasting pairs both semantically and phonologically. In the first stanza of the present song, these words are: "for you" (*unakku*) / "for me" (*enakku*); "*makuḍam* flower" / "*tāṛam* flower"; "folded" (*maḍicci*) / "sewn" (*tacci*); "hidden place" (*māyam*) / "searching" (*tēḍi*).

The two members of each of these pairs of contrasting words occupy parallel contexts in the song. In sound and in meaning, they share many or even most of their features. Their differences, therefore, become all the more significant. Here, they encapsulate in formal symmetry the dominant feeling of the song: the daughter (represented by the second member of each pair) is an image of the mother (represented by the first member), but a changed and lesser one; the daughter is one with the mother but at a crucial point departs from her. In other songs (for instance, the third), such contrasting word pairs serve to highlight other messages.

The themes and characteristics of this first song are not unique to it but flow into other songs, where, however, other themes become central. The cry *ennē petta tāyē*, "mother who bore me," is repeated throughout almost all of the songs, and the bond between mother and daughter is a vital point of reference for all of them. So also is the idea of separation, of division, of cutting off. But the themes of the bond and the severance of the bond have many aspects and lead on to other themes which join them. The following song is one step away from the preceding one and develops in a slightly different direction the vegetal imagery of the mother-daughter bond.

Second Song

Today above the edge of the tank,
O mother who bore me, you sat like a cuckoo.
Today, not knowing you were a cuckoo
That god of borders and edges took you and burned you, mother.

Today on the edge of the pond shore,
O mother who bore me, you sat like a peacock.
Not knowing you were a peacock,
That god of borders and edges poisoned and burned you, mother.

We took root in your belly,
O mother who bore me; if we had taken root in a forest,
We would be colorful trees,
O mother who bore me, we would be flowers for the doorstep.

We fruited on a vine,
O mother who bore me; if we had fruited in a tank
We would be *koṉṟai* trees.
O mother who bore me, after you left, we would be flowers for the temple.

You tied a small reed,
O mother who bore me, you made us a small reed basket.
On the day that you blessed us with gifts,
O mother who bore me, you went to stay in a strange land.

You cut a large reed for us,
O mother who bore me, you made us a large basket.
On the day that you named us,
O mother who bore me, you parted from us and left.

I had a plantain tree on the doorstep,
O mother who bore me; what you grew us was a full body, a beautiful crop.
Now, having grown, we blacken,
In this distant land of Pukkatturai, we have no mother to send us on our way.

[Inaudible] you have done the greatest of wrongs. Since the day you left, the river water is far for us, mother.
For me, the troubles a woman suffers,
For us, what is put on our heads, mother, mother, no one knows.

We are a measure of grain, mother,
O mother who bore me; though we consulted the almanac,
Today, mother, our measure has become chaff.
The almanac we consulted, mother, was a lie.

I am a measure of grain.
Though I, poor woman, observed the signs and astrology,
Today my measure, mother, has become chaff.
The signs and astrology we observed, mother, were a lie.

We took a leather bag.
O mother who bore me, my husband and I left all and came home.
If the mother who bore me was alive,
Today she would take the child of her breast.
As soon as she saw my husband,
She would take a folded mat and lay it out for him.
If she saw us in the distance, if she saw us in the distance,
She would put on warm water for us to wash our feet,
O mother, she would take the child of her arms.

For me, by the river,
O mother who bore me, for us, long ago, came slavery.
The garland put on us when we were five, the garland put on us when we were five
For us, poor girls, was a garland without love, mother.

Today on top of a ten-story house,
We poor girls are the kinds of paddy drying in the sun.
Today without declaring the price of paddy,
Those wrong people, to that treacherous man, declare the price of chaff.

On top of your eight-storied house, on top of your eight-storied house,
O mother who bore me, father, the kinds of sesame dry in the sun.
There, not declaring the price of sesame,
They declared a price to the babbling boy Subramani.

Today for Yama who comes to strike,
O mother who bore me, father, shelter, mother.
Today to Yama who comes to kill,
O mother who bore me, since the day you left, we lift our hands
calling him guru.

Today by the Piḷḷaiyār temple,
If we poor girls boil food,
Since I have no children, since I have no children,
The female crow, mother, will not touch the food we cooked.

Today if we cook, mother, if we cook.
Because today we have no husband,
Today the male crow, O poor people, does not touch our food.

This song was sung by Kamalā, a woman married and in her twenties, with no children. Kamalā is a good friend of Pushpam's. The theme of her song is death before ripeness, and analogous forms of unrealized potential. It is not the severance itself of mother from daughter that is so bad, she is saying, but the fact that so much good could have grown if only our lives had not been broken off from each other so soon. Further, whereas in the first song the daughter blames the mother for leaving her behind, in this song a third person is blamed for the separation, of which the mother and daughter equally are victims.

The singer laments that her mother was seized before her time by death, "the god of borders and edges" (*ōrakkāra teyvam*). This name for the god refers to the fact that he does not treat all equally, but draws lines between people, makes distinctions among them, taking some too soon and leaving others until later. Through this name the injustice of the mother's early death is stressed, and closely tied to this sense of injustice a general aversion to boundaries is conveyed, an aversion that appears often in these songs.

As in the first song, the early loss of the mother is linked to the early marriage of the daughter, and the daughter's marriage is seen as a kind of death, a sudden sharp end to her thriving. But if the daughter's marriage is like the mother's death, a further parallel between their two fates is drawn: the husband who seizes the daughter is the same as death himself, who seized the mother. One is reminded of the Greek myth of Demeter and Persephone.

The singer calls the village into which she has married "this distant land" (*sīmai*), a euphemism for the place of the dead, and she sings that a god of death has become our shelter and guru (ideally, for Tamil woman, the husband should fill these roles).

The singer also links marriage and death with birth, for childbirth is closely associated with death in South Asia and often leads to it. Childbirth, too, is a fate shared by mother and daughter, simultaneously drawing them closer together, for it makes them more similar, and pulling them further apart, for once the young daughter has borne a child, her own childhood is gone forever.

Thus the singer cries to the mother, you made a reed basket to carry us in, you gave us gifts and named us, and on that day you left us. The reed basket is a crib. "On the day you gave us gifts" (*sīruḍu nāḷaiyilē*) refers to the custom of gifts given by parents and others at the time of birth, first menstruation, marriage, first pregnancy, and other auspicious ceremonies, ceremonies of beginning. On the sixteenth day after a child is born is the naming ceremony. They give the child bangles, ankle bracelets, a necklace, and a name, sing to it and bless it. The import of Kamalā's lament, therefore, is that the daughters were cut off from their mother at the very beginning of their lives, and all the possibilities, all their "gifts," were lost.

But the dominant imagery of this song is of plants and foodstuffs that are wasted. The singer and her sisters are these plants and foodstuffs. They are, first, seeds that have fallen on the wrong soil, the soil of this mother's belly, and fruit that has grown on the wrong vine, the vine of this mother's family. Next, the singer complains to her mother, you grew us a full crop, but now that we are grown, we die. "Full crop" (*mēni*) also means "beautiful or perfect body." Evidently both meanings are intended in this song. The mother gave her daughter the gift of a body, but now this body, the daughter herself, like a field of grain parched by the sun or stricken with disease before it is harvested, withers, blackens, and dies. Not only, therefore, was she wasted in the planting (seed fallen on the wrong soil), but she is wasted in the growing.

At the next stage, she is wasted in the harvesting. She sings, I was worth, and I myself was, a full measure of grain. But though I followed all the law books in the husbandry of my grain, my measure has become chaff. The grain of the singer is wasted because although she has harvested it according to the rules, she has spent herself in a fruitless marriage. Following upon the harvest, she sings, we are like the many kinds of paddy and sesame drying in the sun on top of a great house—our value is high. But we poor sinners have been sold by sinners to a treacherous sinner for the price of chaff. Our value has gone unrecognized and we have been sold for the price of chaff.

The word *pāvi* (glossed as "poor girl," "poor people," "cruel man," or "sinner") refers in these songs both to someone who does wrong and to someone who is wronged. However, it does not necessarily always carry both meanings. The singer regards herself as guiltless, innocent as grain. When she calls her husband and parents *pāvi*, it means that they do wrong to her, or that wrong has been done to them, or both. The person named here as "that treacherous sinner, the prattling boy Subramani," is Kamalā's husband, with whom she has recently quarreled. This line is significant because, according to the "rules" of village society (which, however, Kamalā has already questioned), a woman is never supposed to utter her husband's name.

The singer has sprouted on bad soil, grown and withered, been harvested and turned to chaff, been dried in the sun and sold for a low price. Finally, she must be cooked and eaten, but at this stage, too, she is wrongly used. She sings, if I cook food and offer it to the temple, because I am without children and my husband is not home, not even a crow will touch it. (There is a tradition of not accepting alms from a household without children or from one in which the husband is dead or absent.) The food she cooks (the terms used are *ākku* and general terms for "create," with no specification in the song as to what is being created or how) represents the singer's own substance. The food will be wasted, rather than being eaten and so undergoing its proper transformation.

Several stanzas of this song depart from this relentless food sequence that the singer feels herself going through, but these only express in different ways the sense of waste and loss and longing pervading the entire song. For instance, Kamalā sings in the sixth stanza that she goes with her husband to see her mother, but when she reaches her old home, there is no mother there. The mother's absence means a fruitless end to the daughter's own married journey.

The next song concentrates upon a theme that was only an undercurrent, briefly surfacing, in the previous song—the theme of the lonely married journey coming to an empty end. It is sung, not from the perspective of what might have been, but from the perspective of what once was. To a certain extent, then, it reflects the singer's own state, for she is an old woman, just as faint references to childlessness mirror some aspects of Kamalā, the previous singer. The sense of relentlessness is present in this third song also, as it was in the previous one, but here it is even stronger.

Third Song

I was born in a conch shell,
O mother who bore me, and I ruled the ocean.
He took my conch shell, mother, that merciless criminal,
And made me a beggar.

Today I was born in milk,
O God, and in this place I ruled the city.
He took my milk, mother, that scheming man,
And made me a beggar.

For me, four hundred cars would come,
O mother who raised me;
in the middle of them all would come our car.
For me, they would set out a four-legged chair,
O mother who bore me; for me, the troubled younger sister,
four tassels would be tied.
For me, settled in the chair,
O mother who bore me, for me, the younger sister,
did you bother to oil me for my wedding?

Three hundred cars would come for me,
O mother who bore me; for me, the troubled younger sister,
ahead of them all would come our car.
For me, they would set out a three-legged stool,
For this wasted mother, O God,
but today only three tassels, poor girl, would be tied.
As I sat on our three-legged stool, O mother,
O wasted younger sister, O mother that I raised, for me,
Did you not find an auspicious wedding day?

For us, five o'clock strikes,
O mother who raised me; the five o'clock bus comes and stands by me.
If I, who am a lily, told my troubles,
For me, the five o'clock bus would have to wait five days before going.

For me, ten o'clock strikes,
O mother who raised me; the ten o'clock bus comes and stands by me.
If I, who am a poor girl, told my troubles,
My lord, in the distant land that you have gone to, for me,
the ten o'clock bus would have to wait ten days before going.

I am red gram, mother, O mother that I bore;
I am the troubled younger sister; I am unbending, mother, I am gold.
He bent me and took me away;
That cruel man, O younger sister, took the flesh of my shoulders.

I am white gram, mother,
The prey born in your belly, I am unmelting gold.
He crushed me and took me away,
In this town of cruel people, he took the flesh of my legs.

I took a banyan leaf bud,
O foolish mother who bore me as a girl.
At this age I will fetch water from a new well.
I am a ruined widow who gave a golden coconut,
At this age, I am a widow. If I boil food and go,
If I boil food and come outside,
They will call me a poor woman without a daughter, a poor woman without a son.
In this town without justice, even a female crow will not touch what I cook.

For me, I took a banyan leaf bud.
At this age, I am a widow who has seen evil magic,
and I will take water from the well depths.
I am a widow whose vagina is ruined;
If I cook for the Hanumān temple,
If I cook and come outside,
I am a widow with no one,
and even a male crow will not touch what I cook.
For me, I made feed for the elephant,

O poor people who raised me, and the elephant keeper struck me with a stone.
Mine is the sorrow of the elephant.
My husband, since the day you went,
I, who am a lily, have been hurt.

For me, I made feed for the horse,
O mother who raised me, and the horseman threw stones.
Mine is the sorrow of the horse.
O mother who raised me, since the day you went,
I, who am a child, have been hurt.

For me, cattle grazed, climbing the hills;
O mother who raised me, in this town I was Gōpāl's younger sister.
Not knowing the place to which he gave me, this cruel older brother,
In this place where justice is lost, has pushed me into a tank.
For me to swim out of the tank,
For me, a poor girl whose husband is gone, for me, the day will reach noon.

For me, cattle grazed, climbing the hills;
O mother who raised me, I was Gōpāl's younger sister.
Not knowing the place to which he gave me,
this cruel older brother pushed me into a tank.
For me to swim out of the tank,
In this town of cruel people, for me there is only a little day left.

For me, golden millet,
O poor people who raised me, for me, a tamarind-flower road.
For me, for this woman, send a person.
For me, at this age, older brother,
for me, someone to hold, older brother, is scarce.

For me, golden millet,
For me, for this younger sister, send a person,
In this little remaining day,
older brother, for me, the day grows short.

This song was sung to me by Nīlammā, who was about sixty-five years old. Her husband is alive, they are both healthy and continue to labor in the fields, but they have no living children. Nīlammā said that this song would be sung by a daughter when she goes to her mother's house, lamenting that her marriage is no good (*vāṛkkai sariyillai*).

The unifying theme of this song, the basis for semantic parallelism among the stanzas, is the property of waning, of there once having been much and now being very little. The singer laments her loss of wealth, of bodily substance, of time, and of relations. Her wealth was her city and ocean, the riches of her wedding, the cattle of her brother. Her substance is the flesh of her body and the food she cooks, which is now not even good enough for a crow, and which is kept from the horse and elephant. She shares the sorrow of the horse and the elephant, for their deprivation is similar to hers.

She has lost time and relations, for she perceives herself as aged, rejected, and alone. In the end, she sings of things that fall to her—golden millet (ready for harvest?), a tamarind-flower road (the entire tamarind tree is sour; people believe that even to sit under its shade will cause one to lose both weight and intelligence). Finally, even a person to hold (*piṭiyāḷ*, "available person, person grabbed off the street, person to hold") is hard to find (*pañcam*, "famine, scarcity").

Frequently in this song, the idea of decline is signaled not only by individual images but by sequences of contrasting images. In the first stanza, "ruled the city in this place" describes a power not quite as expansive as "ruled the ocean." In the second stanza, the image of "four hundred cars" and "four tassels" diminishes to "three hundred cars" and "only three tassles." In stanza 3, the movement from five o'clock to ten o'clock, and in stanza 7, the contrast between "noon" and "only a little day left," reinforce the sense of time loss. Similarly, the contrasts between "shoulder flesh" and "leg flesh," between "new well" and "well depths," between "elephant" and "horse," suggest a transition from higher to lower, greater to lesser.

The singer calls herself a widow repeatedly: "a ruined widow," "a widow who has seen evil magic," "a widow whose vagina is ruined," "a widow with no one." The state of widowhood is itself a state of decline. It should also be remembered, however, that the singer is in fact not a widow, nor does she say that this is a song a widow would sing. She is saying that she is for all intents and purposes a widow, thus indirectly cursing her husband.

Sometimes in these songs, the singer refers to herself as a water lily (*alli*). The term is used among villagers here to refer to a clever woman. In one version of the Mahābhārata, Alli was the name of a queen of Andhra who would not be conquered by any man. With Krishna's help, Arjuna drugged her and, while she slept, tied a *tāli* (a necklace with a pendant, a sign of being married) around her neck, thus marrying her. When she awoke, she was angry, but she accepted the marriage as valid because the *tāli* had been tied.

At one point, the singer calls herself "wasted mother" and her mother "wasted younger sister." This is not a slip, since Nīlammā informs me that in certain circumstances one's mother can be called younger sister—the term signifies more than a particular genealogical relationship. This information is consistent with what I observed in the village, where an older man might call a younger man *ammā* (mother) or a young man might call a slightly older married woman -*ḍā* (boy) (Trawick 1990b).

The specification of case in these songs, like the specification of tense, is often vague. For instance, the nominative case sometimes appears where literary Tamil would dictate the accusative or dative. The apparent switches which arise as a result of this usage, however, are not random. In this song, they all signify an identity, or even role reversal, of mother and daughter, as do the reversed epithets for self and mother used in the first stanza of the song. In stanza 2, the mother is addressed "O mother that I raised" (*nāṉ vaḷatta tāyē*), rather than "O mother who raised me" (*ennē vaḷatta tāyē*), as is usual. In the fourth stanza she is called "O mother-girl that I bore" (*nān petta ammāḍi*), rather than "O mother who bore me" (*eṉṉē petta tāyē*), which is the epithet the other singers use. This conceptual merger of mother and daughter is expressed in various ways in different songs (e.g., fourth song, fifth stanza; first song, first and second stanzas). Perhaps the merger becomes a reversal here because Nīlammā, who is much older than the other singers, thinks of herself more as mother and protector than as daughter and protected.[6]

Fourth Song

I wore a silk sari.
O mother who bore me, O father, and I went to see the town where I was born.
Today the wife of my first older brother, thinking that I come for my share,
Has set a screen in my way, and has put out two Pariah dogs for protection.

I didn't come for my share, mother;
I, poor girl, came to see the town where I was born, and cry.

I wore a printed sari,
And I, the younger sister, came to see the foreign land where I was born.
Today the wife of my second older brother
Has set a wall in my way and has put out two red dogs for protection.
I didn't come for riches, mother.
I, poor girl, came to see the foreign land where I was born, and cry.

A letter has not come for me, older brother;
A letter, a letter has not come for me.
I bought (paper) and wrote lines to my older brother, to the forest,
A letter, brother, did not come for me.

I bought (paper) and wrote lines to the forest where my brother is.
If I, the younger sister, send it,
Will you take it, older brother, and read it?
Brother, will you hear my sorrow?

For me, older brother, a letter is a hook.
If I, the younger sister born with you,
If I send a letter to where you are, older brother,
Will you put it together and read it?
Will you listen to the pains that I, your younger sister, suffer?

I have a golden nose pin, older brother.
I, the wasted younger sister, have half a bag of beans.
Today she says that the water vessel is not hers, older brother.
If we two lilies come there, she says the river water is far away.

I have a nose pin of straw, older brother;
I have a partial bag of beans.
If we are seated, older brother, and ask for water,
That cruel sister-in-law will say the pot is not hers.
She will say the tank water, mother, is far away.

In the south, older brother, rain would fall for me.
O shameful older brother, shameful older brother, on the south wall
rain clouds would come for me, for your younger sister.
A fruit is sold that is made there.
You didn't seek it for your younger sister, or tie it in the fold of her sari.

In the north, older brother, rain would fall for me.
Your wife says that I, the cruel younger sister, am coming.
Were you not born to stand in the doorway for us,
And to send us on our way?

Do not forget, older brother, my birth,
In my pomegranate garden.
You have listened, older brother, to the speech of Mātavi,
And have you forgotten, older brother, my birth?

Today have you listened to a whore's talk,
O older brother who was born with us,
and have you forgotten us,
your mother and younger sisters?

If I watched, older brother, a bicycle would come for me,
O brother, brother, for my sister and me a nice car would come with a mattress,
Since the day you left, since the day you left,
When we look, older brother, no bicycle comes, no car comes,
older brother with a mattress.
Since the day you left, since the day you left, when we look, older brother,
no bicycle comes, no car comes, older brother with a mattress.

If we waited, older brother, a bicycle would come for us;
For us two younger sisters, a car would come for sleep.
Since the day you left, for me, the younger sister,
If I stand there a bicycle does not come.

We are bush-jasmine, mother, we are vine-jasmine.
Mother, we are jasmine that has blossomed on your vine.
We are only two younger sisters, only two younger sisters.
What wrong have we poor girls done?
Has it surrounded us poor girls?

Poor father, did you beat a Brahman?
O father who got me, did you kill a milk cow?
Today, father, does the sin of a milk cow
Surround us children, us two Sītās?

Did you kill, father, did you beat,
O father who got us, did you kill a pregnant cow?
Today does the sin of a pregnant cow
Meet us two younger sisters and surround us?

The fourth song, sung by Pushpam, differs from the first three in that the mother is not the person addressed, though the themes of mother-daughter continuity and of severance are still present. Instead of the mother, another failed protector is addressed, the older brother, and in him are merged the abandoning mother and the cruel husband of previous songs.

The first six stanzas of this song are about the relation between a man's wife and his sister, as seen from the sister's point of view. More generally, they are about being locked out of a place one once was in, about the severance of a primordial tie.

The wife and the sister are not mutually complementary with respect to the man between them; they are rivals. The sister sees the wife as a usurper and a thief of her mother's and brother's home because she, the sister, was there first. In the fifth stanza, "my pomegranate garden" is the birthplace of both sister and brother, the vagina of the mother, which the sister sees also as hers. The brother has forgotten the pomegranate garden, has forgotten both mother and sister. The wife of the brother is called "a whore" and "Mātavi," the name of an epic concubine (in the Silappatikāram, or Kōvalaṉ Katai in folk variants) who temporarily enticed a husband away from his virtuous and suffering wife and took also the husband's wealth. The implication is that a man's wife is to his sister as a whore is to a wife.

The first through fourth stanzas all contain images of the singer's being locked out of her own place or treated as a stranger in it. That place, the place where brother and wife now are, is called a fortress, a foreign land. Walls and dogs are set in the singer's way. The only link she has with her home (a "hook" to pull her brother to her) is a letter, and the brother will not read hers or write an answer. When she goes there, "water is far away"—nothing is given her to incorporate her into the household again. And when she leaves, the brother does not place in the fold of her sari "a fruit that is made there" to keep a part of her home with her and within her when she is gone.

The last two stanzas of this song are only loosely connected with the first six, asking what sin was committed in the past that the singer should suffer now. As in the earlier part of the song, the singer identifies with her mother and her sisters ("mother, we are jasmine that has fruited on your vine"), and she does not blame herself for her suffering but blames the prior sins of her father. She feels herself surrounded and entrapped by the sins of her father, as she feels herself locked out by the sins of her brother. The next song, also sung by Pushpam, links up with the previous one.

Fifth Song

For me clusters and clusters of eggplants,
O older sister born to me, though they fruit for me on the plant,
With no one to join and embrace us, no one to join and embrace us,
We poor girls rot with the plant.

Today clusters and clusters of eggplants,
O poor girls, though they fruit on the vine,
With no one to hold and embrace us, no one to hold and embrace us,
We rot with the vine, mother.

For me water comes into the tank,
O cruel man, older brother, it circles for us round our pot.
I am your wife's younger sister's water, it says,
O older brother born with me, both of us fear to drink.

For me into the river comes water.
It circles for me round my pot.

Today knowing this is your water,
O older brother born with me, we fear to scoop it and drink.

For us, if a heron took form, and it fruited in the forest—
Today, what would the heron pluck?
O mother who bore me, for us, would the heron's hunger end?

For you, if a crane took form,
O older brother born with me, and it fruited for us in the tank—
Today, what would the stork pluck?
O brother born with me, would the stork's hunger end?

For me, combing the golden threshing ground,
O mother who bore me, for us, beating and stacking the stalks,
O poor people who bore me, poor people who bore me,
For us, if the tax collector comes and asks,
O mother who bore me, to answer him humbly, O poor people,
who have you kept?

For me, combing the golden threshing ground,
O poor people who bore me, beating and stacking the stalks,
Today, if a policeman comes and asks,
In this foreign land of Pukkatturai, to be responsible, who have
you kept?

For me a burnt neem tree,
Before I, who am poor, told all my troubles,
Today the burnt neem tree would send out shoots in front.

Today an injured neem tree,
O mother who bore me, mother who bore me,
Today before I told all my troubles,
The injured neem tree would send out shoots on the side.

For me, a well with golden steps,
O mother who bore me, a room to hold the rope.
Today if I see curd I feel no thirst, if I see curd I feel no thirst.
Today if I see my mother's face, for us poor girls thirst will end.

Today a well with golden steps.
O mother who bore me, a new well, a tank with a float.
If I, a poor girl, go and sink there, girl,
In this town without courage, to be responsible for us, who have
  you kept?

The property shared by all the image clusters of this song is ineffective containment, containment that offers no fulfillment, completion, or protection. The plant holding the eggplant that rots, the water circling but not entering the pot that is supposed to collect it, the forest and tank holding the hungry birds and unguarded fruit, the threshing ground holding the hay unsafe from the tax collector, the burnt neem tree parenting green shoots, the well that the singer feels she will drown in—all are images of wrong containment.

Sixth Song

Today lightning in the south,
O father who bore me, for me a window on the south side.
Today on the south side street,
O father who bore me, for me, honey is sold.
If my father were here, today he would weigh the price of honey,
He would extend his southern hand.

Today lightning in the north,
O father who bore me, for me a northern window.
If my mother were here, today she would weigh the price of arm
  rings,
She would extend her northern hand.

Today a rice scoop and serving plate,
O father who bore me, for me a hall without rice.
Today in the hall without rice.
O father who bore me, I, the lily, sob, father.

Today a rice bowl and serving plate,
O mother who bore me, for me, a hall without beans.
Today in the hall without beans,
O mother who bore me, I, the girl, sob, mother.

Today lime pounded to ash,
O mother who bore me, for me, a built and erected hall.
Today in the built and erected hall
After you, for me to stand and cry there are no kin.

Today lime pounded by stone,
O father who bore me, for me, a mixed and built hall.
Today in the mixed and built hall,
O mother who bore me, for me to bellow and weep there is no justice.

Today green asafoetida,
O mother who bore me, for me, if you stood a weight,
Today I am deficient of weight, mother,
I, the wasted younger sister, am made low by my husband's brothers.

Today fresh asafoetida,
O mother who bore me, for me, if you stood a weight,
Today I am deficient of weight, mother,
I, the wasted younger sister, am made low by enemies.

Today a stone fort encircled eight times,
O father who bore me, for me, a lodge that an ant will not enter.
Today if I rise, it obstructs.
For me, the wasted younger sister, when an eight-headed snake rises up there is fear.

Today a stone fort encircled ten times,
O poor people who bore me, for me, a lodge that a snake will not enter.
Today if I look it obstructs, father,
For me, the wasted younger sister, a ten-headed snake hisses with its hood.

Today lightning in the north,
O father who bore me, for me, a plantain-flower window.
Today on the north side street,

O father who bore me, for me arm rings are sold.
If my father were here,
He would weigh the price of arm rings; he would extend his right hand.

Today lightning in the south,
O poor people who bore me, for me, a palm-flower window.
Today on the south side street.
For me honey is sold.
If my father were here,
He would weigh the price of honey; he would extend his clear hand.

Today ten lakhs of green parrots.
O mother who bore me, for me, they will fly to the sea to the Paramaśivam temple.
If I poor girl told my troubles,
Today without taking food they would fly away.

The sixth song, like the previous one, is addressed to the singer's brother, to tell him that he is not caring well enough for her. This was sung by Muttammāḷ, a young woman in her twenties with one daughter. Muttammāḷ is the wife of Pushpam's older brother, Antony. Both of Muttammāḷ's parents are dead. She is said to have been very close to her father. Two related types of image dominate Muttammāḷ's song: one of edifices and vessels holding hunger and loneliness, danger and entrapment; the other of light and windows bringing riches and the loving care of parents. This song shares with Pushpam's songs a discontent with containment, but it has a different message, for it seems to suggest, through the associations it creates, that perfect containment is itself undesirable, that the best thing is to let in a little light, friendship, and food.

Seventh Song

Today *maṅgam cambā* paddy will grow, *maṅgam cambā* paddy will grow.
O father who bore me, O mother, on the side of the mountain the tied bundles fall.
Today in this town without justice,
To glean rotten paddy is it my, this woman's fate?

Today *cinna cambā* paddy will grow,
O father who bore me, O mother, for me by the side of the hedge
the tied bundles fall.
Today to glean spilled paddy,
Is it my, Sītā's, fate?

Today a crow calls,
O lord who bore me, O mother, like a black voice upon a stone
mountain.
If I take a stone and toss it,
I at this age, O mother who bore me, I suffer this sight.

Today a crow hisses,
O mother who bore me, O father, like a rich voice upon Gingee
mountain.
If I drive it off hissing, drive it off hissing,
I, the wasted younger sister, O mother who bore me, why do I suf-
fer this smallness?

If I make a golden hook
And I, the wasted younger sister, go to break off flowers,
Today it is no crime to break off flowers;
In this town without justice, to enter and beat me, is it right?

If I make a golden hook,
O father who bore me, O mother, and I go to break off the leaves,
Today it is no crime to break off leaves.
In this town, to rush upon me and beat me, is it right?

Today making a road of the sky,
O mother who bore me, and leaving the mango garden behind,
In this town without justice,
To throw a stone in the mango garden, and trap and beat, is it right?

For me making a road of the earth,
O mother who bore me, and leaving the flower garden behind,
In this town without justice, to throw a stone in the flower garden,
And enter and beat, is it right?

This song was sung by Kamalā. Its topic is obstruction, the exclusion of the singer by others from actions and states which she feels are good and right. Rather than contrasting a present with a past state, as all the previous songs have done, this song, which in other respects follows the design of the others, contrasts the singer's present undesirable condition with a more desirable possibility she sees before her. She sees bundles of good paddy fall on the mountainside, but she must glean rotten paddy; she must suffer the taunts and anger of the crow without expressing her anger to it— she feels smaller than the crow; she sees leaves and flowers, but if she plucks them, even with a golden hook, she is beaten.

The final stanza is ambiguous. She may be saying that she must leave the mango garden and the flower garden behind, reject them ("throw a stone" in them), and take a different road or others will "trap and beat" her. Or she may be saying that she is the garden, into which stones have been thrown, where others "enter and beat" her, and then rejecting her, take a different road. Perhaps both meanings are intended.

Eighth Song

Today the green parrots of ten towns,
O mother who bore me, will fly to the sea by the Paramaśivam temple.
If I, a poor girl, told my troubles,
There they would not even feel hungry, mother; they would fly away without eating.

For me the green parrots of eight towns,
O mother who bore me, O father, will descend to the sea by the temple of Yama the punisher.
If I, poor girl, told my troubles,
There they would not even take food.
O mother who bore me; they would rise away without eating

Today in a hut on top of a mountain,
O father who bore me, O mother, they are selling jasmine flowers.
If I, a woman, ask for a flower,
In this town without justice, brother, today the tree has a guard.

Today in a hut with plants at the edges,
O father who bore me, O mother, there they are selling red
  flowers.
If I, a lady, ask for a flower,
In this town without you, brother, today the bush has a guard.

Today white gram, mother;
O mother who bore me, O father, I am an uncrushed body,
  mother.
They crush me and take me away.
In this town without you, they make me suffer harm.

I am red gram, mother;
O father who bore me, O mother, I am gold with an unbending
  body, mother.
They bend me and take me away.
In this town without you, they make me suffer pain.

This was sung by Muttammāḷ, the singer of the sixth song. In the first stanza, the temple of Paramaśivam that the parrots fly from is called the temple of Yama (the god of death), the punisher and separator. Muttammāḷ might for good reason make this equation, since Paṟaiyars have traditionally been excluded from large Siva temples. In the second stanza, instead of being locked into buildings devoid of food and company, she is locked out of buildings where good things are sold. Like some previous songs, this song says that enclosures punish, fail to provide, and are to be rejected.

In the third stanza, Muttammāḷ uses an image that Nīlammā used—that of the singer's being gram and gold that are crushed and bent and carried away. But instead of blaming her husband for the crushing, Muttammāḷ blames an unspecified "they." If the third stanza is connected with the first two at all, it is likely that this "they" is the same "they" who own the Paramaśivam temple by the sea, and who would exclude her from their huts and from the purchase of their flowers. For Muttammāḷ perhaps there is a similarity between crushing and bending and exclusion, or perhaps she has simply departed from the strict semantic parallelism that most of the songs follow.

I have tried to show that the stanzas in a Paṟaiyar crying song constitute, with some variations, a network of Peircean metaphors. The metaphorical relations among the stanzas alone give each song its internal coherence and its overall significance. Furthermore, a particular image within the context of a particular song may acquire a significance that previously was only a possibility for that image. Through parallelism with other images in the song, this significance is brought to consciousness and thus a new sign is created.

To take one important example, the image of enclosure as a sign of deprivation— a meaning-association established in several of these songs—is unusual and perhaps new in the context of conventional Tamil symbolism, where unbroken enclosures (such as bangles, pots, wedding halls, the *tāli* or wedding pendant, the *kōlam* or doorstep design) are preeminent signs of auspiciousness, health, and plenty.

The reader may have observed that there is a metaphoric relation not only within songs but between songs. This tie between songs serves at least two communicative purposes. First, when the same message is repeated from song to song, the intensity of that message, and the likelihood that it will get through to others, is increased. All crying songs share the message that the singer has been hurt by someone in authority over her; correlatively they say that to be junior, "younger sister," is to be innocent, not morally inferior, and to have primordial rights which should not be alienated.[7] The message that the singer has been alienated from others and from what is hers, either locked in or locked out, is present in many songs. Though more specific and individual grievances may be missed, a hearer of even fragments of crying songs could hardly fail to catch these basic ideas.

The second communicative purpose is that when an image is repeated from song to song but some detail is changed, one knows that the details which substitute for one another belong to the same semantic class—that is, that they also have some property in common. Since the contexts of substitution are so specific, the number of features shared by the variant details is likely to be much higher than the number of unshared features. We have seen that within a single segment of a song, the terms which substituted for one another are related in sometimes trivial, sometimes interesting ways. In the first song, first stanza, are substitutions like *kāḍu* (wasteland, also forest) for *veyyil* (heat of the sun); in the first song, fourth stanza, *nilā* (moon) for *maruntu* (medicine); and in the sixth song, fourth stanza, *etirāḷi* (enemies) for *paṅkāḷi* (husband's brothers, literally "sharers").[8]

Similar substitutions take place among images that are shared from song to song. When Muttammāḷ sings in one song about ten lakhs of parrots flying to the sea, and in another song about ten towns' worth of parrots flying to the sea, we know that for her the two quantities are comparable. This is for us a less interesting substitution. More interesting is the fact that laments of alienation, isolation, and separation are directed both against kinsmen—mother, husband, and brothers—and against upper-caste men, for this suggests that the singers perceive a similarity between kinship and caste relations and between violations in both spheres.

Also interesting are the contrasts between desirable and undesirable states that are expressed in the song. In some songs the contrast is between a past desirable state and a present undesirable one. In others the contrast is between two present states physically juxtaposed, one desirable and the other undesirable. Since the expression of tense is nonobligatory, the difference between a contrast of past and present and a contrast of contemporaneous states is usually subtle.

Compare, for instance, the first stanza of the fifth song,

> For me . . . clusters of eggplants . . .
> With no one to hold and embrace us,
> We rot with the vine . . .

expressing a fall from fruitful past to rotten present, with the first stanza of the seventh song, expressing exclusion from a fruitful state and confinement to a rotten one:

> Today, *maṅgam cambā* paddy will grow . . .
> On the side of the mountain the tied bundles fall . . .
> Today . . . to glean rotten paddy . . . is it my fate?

The parallelism between a fall from a higher to a lower state and exclusion from a higher or confinement to a lower state approaches identity in these songs.[9]

I have stated that those who are meant to hear a crying song include those against whom the grievances in the song are directed, but that the route by which a song reaches its target is not always direct. So the intended addressee, the real addressee, is not always the person apostrophized in the song. In the first song, for instance, Pushpam calls out to her mother, long dead, and vents her anger and pain that this mother died and abandoned her so young. But the song also makes the point that early marriage of the daughter entails a separation akin to that of the mother's death—perhaps a warning to other parents not to marry their children so young—and is a general appeal to the world for sympathy and protection. Similarly, the second and third songs are addressed directly to the mother but indirectly to husband and in-laws, and still more indirectly to the hearers of these songs, those surrounding the singer, the "society" responsible for maintaining the tradition which has caused her harm.[10]

Crying songs are protest songs in a general sense; they protest not only the personal sufferings of the singer but the rules of hierarchy themselves. Some of the challenges presented in those songs are gentle and subtle, as for instance the implicit analogy drawn between the neglectfulness of older brothers, who do not allow their sister to come back home, and the exclusivism of higher castes, who deny the singer entrance to their gardens. Other challenges are stronger and more clear.

One of the latter is the challenge to the concept of auspiciousness (*maṅgalam*) held by members of higher castes in the village. This concept involves the idea that for the sake of the whole—family, village, or society—individual members should give up their personal interests. Even words of disunity should not be uttered, and an evil thing should be given a good name, as though if its evil is not socially recognized, it will not be. Auspiciousness dwells in the realm of appearances—a powerful realm. It is expressed most often on doorsteps and before others' eyes. Protection of auspiciousness is above all the duty of the women of the family. To sing a sad song dwelling on an evil fate and an unhappy ending is not an auspicious act, though there are some appropriate contexts for it. For a married woman to call her husband a criminal and herself a widow, for her to give open expression to her sense of her own value independent of and in opposition to the acts and opinions of others is to deny or neglect her duty as guardian of auspiciousness.

High-caste women, as far as I could ascertain, never sang such songs about themselves; their sense of self-esteem often involved struggle and independent action, but it was based ultimately on their fulfillment of the role of nurturer and supporter. Their main aim in life was, ostensibly, to protect their husband's and their family's well-being. They believed that they should never wish their husband dead, and they did all they could to avoid the appearance of such a wish.

For the singers of crying songs, auspiciousness was clearly not so sacred. Their reasons we can only guess at. They may have felt, in the first place, that it was not to their advantage to maintain a hierarchical "whole" of which they were nowhere near the head. In the second place, they may have seen no purpose in making things appear fine when they were not in fact fine, and when they themselves had to suffer the evils that others felt it desirable to hide.

Shortly after Nīlammā sang the third song to me, a woman of the landowning caste who had not been present at the singing or heard the recording came to the place where I was staying. She severely chastised, not Nīlammā herself, but Kamalā and Pushpam, for singing a song about the sufferings of widowhood when in reality their husbands were still alive, though Kamalā and Pushpam were at that point innocent of this offense.

The incident taught me a number of things about communication within the village: that such songs, or reports of such songs, do reach the ears of high-caste people who are not present at the singing; that the high-caste woman (who was about forty years of age) did not feel free to chastise Nīlammā (who was about sixty) and therefore vented her anger on the younger women instead; that the songs are taken seriously; and that the particular message in this song was unfamiliar enough to the high-caste woman, or opposed enough to what she accepted as true, for her to respond strongly to it.

A second challenge to high-caste values contained in these songs is the redefinition of karma (*vinai*) and wrong (*pāvam*) that they advance. I have pointed out that the term *pāvi* (one associated with wrong or *pāvam*) has two meanings in these songs, as in colloquial Tamil generally: first, someone who suffers, who is in a pitiable condition; and second, a wrongdoer. Each of the two meanings implies the other to those who believe that all suffering is the result of the sufferer's own past evil actions.[11]

However, in crying songs the two meanings of *pāvi* are dissociated. The singer refers to herself as *pāvi* and to her tormentors as *pāvi*, but there is little indication that she feels she has done wrong in the past for which she is now being punished; on the contrary, she continually declares her innocence. The concept of *vinai* remains, but in a significantly modified form—it is not the sufferer, but the sufferer's senior kin whose evil actions now come back to haunt her. Nīlammā asks her mother (third song), "Did you not find an auspicious day for my wedding?" and more pointedly Pushpam asks her father, "Did you kill a pregnant cow?" in search of an explanation for her sorrows.[12]

Inasmuch as the doctrine of karma is used to justify a system of rank by birth, the Paraiyar redefinition of karma attacks the underpinnings of that system itself. If, in this redefinition, grievances against senior kin become grievances against senior castes, as we have seen happen in crying songs, the consequences will be powerful, because they are close to the truth.

The last song I wish to consider here is a lullaby that was sung to me by

Nīlammā. It is difficult to decide whether it should be classified as a crying song or not, since it differs rather sharply from the others, none of which, for one thing, are lullabies. It is similar to crying songs, however, in that the singer weeps as she sings; therefore I include it here.

Ninth Song

Ārārō ārārirō ārārārirō
You little eye, sleep, boy.
My eye, O jewel, O jewel of my eye,
Go to sleep.
Who was it here that hit you, my eye?
That did you wrong?
Won't you tell me who hit you as you weep?
For my eye, Nākiṉiṅkam, I'll go away and come again.
For you, *ārārō ārārirō.*
My eye, whose baby could you be?
Did grandmother beat you,
My darling, with her ringed hand?
Did your father beat you, my little brother?
Red-footed cow-grazer,
For you, *ārārō ārārirō.*
Little eye, *ārārō ārārirō.*
When you go out to the forest,
My eye, bears and tigers will catch you.
For you *ārārō ārārirō.*
My eye, whose baby could you be?
Once you said you were going far away.
My little brother, cheetahs and tigers will surround you.
For you, *ārārō ārārirō.*
My little brother, *ārārō ārārirō.*
If you buy a thread of Kāci,
Little brother, and you travel to Kāci and Rāmēśvaram,
For you, *ārārō ārārirō.*
For you swans and parrots will fly,
My eye, for you they will bring fruit to eat.
On you the merchant's son will bestow pearls;
My eye, on you the smith will place a crown.

For you, in the doorway of the smith,
My eye, O you son of a king,
If you stand there,
They will beat you; they will kill you,
My little brother; they will send a servant to watch you.
On you the merchant's son will bestow money;
My eye, for you the smith will open his store.
For you, in the doorway of the smith,
My eye, O you son of a king, if you go stand there,
He will beat you; he will kill you.
My eye, he will send a servant to watch you.
For you, *ārārō ārārirō.*
You go worship the crescent moon of Māsi,
My eye, for you to raise up your mother's brother's family.
For you, *ārārō ārārirō.*
My eye, *ārārō ārārirō.*
On you the son of the merchant will bestow pearls,
My little brother; on you the smith will place a crown.
For you, in the doorway of the smith;
My little brother, you son of a king, if you go stand there,
They will beat you; they will kill you,
My little brother; they will place a servant to watch you.
For you, *ārārō ārārirō.*
My darling, *ārārō ārārirō.*
Your conch shell sounds, boy,
My eye, in your temple of the lord.
Your drum sounds, boy,
My little brother, in your temple of the supreme.
For you, *ārārō ārārirō.*
My eye, *ārārō ārārirō.*
For you, lullabying and caressing,
My eye, [I] have laid you in your cradle.
For you the conch shell sounds, boy,
My little brother, in your temple of the lord.
Your drum sounds, boy,
My darling, in your temple of the supreme.
Ārārō ārārirō,
My little brother, precious parrot, ārārō.

This song is similar to the other songs considered here, in many ways; weeping is only one of the properties they share. It is a song of injustice done to an innocent, and it is a song of contrasts. However, it rings some major changes on the basic pattern established by the other songs as a group, and for that reason it may be considered to belong to a different song type. These are some of the changes: the stanzas have a very different formal design; the actions described are attributed to the future rather than to the present or the past; the person apostrophized is not a senior protector of the singer, but a junior protégé.

However, the most important change is that in this song *uṉakku* (for you) and *nī* (you) take the place occupied by *enakku* (for me) and *nān* (I) in the other songs. The singer communicates to the baby an image of himself identical to that of the singer conveyed in other songs. "You are," she sings to the baby (as "I am" in other songs), perfect and innocent through all changes, but the world is an ambiguous and shifting place. This world is comprised not only of tigers and parrots but of smiths and merchants, who are equally treacherous and benevolent.

Why is this message that higher castes are the wrongdoers so much more powerfully stated in this song than in others? Here only, higher castes are mentioned by name, and here only, actual and serious wrongs of caste against caste are described: the Paṟaiyar boy may not stand in the doorway of the goldsmith, or he will be killed; the conch shell and the drums sounding in the temple are brought by the Paṟaiyar, thus they belong to him, and Nīlammā sings to the baby, the temple is "yours." And yet he may not enter.

To answer the question posed above, it may help again to consider the actual addressee of the song. It is only in part the baby, for a baby could only partly understand what is being sung here. Ultimately the smith and the merchant may also hear this song. If they do, they will recognize that the singer is weeping not for her own past but for the baby's future. They may also recognize that the innocence of the baby, unlike the innocence of adults, is indisputable and that to treat him as guilty from birth is not right.[13] The clarity of the accusation is in proportion to the clarity of the victim's innocence. The song may be read as a strong appeal to the listeners not to treat the child in the future as the singer was treated in the past. The parallelism between baby and singer, future and past, that arises from a comparison of this song with the set of crying songs amounts to such a plea.

As its parallelism with other songs affects the meaning and impact of this one, so this song in turn affects them. The protection that the singer of the lullaby offers the baby substitutes for and contrasts with the lack of protection that the singers of other songs experience from parents, older brothers, husband, and the unspecified "they." The substitution of baby, "younger brother," for self, "younger sister," strengthens the association of innocence with self. Thus, through their parallelism, the songs build upon each other.

In this chapter I have discussed crying songs as vehicles for the individual singer's origination of new image-meaning associations and the propagation upward of these associations as potential new conventions.[14] I have given evidence that some nonliterate female rural members of the Paraiyar caste question not only their status in the social hierarchy but some of the assumptions upon which that hierarchy is based. Inasmuch as these songs oppose conventional definitions of order, the image-meaning associations through which they do so must necessarily be nonconventional. Yet they must also be close enough to the familiar order to have meaning to the listeners. The images appearing in crying songs are ancient, but the significations they acquire through the metaphors of the songs are not the common ones. Enclosures and boundaries, as we have seen, in these songs signify separation and restriction rather than purity and protection. The abandoned younger sister (a major figure in Tamil oral literature) becomes metaphorically linked with the untouchable woman, wrongfully excluded from her primordial home. The divine and innocent child becomes representative of the sinlessness of the lower castes. Among higher castes, participation in struggles for "freedom" (*sutantiram*), the title of "original Dravidian" (*ātiḍirāviḍa*) for hill tribes and untouchable castes, and talk of the "innocence" (in English) of nonliterate laborers, suggest the kind of new conventions that crying-song metaphors, if received, enter into.

I have been most concerned to point out the type of creativity involved in crying songs: the singers are very close to the songs they sing. Though the songs borrow from each other, there is no object mentioned in any song that is not part of the singer's own experience and imagination. The principal referent of the songs is the self, and no other self than that of the singer. The symbols she builds out of the objects of her experience are personal sometimes to the point of seeming private, but they are not private, for they are directed outward. They aim to convince the world that the singer is as she describes herself and not as the world describes her. For while dominant conventions support a strong self-image for most literate groups (which are by and large a subset of high-caste groups), the unlettered Paraiyar woman, unsupported by convention, must create her own.[15]

Chapter 3

Work and Love

The Paṟaiyar women's laments were part of a global genre. They bore the message, "My fate is to lose." The singers were condemned to lives of slow, relentless death, and their songs said this was not fair. They showed not a glimmer of a way out.

The same Paṟaiyar women sang other kinds of songs, however. Here they sang less structured, more diverse songs, including love songs and work songs.[1]

To my eyes, what was most striking about the Chingleput Paṟaiyars was that they were people of the body, a body not unlike the one Bakhtin found in Rabelais' world. (In 1980, I had never heard of Bakhtin but was much influenced by the work of Victor Turner, whose thoughts on the body, the folk, and the carnivalesque in many ways paralleled the thoughts of Bakhtin.) What distinguished the Paṟaiyars more than anything else from their high-caste landlords was their relationship with this body. First, they lived by hard physical labor—labor that they had transformed over centuries into dance, dance often accompanied by song. When they weeded the fields, when they built the roads, when they lifted water, when they guided the powerful buffaloes pulling the ploughs, when they carried great loads on their heads, they were pictures of grace and strength, and they knew this about themselves and were proud of it. But that they did this kind of labor, that they knew how to do it, was a sign—to those who lived by nonbodily work or by not working at all—of their inferiority. "What does the bridegroom know how to do?" said a mocking, double-entendre wedding song of the Brahman community. "He knows how to irrigate fields, he knows how to dig a ditch."[2]

Agricultural workers in the village where I stayed were close to the earth in the strictest, most physical sense of the term. Daily, for many hours each day, their eyes saw, their ears heard, and their hands felt nothing but earth, plants, animals, sky, and each other. Times when I spent the day working in the fields with them, trying to be like them, I would dream vividly all night long of rocks, weeds, mud, and rice seedlings—the objects upon which my attention had been focused for such a long period during the day. The Paṟaiyar laborers' songs of themselves, like my dreams of my days with them, were brimming with vegetative imagery: they called themselves eggplants, lentils, onions, grains, flowers on the vine. They blossomed, they fruited, they ripened, they were plucked and eaten, they were dried in the sun, they were left for seed. In their songs, they did not own the earth around them, they were that earth.[3]

The Paṟaiyar laborers were people of the open and unfinished body in another sense as well, for their traditional ritual occupation was nothing other than to take care of the dirtying processes and products of that body. They handled human and animal corpses, human and animal excrement, the substances of birth, the leftover food, the old clothes. From the point of view of the higher castes, Paṟaiyars were, by birth, untouchable (*tīṇḍā*). There was thought to be something inherently dirty about them, something that demons liked and deities did not, a property that would spread to others who came too near. In face-to-face situations, Paṟaiyars were treated with contempt by the higher castes. Spatially, they were excluded from those places that represented, to the Paṟaiyars themselves as well as to the higher castes, the heart of the human world—the center of the village, the homes of the village magnates, the shops where good things were sold, the places where food was prepared, the temples of the higher deities.

No one of a higher caste would eat food touched by a Paṟaiyar. Paṟaiyar houses were on the village outskirts. On festival nights, Paṟaiyars got wildly drunk and were given to spirit possession, and their loss of control on these occasions, especially their drunkenness, was taken by people of higher castes as one more item of evidence that Paṟaiyars and others near them in rank could never be suited to positions of responsibility, no matter how much legislation was passed in their favor. In Tamil, the word *Paṟaiyar* itself (whence our term "pariah") was, in its associated feeling-tone, much like English "nigger." Hence the preferential use of the Gandhian euphemism *harijan* ("God's child"). The social context of the Paṟaiyar songs was inseparable from the bodily state of the singers, and not only because their social rank was indexed by their bodily labor. Paṟaiyars of the Chingleput area were on the disprivileged end of a massive hierarchical social order that sought to organize all the human variety of a civilization into a single all-encompassing, sacralized system controlled from the top.

They lived in the presence of a powerful vision of a total society that actively, physically, and spatially excluded and exiled certain people from places these people viewed as their own, as home. The Chingleput Paṟaiyars had a keen sense of their exclusion from the center of their world; they felt the injustice of it, the heartlessness of it, and this sense of the injustice of their exclusion was clearly evident in many of their songs. They sang of themselves as driven from their natal homes; confined in lonely, walled, and windowless fortresses; denied entrance to gardens of flowers, fields of rice, orchards, temples, wedding halls. They sang of river water refusing to enter their pots, of animals refusing to eat the food they offered. Most of all they sang of being cut off from love.

Many Paṟaiyars were Christians. Christian missionaries in India have from the beginning concentrated their efforts at conversion on low-caste communities and have been most successful with these communities, largely because Christianity represents itself as a religion of the oppressed. In the kingdom of heaven, the last shall be first. Christian ideology was an important component of the worldview of Paṟaiyars in Chingleput and other areas. The songs protesting exclusion primarily took the form of laments (*ayiṟa pāḍḍu*). In the songs discussed below, most of which are songs of sexual attraction (*kātal pāḍḍu*), I try to show how the singers covertly express their feelings about social hierarchy. The Paṟaiyar singers did not, because they could not, express too openly their rejection of the social order of which they were part.

Aims and Methods of Paṟaiyar Singers

Paṟaiyars of the present day appear to have a much wider repertory of folk songs than members of higher castes. In part this is probably due to their higher rate of nonliteracy, which is in turn a consequence of landless poverty: they cannot so easily afford to take their children out of the workforce and put them in school, as much as they would like to do so. In part, the importance of songs to them is due to the preponderance of physical laborers among them: song does not require free hands, and it can transform labor from lonely drudgery into a kind of art form. Song, like dance, is democratic and communal—the only material needed is the body, and in the very process of creating it, you share it with those around you. Finally, we might say that the songs of Paraiyar laborers were songs of hopeful self-affirmation. Paraiyars knew that times were changing and perhaps they might change in their favor. The singers were ready to make themselves, as individuals, heard.

Paraiyars, as well as women of other castes in Tamil Nadu, have several kinds of songs that express personal sentiments and are sung spontaneously, in relatively protected environments and for select audiences. These include laments, work songs, songs of clandestine love, put-down songs, songs of social commentary, and songs that mix these various themes. Laments are wept song, highly stylized in form and yet unique to each singer. Low-caste women may be hired to sing laments in funeral processions; the kinswomen of the deceased will also sing. Yet the content of the laments often has nothing to do with the person being buried; rather, these laments proclaim the singer's own sorrows, in particular the sorrows connected with her marriage and with her low-caste status. The same laments may be sung spontaneously, in lonely places such as palm groves, before people the singer knows will be sympathetic to her plight. A central theme of all laments is the victimization of the singer by more powerful others. It is necessary for the singer to voice her complaints circumspectly; a little girl who sang a lament while sitting on the doorstep of her house was beaten by her older brother for showing dissatisfaction with her life.

Put-down songs, which criticize or mock particular individuals, together with songs of social commentary, also must be performed with a careful eye to context, lest the target of the song become angered and seek revenge. Yet the content of these songs can be surprisingly bold. One *ēṟṟappāḍḍu*, a song sung by a lone laborer to keep himself company as he lifted buckets of water to irrigate the fields, contained the comment, "There goes the Reḍḍiyar walking over the *bund* in his new white *veshtie*. May he fall in the mud, break both his knees, and have to crawl all the way to God's heaven." The singer's landlord, a pious Reḍḍiyar dressed in white, was standing with me when this song reached our ears. This man was also my principal informant and research assistant. He was powerful, highly educated, and articulate, a professional lecturer.

When we heard the song, he commented to me with a smile that it sounded as though the singer was angry. I wondered, was my presence a shield of some kind? The landlord knew that I had sympathetic feelings for the laborers. Or perhaps the song was sung for my benefit. On the other hand, perhaps my presence made no difference.

"White men" (*veḷḷaikkāraṅga*) were often the butt of put-downs in *kummippāḍḍu* songs. Some of these, evidently originating in preindependence days, were sung by old women in evening get-togethers with a group of Malayāḷi Catholic Sisters who ran a clinic near the village. The women were all Paṟaiyars whom the Sisters were seeking to convert. There were no men present at their gatherings. When I joined them with my tape recorder, these anticolonial songs were among the first they sang. One such song begins,

> The white man sits on his porch;
> he has a woman in every corner;
> pee into his drinking pot, girl;
> pour it into his rosy red mouth.

Another *kummippāḍḍu* comments upon the white man's role in the transition to a cash economy:

> One man, one man in the garden,
> he alone planted his cucumbers.
> Saying "Sell them at two for a coin,"
> the white man is writing
> a letter . . .
>
> The white man's coin is a silver-white coin.
> It's playing a joke on us, that little coin

Love songs were often equally songs of social commentary and put-down songs. They might take the form of festival songs, devotional songs, lullabies, or most frequently, work songs. A woman sang, as she worked on a road crew, carrying baskets of earth on her head, keeping count of the baskets:

> One load of earth, lift it lift it, lifting earth,
> O it's easy, lifting earth, lift it, lift it,
> the road I'm building,
> O it's easy, the golden road.
> Boy who's walking, lift it lift it, on my road,
> O it's easy, on my road,
> what's your smile for, lift it lift it,
> what's your beauty for, O it's easy,
> what's your nerve for.

Two loads of earth, O it's easy, lifting earth,
lift it lift it, boy who's walking,
O it's easy, on my road
. . . in your pocket, O it's easy,
there's no money, lift it lift it, you're a baby,
from store to store, O it's easy,
you go walking, you pluck your treasures,
O it's easy, you sleep on the porch . . .

Pounding rice into flour with a mortar and a long wooden pestle, singing in time to her pounding, a woman complained to her husband about two kinds of want:

I have no mortar to pound in,
you clever boy who took me away;
with a little little mortar, *tillālē*,
we can pound without spilling, *nannānē*.
I have no oven to cook in [and so on] . . .
I have no stick to stir with . . .
I have no pot to mix in . . .
I have no sari to wear,
you clever boy who took me away;
with a little little sari, *tillālē*,
we can wear it without spilling, *nannānē*.

Tying sheaths of cut paddy, another woman sang the story of a worker who flees his overseer, finds a girl who pities him, and leaves her pregnant.

By the stream at harvest time, tying one, tying two.
He yells, "You didn't carry your bundle."
He's running, see girl. Crying, "He's running,"
he takes a stick in his hand, takes a stick in his hand.
Girl going to the village with pots stacked on your head,
put your pots down, say a kind word before you go on your way.
Tying a swing in the coconut orchard, bearing a child by the edge
of the road,
tying a hammock at the edge of the trees,
"Uncle leaving for Tirupattur, pick up the baby, give it a kiss."

Ellipsis and understatement alone soften the pointed observations of this song: that violent treatment of workers results in vagrancy, that vagrancy yields fatherless children.

When we hear songs such as these, we might ask, are they about love or about poverty, about personal and immediate experience or about general and global processes, about relations between individuals or about relations between classes? Such questions answer themselves. These songs are both social and personal, both local and global. One characteristic that distinguishes them from the kinds of songs we are used to is the degree to which they are integral to particular but undemarcated social situations, and active within those situations. They are not necessarily sung on "ritual" occasions. Even when they are performed at, for instance, funerals or festivals, they are tailored to specific interpersonal concerns: this particular laborer addresses this particular client, this particular wife addresses this particular husband, referring directly or obliquely in her song to this particular event. Yet to the extent that the problem addressed by a song is a common one, the song will be remembered by other singers and sung by them again in new variations. Through the specific, the singer reaches the general.

The creation of song and other sorts of poetic language in response to specific interpersonal situations is not unique to Tamil Paṟaiyars. Similar uses of verbal art are reported from points all around the world (Tannen 1982; Emeneau 1958; Feld 1982; Heath 1983; Abu-Lughod 1987).

In the Tamil context, a focus on the personal and situational nature of songs recorded in the field raises a number of important issues. First, it seems clear that if such songs have a purpose it is not, as a rule, to maintain the status quo or commemorate it, but, more often, to effect some kind of change in the singer's situation by moving some particular party in the audience to feel and act differently from before. Laments, criticisms, and entreaties are much more common than songs of praise or thanks.

Second, many songs are deliberately ambiguous. Double-entendre love songs are one obvious example: a song may be both a complaint about material deprivation and a sexual invitation, both a criticism of leisured arrogance and a teasing appreciation of a desired boy's body. By the same token a song may simultaneously protest both a general social problem and a specific example of that problem as experienced by the singer. In some situations, a singer may most safely protest a general social problem by couching her protest in strictly private language. In other cases, a singer may most effectively get her personal message across if it is stated in general terms. The more powerful is her intended audience and the object of her criticism, and the more counter to social codes is her message, the more careful the singer must be and the more she must resort to subtle, even subliminal, means of persuasion.

Third, if a scholar from the West comes with her tape recorder to live among people whose songs are commonly spontaneously performed, composed by the singer and immediately interpersonal in nature, the scholar should expect that at least some of the songs will be addressed, at least on some level, to her. I would contend that this fact is not a problem—or rather, it is a problem only if we treat it as one, either by ignoring that aspect of the song that is addressed to us, or by pretending that we are not part of the social situation we are documenting.

Rather, we should make an effort to comprehend what the singers are trying to say to us. We should understand that this may not be an easy task. We are very powerful and for that reason the singers will be trying hard to get us on their side, and at the same time their approach to our hearts may be very roundabout. Their method of trying to move us—precisely the stylistics and poetics of their message, as opposed to its bare referential content—may be both the most significant and (because of their difference from us) the least easily accessible aspect of their message to us. We need more than literate common sense to get at this message. We cannot assume that it will be simple or obvious. Moreover, inevitably the singers will try to tell us things that we do not want to hear, and inevitably they will compete with each other for our attention and say bad things about each other. Often their values will conflict with our own. None of this excuses a refusal on our part to listen carefully to them, or a muting of their voices by ours.

The songs discussed below were all sung directly to me by their composers. The situation was intimate; there were usually only one or two other people around. The singers came to my house when they chose and sang what they chose. I tape-recorded their songs and rewarded them materially with various kinds of gifts including cash, which was certainly one of the main incentives of their singing for me. But I would not call this situation unnatural. The singers had grown up in the presence of electronic media, of Western (or at least Westernized) professionals, and of an urban, cosmopolitan cash economy (public transportation to the city was fast and cheap). The idea of selling their songs for money was not strange to them.

But there was another dimension to my relationship with the singers, having to do with our shared womanhood, with money, and with the intimate and direct nature of the messages purveyed by the songs. Young, low-caste, moneyless, laboring women with hopes that they might be better off in the future had to confront the knowledge that one of the easiest ways, in the short run, for them to pick up cash was to sell their sexual services. The combination of sexual hierarchy, caste hierarchy, and economic inequality bore down hard upon the young Paṟaiyar woman. This was a problem that she did not share with her brothers. If one of the big men in the village called her to his bed, what should she do? A number of the songs below address this question, and answer it. I will not claim that by paying for their songs I saved these young singers from a life a prostitution—they did not need me to save them. But I would like to think that by giving them good money for their artistic work I lent support to an idea they may already have had: that their own creative minds were by far their most valuable resource.

Multivocality and the Nonautonomy of Selves

A well-known old Tamil poem comments upon the fusion of souls that happens in love:

> My mother and your mother, who are they to each other?
> My father and your father, how are they kin?
> I and you, however we knew,
> like the fine soil and the falling rain,
> our very hearts are
> mixed past parting.

The sense that those who love are commingled in both body and soul (body and soul themselves being commingled) is strong among Tamil people and is enacted and articulated in many ways among them. Feeding the beloved from one's own dish with one's own hand and being so fed, deep gazes, sexual intercourse, conversation, caresses—all are commonly described by Tamil people as a mixing (*kalattal*) of the substances of life and self. Love (*anbu*) entails the melting (*urukutal*) of the heart, a dissolution (*karaital*) of the hard boundaries of self (*āṇuvam*, *timir*), the latter conceived as both bodily strength and mental invulnerability. All of this is Tamil cliché, a set of "metaphors" deeply embedded in common usage.

There is, perhaps, a peculiar astigmatism in the Western eye, or more specifically in the eye of the modern Western literate elite, which makes us see such phrases as "the mixing of hearts" as metaphor, which is to say, not real or even possible. To us, "I" am only I; "you" are only you. This is our own, largely unquestioned view of the reality of the human self, and our unconscious, evidently very strong, expectation is that other people will have the same view or should come to have it. Each self is inviolably bounded and separate from each other self. The integrity of each self is sacred. When I say, "I went home," the subject of that sentence can be only one person. Or can it? Does everybody share the same limitations on "I" that restrict our academic vision? There is no reason to assume so. Perhaps if we were able to free ourselves from this restriction, we might perceive meaning and pattern where previously we saw none. If there are people on earth whose experienced selves are less holy than ours, we might, having removed our blinders, be able to see what these people are trying to show us, or (to return to the verbal medium) hear what they are telling us, more clearly.

In 1980, when we tape-recorded and transcribed songs sung by the workers of our village, I and my scholarly Reḍḍiyar assistant set aside a number of these songs as being confused or incomplete or not coming out as the singer must have intended.

To us, these particular songs had no aesthetic appeal. They contained apparent grammatical errors, including errors in pronominal usage, which were annoying to us with our shared love of linguistic precision. Charitably, we surmised that each singer had her occasional off days. I kept the seemingly flawed songs and my notes concerning their performance, but I never attempted to do anything with them; I never published them or wrote anything about them because they were opaque to me; they told me nothing about the singers, exemplified nothing interesting. I lacked the tools that might have enabled me to understand them. I had studied many Western descriptions of Indian society, some saying that it was monistic, others that it was pluralistic; some claiming that it was hierarchical from top to bottom, others that it had a strong antihierarchical, egalitarian component; some describing Indian villagers as possessed by an almost obsessive concern with boundary maintenance, others describing the thought of such villagers as fluid, relativistic, and ambiguous with respect to all entities, categories, and boundaries including that of the person.[4]

In the remainder of this chapter, I examine the lyrics of a few such songs, with an eye to the relations between voices contained in the songs. I try to suggest that what I perceived as inadvertent confusion on the part of the singer was not inadvertent at all but was a way of trying to get me to comprehend a specific emotional message.

Among the songs that I recorded, one very common type consists of a dialogue between lovers or potential lovers, in which one of the pair is inviting, the other refusing. For instance, one young woman sang a song that began,

> I'll give you one lakh of gold,
> I'll give you a single nose pin,
> dancing girl, little girl,
> why don't you come here,
> girl, little girl,
> why don't you come here, girl.

To this invitation comes the reply,

> I don't want one lakh of gold,
> I don't want a single nose pin,
> go put your foot in a cow pie,
> temple owner,
> go put your foot in.

In the next verse, two lakhs of gold and two nose pins are offered, and the suitor is told to put his foot in two cow pies, and so on up to ten. Counting songs such as this one have no time when they are "supposed" to be performed, but they tend to accompany repetitive activities—anything from weaving mats to winnowing. They are often more internally varied than this song, as for instance the road-building song given above. This song would not be addressed to any particular person; it would be heard by whoever was nearby—fellow laborers, stray "others." But the rather angry social message it conveys is quite clear.

Among my collection of songs, this song is closer than most to the symbolic, or boundary-maintaining, end of the stylistic continuum. Although there is no objective narrator, the characters are objectified in that their speech is mechanical and their voices are very clearly demarcated from one another, to such an extent that neither character is moved at all or changed at all by the other: each sticks to his or her own invariant little speech right through to the end.

The style is hierarchical in that the singer controls her characters like puppets, and she herself shows no emotional involvement in the song. As a piece of art, this particular song, after the first verse, is so predictable as to be boring. It is also atypical; only three or four songs in my collection of several hundred were as highly patterned as this one. But as a member of the whole set of songs that were sung throughout the village, this one serves the important function of setting up a model of the expectable and the predictable against which the others may play.

Another song of the same type, but slightly more dialogized, was sung by another young woman of the same community as the first. The song begins, "To the limit of my knees, or to the limit of the water, shall I plunge in, prostitute girl?" (Water is a common Tamil image for female sexuality and for the slaking of passionate thirsts.)

To this question, the other replies, "O merchant, O temple owner, O king, O my darling, you should move a little farther away [*unnum koñcam oḍḍi pōnga*]." The suitor continues asking, setting the limit higher and higher, and the girl continues giving him the same reply. But this reply is an ambiguous one, following endearing and inviting terms of address with a request that the addressee go away, and using both the familiar and the respectful *oḍḍi pōnga*, in the same breath, to make this request.

In the story of Valli and Murugan, the god Murugan, who already has a wife, falls in love with the forest-dwelling mortal girl Valli. Disguising himself as an old mendicant, Murugan comes to Valli to beg for food. She gives him millet flour and honey to eat. It sticks in his throat and he asks for water. Reluctantly, she takes him into a deep and dangerous part of the forest to show him where clear water is, and eventually he wins her. This well-known romantic tale was sung to me in narrative form by a young Brahman woman of the village. The singer, nearing the end of what was clearly a burdensome pregnancy, said without enthusiasm that it was a song to be sung at weddings. She had learned it from her mother, who had learned it from a singing master. The song as she sang it—sweetly modulated, flowing and melodic—told the whole story of Murugan and Valli in detail from beginning to end. But the version sung by a Villi woman, as a hymn to Murugan himself, and addressed to him, confined itself to one fragment:

Honey and millet stick in my throat, Valli.
[Repeat]
There's water stirred up by goats and cows;
Scoop it and drink it, son of a priest.
[Repeat]
There's canal water flowing over there;
Scoop it and drink it, son of a priest.
[Repeat]
Water stirred up by goats and cows
Isn't what I want, Valli.
[Repeat]
Honey and millet flour stick in my throat, Valli.
[Repeat]
There's pond water over there;
Scoop it and drink it, son of a priest.
[Repeat]
Water mixed with the urine
and dung of goats and cows
Isn't what I want, Valli.
[Repeat]

This song takes us somewhat further toward what I have labeled the expressive end of the stylistic continuum. Between the two voices, there is no strict turn taking, so that we can only know who is saying what on the basis of the content of what is said. The whole song is looser than the others, less strictly patterned and controlled. Nevertheless, the voices of the two characters in dialogue remain clearly distinct, and although they respond to each other slightly, for the most part they seem to speak past each other: neither significantly changes his or her message to the other.

The three songs described above all represent dialogues in which a hierarchical social relationship obtains between the quoted speakers, the man and the woman. Perhaps this has something to do with the firm refusal given by the woman to the man in each of these songs, and the clear boundaries maintained between the voices.

But there are other songs reporting dialogue between lovers or potential lovers who are social equals, and here the total patterning of the songs becomes much looser, the behavior of the voices less predictable, and the boundaries between them less precise. The boy addresses the girl by familiar and intimate terms, such as *ḍī* and *ponnē* (both glossed here as "girl" or "little girl"), but so does the girl address the boy, reciprocally, as *dā* and *payyā* ("boy" or "little boy"). She also addresses him as *māmā* "mother's brother," a term indicating familiarity, and most importantly, a sense of kinship—a feeling that the two lovers are made for, and of, each other. In some of these songs, the dialogue begins to resemble actual conversation:

If it's a lake, it's just a lake, *māmā*,
and the thorn fruit trees grow in a row,
and the thorn fruit trees grow in a row.
I'll climb high and shake one hard, girl,
you leap wide and grab it tight,
you leap wide and grab it tight.
And if I leap and grab it tight, *māmā*,
and my husband asks, what shall I say?
and my husband asks, what shall I say?
When you were stooping for some dung, girl,
a single bangle broke in two,
a single bangle broke in two.
And you who broke me, too, *māmā*,
you who gave me such wise advice,
you who gave me such wise advice,
you whose magic gave me a secret baby, *māmā*,
tell me some healing before you go,
tell me some healing before you go.
Cut some wild basil, girl,
cut some bark from the black-to-white tree,
cut some bark from the fetus-outing tree [*karuveḷḷām*].
Boil it all and drink it down, girl,
your baby will fall away like a tear,
your baby will fall away like a tear.
And if a secret bicycle came for me, *māmā*,
magically I would disappear.
magically I would disappear.

In the village where this singer and I lived, there actually was a lake (dry most of the time),with a row of thorn fruit (jujube) trees growing at its edge. My house was on the opposite edge. The lake bed was a lonely place; people would graze their goats and cattle on the sparse grasses that grew there. A number of love songs (*kātal pāḍḍu*) sung in this village began with a mention of the lake and the thorn fruit trees. All of these songs were wistful, quiet, and slow. Often they contained mention of goat herding or cattle herding, as in the next song below. Herding a small flock of goats is an easy, leisurely job, which children enjoy doing. Adults will also do it when they want an excuse to be alone, or, some say, when they are in search of a trysting opportunity. These gentle songs are sung, so I was told, to the grazing goats, to aid their digestion.

Another song representing dialogue between lovers who are equals takes off from the ancient mythological motif in which one member of the couple, in order to elude the other, takes the form of various animals, and the pursuer also changes his (or her) form in order to match, and catch, the fleeing beloved. Two variants of this song were sung by Muttammāḷ, who sang the song above, and her husband's sister Pushpam. They were Paṟaiyar women in their mid-twenties. The first variant, sung by Muttammāḷ, goes as follows:

> Goat-herding Valli, vine-like girl,
> how shall I come, girl, *tillālē*,
> how shall I come girl, *nannānē*,
> I come girl.
> And if water flows in the river,
> taking a crab's form, skittering,
> I'll come girl . . .
> And if you come as a crab,
> taking a fish's
> form, wiggling,
> I'll come girl . . .
> And if [you] take form as a fish,
> I'll cast out my net girl,
> I'll cast it out girl . . .

This song was one of those that I thought of as confused when I first heard it. It starts with the boy pursuing the girl, and becoming a crab in order to get across the river to her. After he proposes his metamorphosis, the next verse begins, "If you come as a crab." Hearing this, one imagines that now it is the girl talking, to say that if her suitor comes as a crab, she will become something that he cannot catch. But no, it is still the boy talking, saying to the girl that if she becomes a crab . . . wouldn't it make sense for him to stay a crab? No, he will change again, into a fish. This makes a kind of sense, however, because if he becomes a fish, the crab will desire to catch him. Still, after he becomes a fish, she becomes a fish, but now he will not stay a fish, but becomes a fisherman, in order to catch her. As the song progresses, it becomes increasingly unclear who is the pursuer and who is the pursued. Finally one has to accept that these two are just playing games with each other. But this was a realization that was (in retrospect) surprisingly difficult for me to come to. My confusion was compounded by my expectation that this was a song in which the lovers would take turns speaking to each other. And it was further compounded by the absence of internal clues up until the end of each stanza as to who was supposed to be speaking. Am "I" the boy and are "you" the girl, or vice versa? In this song, at least this question is answered at the end of each stanza by the term of address that appears there, *ḍī* (girl), indicating that it is the boy talking. Or is it?

Bakhtin says that at the extreme end of the stylistic continuum where boundaries between voices dissolve, the distance between an author and his characters decreases, and the integrity of the author's own selfhood is on the line—at this end of the continuum various different relationships between embedded voices may obtain. One of these relationships he calls "hidden dialogue," dialogue in which the statements of the second speaker are deleted, but in such a way that the general sense is not disrupted. "We feel that this is a conversation of the most intense kind, because each uttered word . . . responds and reacts to the invisible partner, referring to something outside itself, beyond its limits, to the unspoken word of the other speaker" (1978, 189).

The variant of the crab and fish song given above may be considered a hidden dialogue of this kind. One experiences the very powerful illusion that not one person is speaking but two, because the single voice one hears is so responsive to a silent other.[5]

In the second variant of the crab and fish song, sung by Muttammāḷ's sister-in-law Pushpam, there are actually two voices speaking, but here again they refuse to take proper turns, and as pursuer and pursued exchange places back and forth within the song. What signals a change of voices is nothing but an exchange of the pronouns, *nī* and *nān*, "you" and "I," and terms of address, *ḍī* and *ḍā*, "girl" and "boy," so that as narrative voices become intermingled, so do persons (I and you) and sexes (boy and girl):

Valliammā grazing goats by the river,
if water goes in the river,
how will you come, girl?
If water goes in the river,
I will make a boat;
on the boat I will come, boy.
If you come on a boat, taking the form of a crab,
I will run scuttling, girl.
If you come on a boat, taking the form of a fish,
by the river, I will come, girl.
If you come by the river, taking the form of a fisherman,
I will cast my net, girl.
If you take the form of a fisherman and cast your net,
taking the form of a crab, I will run scuttling, boy.
If you take the form of a crab, coming with a net,
I will come and cast the net, girl.
If you come to cast a net, taking the form of a chicken,
I will run like a chicken, boy.
If you take the form of a chicken and run like a chicken,
with cash in my hand I will come to buy the chicken, girl.
If you come to buy the chicken, by the Piḷḷaiyār temple,
I will make an offering, boy,
If you make an offering, in the Kāliammā temple,
If you make an offering, I will get up in the morning,
washing my hands and feet, I will come to pray, girl.

Finally, when one sets the two variants of this song side by side, further exchanges of place become evident. For instance, in the first variant of the song, it is the boy who crosses the river first; in the second variant, it is the girl. Now, this way of mixing up persons, sexes, and voices in dialogue was not unusual for songs sung in the village where I worked, and whereas at first I attributed the apparent confusion to some sort of persistent singer error, I am now convinced, as I have indicated above, that it was not an error at all.[6]

As evidence that the singers, in mixing voices and persons, knew what they were doing, I will discuss one other love song in dialogue form that came to me, like the crab and fish song, in two variants. Both variants were sung by Pushpam, with a time interval of several weeks between the two performances. The first variant of the song begins, "On the black mountain where black stones are broken, girl, is your mother's house, made of black stone." The second variant of the song begins in almost the same way, except that the person addressed is not "girl," but "mother's brother" (*māmā*). The theme of one lover or spouse criticizing the other for coming from a hard, black mountain, implicitly suggesting that the lover's body is hard and black, too, is a common and ancient one in India. Each variant of the song continues with the girl inviting her lover to "come gently inside the harbor," and to stay with her when the sun goes down. The girl addresses her lover sometimes as *dā* (boy), sometimes as *payyā* (little boy), sometimes as *māmā* (uncle), and sometimes as *ayyā* (lord), covering virtually the whole range of degrees of respect and distance, intimacy and contempt. More interesting are the slides between "I" and "you." One stanza says, "For desire I grew my hair long, uncle, for beauty I made a bun." Another stanza says, "For desire you grew your hair long, girl, for beauty you made a bun." And yet another stanza, coming between the other two, says, "For desire I grew my hair long, girl, for beauty I made a bun." Is the boy, who is addressing the girl, saying that he grew his hair long and made a bun? This seems to be a mistake. But perhaps it is not. The ambiguity between "I" and "you" is facilitated by the near homonymy of the first-person ending, a slightly nasalized ē(*n*), and the second-person ending, the same *ē* with no nasalization. If the pronoun is omitted, as it often is, the listener has to seek other clues as to what person the verb is in. Otherwise, as the song goes by, the distinction between *vaḷarttē(n)* "I grew," and *vaḷarttē* "you grew," is easily lost, even among different singers of the same song. In one variant of the black rock song, as we have seen, the girl accuses the boy of coming from a house of black stone. In the other variant, the boy accuses the girl of the same. The first stanzas of the two variants of the crab and fish song contrast in an identical fashion. In one variant of the black rock song, only the boy is addressed, so only the girl is speaking, but there is—again as in the crab and fish song—a hidden dialogue; the voice of the other lover is silent but powerfully present. In the second variant of the black rock song—as in the second variant of the crab and fish song—the dialogue is overt, both lovers speak, but the two voices become "confused" with each other through a confusion of pronouns; they trade places in unexpected ways. So there are some striking formal similarities between the pair of crab and fish songs, as a set, and the pair of black rock songs, as a set. If the confusion of voices is an error, it is a highly patterned error. However, the strongest evidence that the confusion of voices is not an error but deliberate comes in a stanza of the black rock song in which the singer refers directly to the confusion of personal pronouns, by asking outright, *nīyā nānā*? (you or I?), even though there is nothing in the preceding stanzas, save the strange use of pronouns and terms of address, to suggest that this question needs to be asked. And immediately upon asking the question, the singer herself answers it:

nīyā nānā jōḍu tāṇḍā māmā
nīlakkāra mōḍu tāṇḍā

Is it you or is it I? It's both, a matching pair, uncle.
We are of the house of dark people, boy.

Here the singer gives overt expression to the idea that the confusion of voices conveys only somewhat less self-consciously: the singer and her lover, the "you" and the "I" of the song, are mixed persons—they are of the same dark house, they have the same dark body, the same name. But this commingling of name, place, and substance of people who are kin or who are joined sexually is a quite ordinary way for Tamil speakers to describe the processes of love.

In Bakhtin's terminology, the black rock song would be an example of "uni-directional discourse." It is multivocal but the different voices share a common intent; they are in harmony with one another. In this kind of discourse, as there is a decrease in objectification of the embedded speech act, there occurs "a merging together of the author's voice and the other voice. The distance between the two is lost" (1978, 190).

In the songs discussed above, the voice of the author, the singer, is in harmony with both the voices she reports. Her feelings are their feelings. She, too, is of the house of dark people. So it is hard to distinguish her from them as she sings. Moreover, the two embedded voices are in harmony with each other, so that they, too, merge. The stylistic relationship between voices mirrors the social relationship between the persons to whom they are attributed.

Multivocal discourse is not always harmonious, however (just as among Tamil kindred, people whose personhood is mixed, who share one body, may yet be at war with each other). When two or more voices are merged and yet are discordant, having different intentions, the resulting speech is what Bakhtin calls "vari-directional discourse." "In such discourse," he writes, "the author's intention no longer retains its dominant hold over the other intention; it loses its composure and assuredness, becomes perturbed, internally indecisive and ambiguous" (1978, 190).

Among the collection of counting songs sung in the village, one song, about incest between mother and son, exemplifies this sort of vari-directional discourse. This song, like others discussed here, came to me in two variants. One variant was sung by a woman of about twenty, who could not herself have had a grown son. As this young woman sang the song to me, it was a clear-cut, monotonous, back-and-forth dialogue in which the son offers the mother (whom he addresses as "girl," *ponnē* or *ḍī*) "one chili pepper" and "one lakh of gold." The mother replies.

> Whatever you give,
> whatever you put down
> boy, my son, Dharmalingam,
> my heart goes far away.

The boy then offers two chili peppers and two lakhs of gold, and the mother refuses with the same words. The song continues to repeat this pattern up to ten chili peppers and ten lakhs of gold. There is a break in the pattern only at one point, when the son offers the mother "a ladder to climb up on and a bed to climb down on," and the mother answers with her stock refusal.

In its clear separation of voices and its near total predictability after the first verse, the song resembles those containing dialogues between dancing girls and temple owners. The singer's decision to keep the two protagonists, and their two voices, separate, is firm and absolute. By the same token, the specific content of the song has virtually nothing to do with the immediate context in which it is sung, and it also has nothing to do, as far as I could tell, with the singer's own life. Thus her relationship to the song is distant. This song about incest is cast in the same mold as the prostitution songs; thus incest and prostitution are classed together. For this singer, both are equally out-of-bounds. She keeps herself completely out of the songs she sings.

The other variant of the incest song was sung to me by Nīlammā, an old woman in her sixties or seventies, whose songs characteristically were subtle, richly imaged, well organized, and conveyed some powerful emotional messages. But the incest song as she sang it was baffling. Its first stanza was identical with the first stanza of the variant sung by the younger singer:

I'll give you one chili pepper, girl,
O girl, O little girl,
I'll give you a lakh
of gold, little girl.

But the answer is subtly different from the answer in the other variant:

O whatever you give, you may give and go.
My lord, my son, Dharmalingam,
my heart goes far away.

Ayyā (lord) is a respectful term of address a woman would use for her husband or father but not for her son. To the mother's not-quite-total refusal comes the response:

O girl, I'll give you a ladder
to climb up, girl,
O girl, O little girl,
To climb down on I'll give you a bed, girl.

The following stanza says,

tārēnyā
I'll give two chili peppers,
lord, my lord, my son, Dharmalingam,
I'll give two lakhs of gold, my lord.

This is followed by a repetition of the initial refusal. The term *tārēnyā* I have glossed as "I'll give, sir," but it might also be heard as "You'll give, lord," or even, perhaps, "Will you give, lord?" The song continues in this vein, up through five chili peppers and five lakhs of gold, with the mother herself, apparently, making the offer, and the mother herself, apparently, refusing.

When we first transcribed this song, my literate assistant refused to believe that it was a dialogue between a mother and her son, and explained to me that it must certainly be interpreted as a dialogue between marriageable affines instead. What I heard as *ayyā*, *makanē* (my lord, my son), my assistant said must be *āyā makanē* (O son of my grandmother), that is, mother's brother. After we listened to the younger woman's much more clear-cut variant of this same song, my assistant still could not believe that it was a dialogue between mother and son, and classified this variant, also, as confused. To settle the matter, the next time we saw the young woman who had sung the song to us, we asked her what it was about. She matter-of-factly replied that it was about a son propositioning his mother and the mother refusing.

The semantic content of these two versions of the incest song, the choice of words and phrases, is rather less exciting than the topic would lead one to expect. But the contrast, between the rigidity of the one and the disorganization of the other, is much more interesting if one thinks of it as a contrast between the ways the two singers had chosen to manage the relationship between self (as singer) and song. The younger singer had sung the song in such a way as to maintain a healthy distance between her own voice and the voices of the characters in the song. She had objectified them and kept them under tight control. The older singer, I surmise, had let them loose. Given the powerful and vari-directional emotional forces that underlie this song, the singer as an artist who had given these voices their freedom might have had good reason to feel, as Bakhtin puts it, "perturbed," and to let this perturbation come out in the apparent indecisiveness of her song.

Nīlammā, the old woman who sang this perturbed version of the incest song, specialized not in songs of love between lovers, but in songs of love between mother and child. Love between lovers, as many singers represented it, was a symmetrical love, and so it was reflected stylistically in symmetrical transpositions of first- and second-person pronouns and male and female terms of address. Love between mother and child was an asymmetrical love, so that the unity between the two members of this dyad had to take the form of something other than a dialogue between equals.

Love between mother and child was expressed most fervently in laments and lullabies (for full texts see the previous chapter on this book). In neither of these genres was dialogue, in the strict sense of the term, possible, because in a lament, the addressee was dead, and in a lullaby, the addressee was too young to speak. Typically, in a lament, a singer would have a set of terms by which she would refer to herself and a set of terms by which she would address her dead mother, and these sets of terms would often be interposed.

Nīlammā, in her laments, would call herself "wasted younger sister" (*naliñcu pōna taṅgāḷ*) or "poor sinner who has wasted away" (*naliñcu pōna pāvi*). Her mother she would call, "o mother who bore me" (*ennē petta ammāvē*), or "o mother who raised me" (*ennē vaḷatta tāṟē/tāyē*), or sometimes "o poor sinners who raised me" (*ennē vaḷatta pāvingaḷē*), grouping the mother with other senior kin.

As the laments were patterned, the singer's references to herself would regularly be in the dative case, and whatever term she called her mother and other failed protectors by would be in the vocative, as in *enakku kunnēṟi māḍu meyyum, ennē vaḷatta pāvingaḷē*, "For me, cattle grazed climbing the hillside, o poor sinners who raised me."

Most commonly, a stanza of a lament would begin with *enakku*, "for me," and end with *ammāvē*, "o mother." But sometimes, within a song that had been following this pattern, Nīlammā would unexpectedly address the absent other as "younger sister," *taṅgāḷē*. She would also replace dative-case references to herself with dative-case references to her mother: *enakku naliñcu pōna pāvikki*, "for me, for the poor wasted sinner" would become *naliñcu pōna tāṟikki*, "for the wasted mother," so that it sometimes seemed that Nīlammā had forgotten whether she was the mother or the daughter of the lamented one. Often, rather than addressing her mother as *ennai petta tāyē*, "o mother who bore me," she would address her as *nān petta tāyē*, "o mother that I bore."

Nīlammā, in her laments, regularly used this technique of changing the cases of nouns and pronouns and so conflating the persons that they referred to. None of the younger singers used this technique at all. Nīlammā herself used it discriminately. In laments, she would merge the identity of herself (as plaintiff) and her mother (as addressee), but she would never merge herself and her older brother, though in laments she sometimes did address him, and accuse him, as she accused their mother, of abandoning her.

In lullabies, Nīlammā conflated persons by means of a slightly different technique, for the achievement of slightly different ends. In such songs, she would address the baby, ask him questions, predict his future, give him advice. Systematically in Nīlammā's lullabies, through an apparent looseness in her use of pronouns, the baby became the subject of actions that in the real world he would have been the object of, and owner of institutions that in the real world owned him. "Who hit you and made you cry?" (a standard lullaby question) became "Tell me who did you hit? "If you go to the forest, lions and tigers will surround you," became, "You will surround lions and tigers."

At the end of one lullaby, Nīlammā makes a bolder transposition, singing,

unakku caṅgē muṟaṅgutaḍā
en tambi anga
sāmināta kōyililē
unakku molam muṟaṅgutaḍā
en tambi unnuḍē
moliyār kōyililē

For you the conch shell sounds, boy,
my little brother, there
in the Swaminathan temple.
The drum sounds for you, boy,
my little brother in your
Mudaliar temple.

The two temples mentioned in this song were ones from which Paṟaiyars of the village were excluded, but for which they were required to supply conch shells and beat skin drums on ritual occasions. The beating of the skin drum signaled a death, hence it was a duty relegated to Paṟaiyars.

As laments were complaints against the injustice of abandonment, Nīlammā's lullabies were also complaints against the future injustices that would be perpetrated against the baby by more powerful creatures and people. But, as in laments the separation was softened by a transmutation of the persons of mother and daughter, so in the lullabies the sense of victimization was softened by a transmutation of the persons of victim and victor.

And as laments rocked back and forth between "me" (the singer) and "you" (the mother), sometimes intermingling the two, so lullabies rocked back and forth between "you" (the baby) and "me" (the singer) continually. A lullaby of Nīlammā's began,

nī kaṇṇē, oraṅgappā
aḍiccavaṅga cevviyārē
en kaṇṇē, maṇiyē
kaṇ maṇiyē
nittirappō
iṅgāraḍiccavanga
en kaṇṇē unnē
aniyāṟam ceytavaṅgō nī

aḍiccavaṅga cevviyārē
en kaṇṇē Nāginiṅgam
pōḍḍuvārē(n)

You darling, sleep boy.
Say who hit you
my darling jewel.
jewel of my eye
go to sleep.
Here who hit you.
my darling to you
did injustice. You
say the ones who hit you
my darling Naginingam,
I'll say good-bye for now

Conclusions

Bakhtin is most criticized for his seemingly mystical view that in a piece of verbal art, the "voices" of characters created by an author can have their own personhood and will, independent of the author himself. But for ethnographers of South Asia, this view is not so unrealistic, just because it is so common for people in South Asia to see themselves as composed of multiple and independent voices, which may speak to each other in dreams or in trance or in songs.[7]

No single will made the voices inside a South Asian person; no single will controls them. If I am a person of that world, words that are uttered through my mouth are not necessarily owned by me. All of this goes without saying. Moreover, the kind of song that we have learned to call a folk song is distinguished from other kinds of songs principally by the recognition (on the part of both singers and folklorists) that such a song is not the property of a single author but is itself as divisible and recombinable—as collectively owned, or as unowned, we might say— as the persons who gave their voices to it. Like singers in many other parts of the world, the singers in the Tamil village where I worked freely borrowed fragments of songs from each other, each piecing the fragments together differently to form unique, whole songs. For the understanding of such songs, the notion of an original multivocality in verbal art, which may be either objectified and deadened or left alive, is even more salient than it is for the kind of written literature to which Bakhtin himself applied it.

We are left now with the question: What were the village singers trying to say to me? I have tried to show that the singers in my village were in the habit of purveying personal and social messages, sometimes troubling ones, obliquely by way of song to more powerful others.

In seeking to understand these songs, I have been aided by Bakhtin's insight that discursive style, in and of itself, can carry an ideological message. A style-borne message can promote hierarchical control, leveling of differences, and objectification of others, or, at the other extreme, it can advocate love, freedom, and plurality. Bakhtin himself preferred a style of the latter kind, a style which aimed "to affirm someone else's 'I' not as an object but as another subject . . . to . . . transform the other person from a shadow to an authentic reality" (Frank 1986).[8]

The singers whose work I recorded showed similar preferences. Through their choices of style, they expressed particular feelings about particular kinds of human relations. Certainly one general message conveyed to me by their songs was that the kind of participatory understanding of the singers' lives that I was seeking was not consistent with the tremendous power and wealth differential that separated them from me. Such a differential—like that between god and mortal, temple owner and temple dancer—only evokes antipathy and hardens the boundary between self and other. Understanding is possible only when the substances of life and selfhood are shared. The field laborers in Pukkatturai created dialogic practice from the inside. Feelings of love come through only where walls between voices dissolve, and the fundamental pair, "I" and "you," face each other as kindred spirits, needing no mediation.

Chapter 4

On the Edge of the Wild

> "What he [Modi] will be called upon to do is not to attack Muslims, it will be to sort out what is going on in the forests, to sweep out the resistance and hand over land to the mining and infrastructure corporations," explains Ms. Roy. "The contracts are all signed and the companies have been waiting for years. He has been chosen as the man who does not blink in the face of bloodshed, not just Muslim bloodshed but any bloodshed." India's largest mining and energy projects are in areas that are inhabited by its poorest tribal population who are resisting the forcible takeover of their livelihood resources. Maoist militants champion the cause of these adivasis and have established virtual rule in many pockets.
>
> "Bloodshed is inherent to this model of development. There are already thousands of people in jails," she says. "But that is not enough any longer. The resistance has to be crushed and eradicated. Big money now needs the man who can walk the last mile. That is why big industry poured millions into Modi's election campaign."
>
> —"'Now, We Have a Democratically Elected Totalitarian Government'—Arundhati Roy," 2014

The fact that certain groups of people in India have been designated as "tribals" or "Adivasis" by British colonial administrators, government officials, and others represents the idea that the people so designated have always been "primitive," "backward," and "criminal" by nature. In modern, postcolonial times they are considered to be just now facing the light of civilization, seeking to enter this light, or alternatively, doomed to remain forever in the darkness of the past. They are thought to be like children and in this sense "undeveloped." A bit of thought will remind us that children are the smartest people in the world, and that forever is a long time.[1]

The title of this chapter, "On the Edge of the Wild," means just that. Some of the people who once lived in the forest, which was owned by nobody, now lived in rural villages, although they were not exactly "in" those villages, and they were not exactly living. They had lost everything, including their bodily health. They were on the edge of survival and they were on the edge between the wild and the cultivated land of the village. The woman called Kanyammā was among the lowest of the low in the village of Pukkatturai, near the city of Chingleput (Chengalpattu) in Tamil Nadu. She and her family were impoverished and despised by those who ranked above them, and that meant everyone. She and her family were classified as members of a "scheduled tribe." My host called them Villiyars, "bow people." More commonly they were called Iruḷars, "people of the dark." Some say their name is because they originated as pagans and became "seekers of the light." Others say they have their name because earlier they lived in caves. Edgar Thurston (1907) says that the name of the Iruḷars was given them because their skin was dark or because they lived in dark jungles. The Villiyars' name suggests that at some point in the past, they hunted with bows.

The traditional occupation of Iruḷars, as I learned in Pukkatturai, was as snake catchers, gatherers of wild honey, and rat catchers. Catching poisonous snakes, gathering wild honey, and catching wild rats are all difficult and dangerous jobs. The fact that the Iruḷars ate the rats they caught caused them to be viewed as deeply polluted, more so than other untouchable groups. Their numbers were small. In Pukkatturai they had no home or shelter.

If the caste system in India did not exist, the Iruḷars' situation might have changed by now from the way it was in the nineteenth century. It probably has changed for some but not for all. The current situation of one family of Iruḷars is discussed later in this chapter. The Iruḷars' situation of over a hundred years ago was described by Thurston.

Edgar Thurston, who lived from 1855 to 1935, probably most of that time in India, wrote a seven-volume work called *Castes and Tribes of Southern India*, which contained accounts of the more than three hundred castes and tribes he found there. For many, he provided detailed descriptions of both the physical and cultural aspects of that group. Among the groups Thurston wrote about were the Iruḷars.[2]

There is no way of knowing how precise were the reports of Thurston and his colleagues, but both the continuities as well as the changes between that time and now are evident. Thurston saw himself as a hunter of wild creatures, accepting the aid of planters, entrepreneurs, and hunters like himself, writing in his own fashion of the natives he stalked and observed. One of his vocations was that of anthropologist, but he would never have imagined viewing or treating the less privileged natives as his equals, or as fellow human beings. Some of the words and phrases in his volume can make a person flinch.

Nevertheless, it is possible to see things through his eyes, to filter out the condescension, to understand that he was trying to be objective and scientific, and to accept that he saw what he says he saw. He just saw things differently from the way someone like me would see them now.

From what Thurston wrote in the nineteenth century, one learns some things one may not have already known. I knew something about the Nilgiri Mountains because I had been there. I knew something about Iruḷars because I had met them in the village near Chingleput where I lived. I did not know there was a connection between that place and these people.

Thurston wrote of the Nilgiri Iruḷars that they grew their own fruits and grains in the forest and sold some of their produce; they managed the cattle of the ranchers; they ate a variety of wild and domestic meat; they worshipped Māriamman, for whom they performed animal sacrifices, as well as worshipping Kanyammā. They gave festivals with elaborate outfits and dancing, where also they performed animal sacrifices. They threw big parties when their corn was harvested. Their women had multiple sexual partners, and in general everybody had a good time. The saddest thing was that in periods of hunger, some of the women had to let their babies die. This still happens among the poorest in India.

The Chingleput Iruḷars, by contrast, were considered "more civilized" than their Nilgiri counterparts. In addition, they were said to be "semi-Brahmanized" and to speak "a corrupt form of Tamil." But they had little to eat. Their main job was husking rice. They made a gruel of the bran and ate that. To supplement their diets, they killed field rats, and made meals out of the bodies of the rats and the rice the rats had eaten. They also ate white ants (termites), not only because termites are edible but possibly because termites liked to eat silk saris that were stored in wooden chests, and the women who owned those saris would have been happy to have the termites gone. While husking rice, the Iruḷars stole as much of the rice as they could. And yet they refused cooked rice, even when it was offered. It is not hard to imagine why they did this. Iruḷa women of Chingleput, as in the Nilgiris, had multiple sexual partners.

Thurston wrote of the Chingleput Iruḷars, "Some Irulas are herbalists, and are believed to have the powers of curing certain diseases, snake-poisoning, and the bites of rats and insects. . . . They have no fixed place of abode, which they often change. Some live in low, palmyra-thatched huts of small dimensions; others under a tree, in an open place, in ruined buildings, or the street pials (verandahs) of houses."

In Thurston's writing from the nineteenth century, the contrast between the Nilgiri Iruḷars and the Chingleput Iruḷars is striking. More striking is the fact that the Chingleput Iruḷars of the late twentieth century lived in the same way as their ancestors had in the nineteenth century.

Caste was not always a system of rigid boundaries. Some people rose in status, others fell. More people fell than rose. The people now living on the margins of the caste system in India may at some point have been closer to the center of one or another civilization than they are now. They may, at some point in time, have been members of the ruling family of a great or small kingdom, or they might have been landowners or cattle owners. Or they might have been respected bow hunters or warriors. The realities of the past are largely unknown. However, it is not improbable that royalty were ousted into the wilderness by competitors more than once, in more than one location. Both the Mahabharata and the Ramayana centered on exile of ruling families to the forest.

Exiles may or may not have returned to something like their original position. Those who did not may have stayed in the forest, becoming adapted to life there. Before cultivation was introduced, it is said that the whole of the Indian subcontinent was densely forested.[3] If this is true, then it is more than probable that the whole human population of the subcontinent consisted of hunter-gatherers for tens of thousands of years, before there were temples, palaces, kingdoms. The hunter-gatherers of South Asia today are almost gone.

The forest-dwelling Nayaka people described below lived in the Nilgiri Mountains. There were several Nayak dynasties in southern India during the sixteenth, seventeenth, and eighteenth centuries. In Karnataka they were called Nayaka. In Kerala they were called Nayars. In the Tamil area, they were called Nayaks. One by one, these dynasties dissolved or were conquered, but castes with those names remained.

A remnant of the Nayaka people of southern India were forest dwellers in the Nilgiri area where Kerala, Karnataka, and Tamil Nadu meet. In 1979, only seventy individuals remained. They spoke a Dravidian language cognate with Tamil. They worked as laborers, therefore they were not entirely dependent on the forest for subsistence. But they did depend on the forest for their spiritual lives, or as Nurit Bird-David (1999) says, their personhood. The Nayaka people viewed relationships as more important than individuals. They perceived and attended to events rather than objects; the forest was their generous mother and father. They shared not only with each other but with the animals, trees, and spirits among whom they lived. They conversed with these others as they conversed with each other.

Eduardo Kohn (2013) describes "an ecology of selves" living in the Amazon region—an ecology of subjects, beings with souls, who can perceive as well as being perceived. In an ecology of selves, through complex processes, a subject may become an object that can be eaten. But the change of subject to object is always tricky.

Kohn develops his understanding of an Amazonian ecology through the philosophy of the semiotician Charles Sanders Peirce, whose thoughts Kohn uses both as scaffolding and guide. Peirce wrote that there are three kinds of sign: icon (a sign that resembles its object), index (a sign that points to its object), and symbol (a sign that is arbitrary, in that it neither points to nor resembles its object). The word "dog" is a symbol in that different languages have different words for this animal. For instance, you cannot tell what the word "dog" means if you know only Tamil or French. Kohn wrote that only human beings make and use symbols. Other animals communicate only through icons and indices.

Kohn says that a forested area speaks many languages and those human beings who live as part of the forest have less need for the symbolic than those who live as part of a city. Communication in the forest is through iconic and indexical signs as much as through symbolic ones, because animals and plants do not communicate with symbols but only with signs. There are more subjects than objects in such a world. Nonhuman selves, such as animals, are cognizant of iconic and indexical signs, but only humans use symbolic ones—signs that have no connection, by either proximity or resemblance, to their referents. In an ecology of selves, where wild animals are more prevalent than humans and humans occupy a status no higher than animal predators, the symbolic is of little use in communicating with and about the nonhuman beings all around.

Vast differences prevail between the people of the Amazon region in South America and the places and people of southern India. The ecologies of those two areas are different. For almost all people in southern India, living by hunting wild animals and birds is no longer a viable option. For a large number of people in the Amazon, hunting remains a way of life. Despite the differences, there are peoples in southern India for whose not-so-distant ancestors hunting of wild animals was a way of life. They lived in forested areas, hunted wild animals, gathered wild plants, and subsisted entirely by what the forest offered. Iruḷars were one such people.

The young Paṟaiyar women that I knew in Pukkatturai sang songs in which they identified themselves with cultivated plants. Their suffering was the suffering of fruits or vegetables left to wither on the vine. The singers in Pukkatturai did not claim that they were like the plants they worked with. They *were* these plants. With older Paṟaiyar women, the songs involved modern objects such as buses and chairs.

The laborers I knew in Darisanamcope in the Kanyakumari District of Tamil Nadu in southern India described the processes of rice plant growth with words that were also used for human growth, and vice versa. The farm laborers in Darisanamcope spoke of the plants as they spoke of children. Left in the sun, they would dry out, wither, blacken, and fail to thrive. In fact something like this happened to one of their own small children. Left in a hammock tied from a tree branch day after day while his mother worked in the fields, he was darker than his cousin, was too thin, and had constant diarrhea. The rice plants, like children, were tender. One should not wear shoes or sandals while working in the paddy fields because they would hurt the plants, harden the bed from which they grew. When I joined them one day to help weed the paddy, I could not tell the difference between a sprouting rice plant and a sprouting weed. One had to pay close attention to see the difference. The field laborers had close, everyday familiarity with the plants. A sprouting plant was called *piḷḷai*, "child" (Trawick 1978). It was not that the tender plants were *like* children. They *were* children. Plants, though having no nervous system, are sentient in that they respond to their environment and send out chemical messages to other plants and other kinds of messages, such as thorns, bitter taste, and poisons, to animals, including human ones, who might eat them. The rice plants were, as I have suggested in previous chapters, people to the women who worked with them.

Timothy Ingold (2000) writes that a person is not distinct from his or her environment. A person *is* their environment, as much a part of the environment as anything or anyone else. I am one animal in an environment that includes not only me but other sentient beings that perceive me when I am near them, whether they are other human beings or crows or cats or cattle or even plants. The more time we spend together, minding each other, the more we will understand each other's habits, and the more appropriately we will respond to each other.

Iruḷars in the villages around Chingleput had been torn from their old environment. Only remnants and memories remained. They were noted for their familiarity with rats, poisonous snakes, and bees. They definitely had no sympathy for rats. Snakes appeared as protectors and persons in one song. Iruḷars were also familiar with certain wild plants, for which they showed sympathy and longing. And through their songs, they showed they were familiar, through what others told them, with the faraway West, its machinery, its riches, its knowledge, and its dangers.

Kanyammā's Story

In the place where I worked,[4] Paṟaiyars were the most numerous and powerful of the untouchable castes. Though most of them were landless laborers, they had organized themselves politically, had achieved some major successes in improving their economic situation, and had high hopes for their children's future. Bodily they were healthy and strong. Iruḷars were not so fortunate.

In the village of Pukkatturai such people were called Villiyars, "bowmen," or *kāḍḍukkāraṅgaḷ*, "people of the forest/wasteland" (the word *kāḍu* generally means wilderness, forest, jungle, or wasteland). In that village there was just one family of Villiyars, camped out across the pond from the village school. They were called bowmen and people of the wasteland because, my landowning host told me, they had once been hunters living in the forest. Now they acted as night watchmen for the orchards; they gathered wild honey; they captured and dispensed with poisonous snakes; they captured rats infesting the fields and houses and ate them.

My host's wife's sister said that the Villiyars of this place were dirty compared to the Villiyars of her home village back in the mountains, and indeed to me also they looked ragged, sick, and unhappy. They were by far the poorest people in this village full of poor people.

A certain ghostly, romantic mystique was attached to the Villiyars. They had a secret potion, my host told me, which they rubbed on their hands when they went to catch a poisonous snake; it would keep the snake from biting. The snakes they caught lived only in *tāẓam* flowers (a big white flower with a strong scent and spiky leaves—a favorite of the goddess in her form as a lone and angry woman). These snakes were the cobra (*nallappāmbu*) and the Russell's viper (*viriyampāmpu*). The former was always female and the latter always male, my host believed, and when they mated they twined in a helix upwards. Anyone who watched them mating would not escape alive. But Villiyars had a certain power over them, my host said. Also Villiyars knew how to gather wild honey without being stung. They were suited to be guardians of the orchards because demons haunted the orchards at night and no one else was willing to go there then. The Villiyars were also not monogamous, my host told me. The head of the family of Villiyars in this village was an eighty-year-old woman who was on her sixth or seventh husband, who was about thirty or forty. As for the food the Villiyars consumed, their diet was their own choice, my host said.

I stored all this information away, planning to go talk with the Villiyar family themselves sometime. Then one day a granddaughter of Nīlammā's, a young woman of about sixteen, came up to me and asked me if I would like to hear a "Villi song." I said sure. She began a song of a kind I had never heard before. The words were simple: "Want *kāra* flowers, Kanyammā? Want *kāra* fruits, Kanyammā?"

The *kāra* vine grows in uncultivated areas. Kanyammā is the name of the village goddess. Whereas most of the Tamil songs I had heard had a moderate or slow tempo, and were sung (when they were done by women) in a thin childish soprano, this song had a fast, difficult, syncopated rhythm, and was delivered in a powerful percussive alto that struck me as almost jazzy. I liked it, but at the end of a few lines the singer ran out of breath, burst into giggles, and ran away. That afternoon I went to the Villiyar camp to find out more about their songs.

They would sing only at night. The forty-year-old man whose name was Little Boy needed a fire over which to tune his drum. All of the Villiyars were there around the fire: about eight of them, including the children. It was the rainy season; they all had coughs. Little Boy would sing as he played his drum. It was an unnatural situation for them. I was there, and so was my host, their patron, the person upon whose good will their living depended. They were nervous and uncomfortable. What did we want?

"It's okay," I said. "Whatever you feel like doing is fine. Try to pretend we're not here." (Children giggle. Adults quickly hush them up.) "Or maybe I could come another night; there's no hurry," I said.

"No," said one of the women. "You're here now. It just takes us time to warm up."

Little Boy started, beating his drum slowly, singing quietly, words that I couldn't hear, sentence fragments, groans, pauses, sniffs, chuckles, occasional spoken narrative. The steady drumbeat stopped, then started again, a beat at a time.

The old woman told him, "Lift it up and sing it." She started to sing herself. He picked up the tune and sang it loudly. His song drifted back into moans. The old woman tried to help again, giving him a tune. He shouted the tune then paused. She sang some more. He picked it up and then dropped off, singing, "Tell me how it goes, woman," as though this were part of the song. This went on for a while. They paused.

"Do you know any other songs? Songs about Kanyammā?" I asked, trying to be helpful. The old woman tried to teach Little Boy some more; they alternated back and forth.

"Would you like to rest a bit?" I asked, feeling embarrassed for them. They passed the songs and the conversation around among themselves.

"Let's sing all the songs we don't know," one of the women suggested.

"I'll sing," said another.

"No," said the first. "Okay, go ahead."

She began a song about the chief minister of Tamil Nadu.

"No, not that," said Little Boy, "She knows all about that. Kids, you sing."

"The kids don't know any songs."

"Try singing about Kanyammā," I suggested again, "about *kāra* flowers and *kāra* fruits."

"What is this *kāra* flower *kāra* fruit stuff?" one asked. "We don't know any songs like that."

"The one about the *onan* vine, that's about Kanyammā," said another.

"Okay, do that."

She began again, and Little Boy picked up the rhythm with his drum. It was the same fast, syncopated rhythm that I had first heard from Nīlammā's granddaughter. This singer's voice was shrill and harsh, but she kept the beat and her words were clear:

Friends playing ball, girlfriends playing ball,
to my forest who has come running?
Find an *onan* vine, friends playing ball, girlfriends playing ball.
Tie up his hands and feet, girls.
Make him stand—stop him.

Here was an interesting song. Was it the goddess Kanyammā speaking? Was she a goddess of the forest? The village goddess named Kanyammā had no connection that I knew of with forests. Was this a different Kanyammā? Was there some old custom in which girls would chase boys through the forest and capture them and tie them up with vines and torment them in some delightful fashion? The name Kanyammā means virgin-woman. I thought of Diana. Romantic sylvan images frolicked through my mind.

As soon as the song was over, Little Boy said, "Now let the kids sing." One child volunteered to sing, started, then changed her mind. I praised the song about the vine that had just been performed and asked the singer to do more. Little Boy was nonplussed. "Let this woman sing her woman's songs," he said.

For the rest of the evening, "this woman" did most of the rest of the singing. I learned a little about her during that time, mainly through her songs and her delivery of them, and I learned a little about her thoughts. I believe that she probably composed some of the songs she sang, as many of the people in this village composed their own songs. Each singer that I knew in the village there had a unique repertoire and a few songs that were uniquely her own. Songs were often very personal in nature, that is, they expressed the feelings of the singer about her own life and her relations with others. A number of communities in South India have well-developed traditions of composing personal songs to comment upon emotionally significant events in the singers' lives. Among the Todas, for instance, every man, woman, and child used to compose such songs. Murray Emeneau (1970) recorded thousands of them. Thus I believe that Little Boy was telling me the truth when I asked him about the origin of the songs that were sung to me by the Villiyars that night, and he replied very emphatically, "We ourselves! We ourselves created them all!"

The main singer's name, it turned out, was Kanyammā, after the goddess. It was hard for me to guess her age. They said she was in her twenties, but she looked older. She was quite thin. Her style of singing was fast, intense, and loud, and her voice was like a steel wire pulled very tight. I imagine it took a great output of energy to sing the way she did. After the third song she asked for me to turn off the tape recorder and wait a while until she caught her breath.

One of the other women said, "She isn't well, so she sings haltingly. Her breath runs out."

One of the children said quietly, "Blood will come."

Often throughout the night, Kanyammā would finish a song with a gasp, and sometimes a curse. It did not occur to me to make her stop singing, since I liked her songs so much. Only a few days later did my host explain to me that Kanyammā really was very sick; she had tuberculosis.

The songs that Kanyammā sang for me were basically of two types. First there were the songs she sang about the goddess Kanyammā, and about other, unnamed goddesses and young women, possibly all of them forms of this one goddess, goddess of the forest and of virgins. Then there were songs of social commentary, songs about the changing world. Most of the songs of this latter type were sad, some of them deeply so, some of them also very clearly angry. Taken as a whole, the corpus of songs left to us by Kanyammā the woman portrays the death of Kanyammā the goddess and laments this death—the death of the forest, the death of a better form of womanhood, the death of a way of life. At the same time it tells of the birth of a new way of life and new values, values the singer does not like and cannot fully accept.

Among the songs concerning Kanyammā the goddess, a number of them simply describe images and acts associated with her, images and acts of a world that no longer is. The first song Kanyammā sang is a song of this type. Maybe sometime in the past girls played ball in the woods and attacked men who came there and tied them up with vines, but this does not happen anymore.

Other songs in Kanyammā's corpus reveal other details of this world where the virgin-goddess reigned:

> On the mountain the rain falls.
> the water from the mountain runs down.
> At the edge of the river waits a virgin girl.
> For the flower garden's watchman to pick a flower
> how many days will it take?
> A plantain tree is in the wagon,
> in the girl's hair is a *tāṛam* flower.
> He is coming into the scent of the flower, mother.
> He will give a gift.

Until very recently, many lower castes in South India paid a bride-price at weddings. Now, in imitation of higher castes, who in turn imitate North Indian trends, lower castes are paying a dowry, a custom which devalues women (you have to pay the other family to take your girl) and which many people abhor, though they feel compelled to adopt it. The song above is about the older custom, and about the sexual power of a young girl, which by itself is enough to attract a suitor. Having been drawn into "the scent of the flower," he will pay a price in order to marry its wearer. The plantain tree in the wagon is being taken to build a wedding platform (they make them out of these trees). The *tāṟam* flower appears in many other women's songs, narratives, and ceremonies in South India. This is the flower said to harbor poisonous snakes, the one signifying lone, independent, and aggressive femininity. My host told me that "only Villiyars" use this flower at weddings; at the weddings of higher-caste people it is forbidden.

Kanyammā's songs, like many other Tamil songs, are spare and evocative. When there is a story to be told, they do not tell the whole of it but depend upon a few key images to make the listener feel their meaning. As in the séance songs described by Feld (1982), the indirection of Tamil songs, especially laments, is in itself a powerful emotional device—suggesting but not stating the truth, it gives the feeling of something hidden, something just out of reach, something tormentingly present in memory but unable to be touched, like the spirit of a dead kinsman, or a way of life lost. I have argued earlier in this volume that indirection also protects the singer of critical messages against vengeful abuse. If her message is questioned, she may always say, I didn't mean that.

Paronomasia (a word or phrase having two or more meanings) has similar uses. Several singers in Kanyammā's village started songs about secret sexual liaisons with the word *ēṟināl*, which means both "if the lake" and "if one mounted." The word *ēṟi* by itself means "lake." Such songs would then go on to celebrate (or bemoan) a lakeside tryst in which the woman "mounted" the man's "tree." Kanyammā started one of her songs in this way, but this song is not about a tryst. Rather it is about a goddess of serpents living in an anthill at the edge of a village called "Woman Mounted." In this song, it is suggested that there is a place where a woman is on top. Recall that Kanyammā's people, the Villiyars, now live as the village snake catchers. Poisonous snakes are a sacred animal for many people in India; their association with anthills and with female divinity is ancient and well known.

Say lake, the mounted lake bank,
woman mounted, at the edge of Woman Mounted
a great tree, mother, at the great tree's base,
an anthill whose flesh is swollen. Like the anthill,

the king of serpents, a woman king,
the woman king of serpents has
a great snake as her protector, so they say.
Say lake, the mounted lake bank,
woman mounted, at the edge of Woman Mounted,
an anthill whose flesh is swollen. Like the anthill,
the king of serpents,
a woman king.

None of the songs given above can be taken, by itself, as a lament. Each of them describes an event or a condition upon which the singer offers no comment but which we may safely assume she does not find lamentable. I would argue here, however, that taken as a whole, Kanyammā's performance of that evening was indeed a lament, albeit a loosely constructed one, of which each individual song, including each of the three above, formed a part.

In the tightly constructed Paṟaiyar laments that I recorded in Kanyammā's village, a number of conventions were common. One very commonly employed convention was to contrast a happy condition of the past with a sorrowful condition of the present. A related convention in Paṟaiyar laments consisted in the listing of a series of diminishing conditions, representing or paralleling the diminishment of the singer's own state.

Consider two other songs in Kanyammā's performance, which make use of both of these conventions:

Lifting one foot and dancing, what will Lord Murugan do?
In one hand a holy skull,
in one hand, an angry fire, they say.
What will Lord Murugan do? [repeat 3 times]

Lifting one foot, what dance will he do?
In one hand, a drum and an ankle bracelet,
in one hand, a holy skull, they say.
In one hand, an ankle bracelet,
in one hand, a skull, they say.

Lord Murugan is a charming young boy, god of war and beauty. His tokens are the spear and the peacock. In this song, he assumes the characteristics of his father, Lord Siva, the dancer, in the latter's form as destroyer of the universe. In contrast with songs sung earlier in the performance about the domain of Kanyammā, songs describing happy states of the past, this song about the actions of Siva-Murugan suggests that destruction of the world is near at hand.

Could it be a crow that's calling, girl,
in my two forests?
Could it be Māyā's doing, girl?
Māyammā goes there.
The gods dance on the south street.

Could it be a blackbird calling, girl,
in my two forests?
Could it be Māyammā's doing, girl?
Māyammā goes there.
The gods dance on the south street.

Could it be a sparrow calling, girl,
in my two forests?
Could it be Māyā's doing, girl?
Māyammā goes there.
The gods dance on the south street.

I offer here some observations which may help to explain this deceptively simple song. First, there is an echo of the first line of the first song translated above, "Who has come running to my forest, girlfriends?" But the echo is ominous. The crow is an inauspicious bird, a carrion eater, bird of hunger, winter, and death (Trawick 1990).

Second, south is the direction of cremation grounds, of ghosts, and of the temple of Yama, god of death. For that reason, "good" gods and their temples are not usually situated on the south side of a village or a town. But in this song, the gods are dancing on that side, and we have just had a song about Murugan's performing a dance of destruction. The direction south is often mentioned in Tamil laments, precisely because of its association with death.

Third, the crow, the blackbird, and the sparrow form a series of descending (successively smaller) items, similar to the descending series found in laments. Crows are sometimes mentioned in Paṟaiyar laments, as in the line,

"Not even a female crow will eat what I cook." The blackbird and the sparrow are similarly considered birds of no account.

Fourth, *māyā* can mean darkness, magic, or illusion. Māyammā is also a name of the dark goddess after whom many low-caste people name their daughters. (Other names for her are Nīlammā and Karuppāyi; all three names translate roughly as "dark woman.")

I cannot say what the basic meaning of this song is, if indeed it has one. It forms a contrast, or an answer, to some of the songs surrounding it. Darkness, decline, and death in the forest of Kanyammā are surely suggested. It could also be that the singer is making derogatory reference to the color of her own face and the sound of her own song. Perhaps she does feel like just a crow cawing in the woods.

A later song in Kanyammā's presentation is addressed to a powerful woman of a different kind. She is not adorned with flowers; she is adorned with jewels. All the creatures are drawn to her. The direction she is associated with is the West. The tune addressed to her is bright and dancing, but the message is ambiguous:

> There a chaste woman is singing hymns.
> She empowers the cause of sin [*pāva kāraṇam patittirāḷ*].
> There a chaste woman is singing hymns.
> She empowers the cause of sin.
> Pearls and great jewels and workmanship glitter.
> Pearls and great jewels and workmanship glitter.
> When one sees you, desire takes hold.
> When one sees you, desire takes hold.
> All the species of water animals
> are gathered in crowds and crowds,
> are leaning in armies and armies.
> When they see you, desire takes hold.
> When they see you, desire takes hold.
> All the species of forest animals
> are leaning in crowds and crowds,
> are leaning in armies and armies.
> When they see you, desire takes hold.
> When they see you, desire takes hold.
> When one sees the West, it seems very far away.

It comes bearing thunder and lightning.
When one sees the West, it seems very far away.
It comes bearing thunder and lightning.
When one sees you . . .

Here the song suddenly ended. "Your breath?" I asked.

"Her breath," said Little Boy quietly.

The last song that Kanyammā sang about young girls and flowers seems to me to be self-explanatory:

The roses and jasmine bought just yesterday have faded in the box.
To gather them up in their hair and wear them there are no divine
young girls,
not a single one to be found.

I have said above that Kanyammā sang two kinds of songs, the first kind having to do with goddesses and young girls and women, the second kind having to do with changes in the world. It should be clear at this point that songs of the first kind are not really separate from songs of the second kind. The songs about goddesses and womanhood seem to be songs of longing, anxiety, desire, doubt, and confusion—all these and other feelings consequent upon change. With the changes in the world, something is dying. This death is signaled by the war gods' dance, the crow's call, the flowers fading. What is dying is the kind of being that the singer is named for, her "identity" we would call it, her way of life, her self. It seems clear that there is grief and mourning in her songs for this loss.

I have also said above that it is part of the ordinary discourse of Hindu villagers to express rage against more powerful others. A more old-fashioned way of putting this would be to say that such expressions of rage are part of tradition. In many Tamil villages, including the one I worked in, there was and is a tradition of lower-caste women going from house to house during certain festival times and singing songs before the homes of the wealthy, which songs were intended both to flatter and to shame the wealthy into treating their wards with more respect and paying them better. No punches are pulled in these songs.

Other songs are more subtle but very astute and stinging; there are quite a few about state-level politics and about money. I see this tradition of delivering critical songs in Tamil villages as being similar in some ways to the Holi festival in North India. During this festival, for one day, the oppressed are able to get back at their oppressors—sweeper women, for instance, are permitted to dump buckets of buffalo urine on the heads of their landlords and to beat them with cudgels. Ethnographers portray the Holi festival as a day of *communitas* and light-hearted camaraderie among people ordinarily separated by hard social boundaries (Marriott 1966), but the violence that occurs on that day strikes me as something a bit other than light hearted; or rather, the sweepers' hearts may be lightened in the Ilongot sense (Rosaldo 1984) by thrashing their landlords, but I doubt that they carry out their revenge in what we would call a light-hearted manner.

I would suggest here that Tamil village women get their revenge and so lighten their hearts not through the strength of their arms but through the strength of their songs. And just as North Indian sweeper women reportedly spend weeks in training, building up their biceps for the day when they will get to use them against the people they hate, so Tamil women pour much creative energy into the composition and delivery of their biting verbal art.

Now Kanyammā happened to be one who was very good at composing and delivering this kind of song. The night she performed before me, she sang three of them in a row, followed by a fourth toward the end of her performance. At first she was hesitant. Neither she nor anyone else there was sure "what I wanted." She sang her first songs, none of them critical except in that they portrayed with longing a lost past to which the present compared unfavorably. Then she stopped for breath. There were long uncomfortable minutes during which more discussion occurred on the topic of what there was left to sing, and a few of the other adults began singing weakly then tapered off. Then without warning Kanyammā's voice stabbed the darkness and the others fell instantly silent. This happened again and again throughout the evening. Each song came out suddenly, fully formed, as though Kanyammā was drawing it all together inside her mind, gathering tension, before letting it go. She sang with a feverish energy, loudly and powerfully, while Little Boy followed her beat with his drum.

Of her three critical songs, the words of the first were the least pointed, the words of the second were more so, and the words of the third were sharp and direct. The first song began with the names of the former chief minister of Tamil Nadu, who was also a popular movie star, and of this movie star's comic sidekick, Bālayyā:

M.G.R. is acting,
Bālayyā is laughing,
all the little children
are going to school.
When they go to school, lady,
please teach their lessons well.
All the big children
are in the first grade.
When they're in the first grade, sir,
please teach their lessons well.

The irony of this song lies in the fact that the Villiyars were camped across the pond from the village school, where they could see all the children coming and going, but they were far too poor to send their own children there. Tamil people of all walks of life nowadays see schooling as the one usable ticket to a secure life. For those who own no property, schooling is especially precious. The reference to the Chief Minister M. G. Ramachandran is perhaps to point out his role in social reform, including attempts to institute universal childhood education. The Villiyars can observe such reforms, but are not assisted by them.

Make a *kōlam*, lady, make a *kōlam* out of rice.
Make a *kōlam*, lady, hide this *kōlam*, lady.
Who made this one here?
Saccakkā made this one here.
Make a *kōlam*, lady.
Who made this one here?
Saccakkā made this one here.
Hide the *kōlam*, lady; sprinkle water, lady.
Make a *kōlam*, lady; make a *kōlam* out of millet.
Who made this one here?
Rukmaṇi made this one here.
Make a *kōlam*, lady. Hide this *kōlam*, lady.

Little Boy started this song, then Kanyammā took over. Her voice was higher, louder, and shriller than before, almost a shriek, and she sang the song frantically and breathlessly. The words of the song, by contrast, seem gentle. A *kōlam* is a design drawn by high-caste women on the thresholds of their houses every morning to indicate that their household is in an auspicious condition. Usually they make the kōlam out of chalk powder, but sometimes, ostentatiously, they make it out of rice flour. The next morning, they erase the kōlam of the day before by sweeping it away and sprinkling water over the spot. Sweeping it away could be the meaning of "hiding" the kōlam of the day before. I don't know if making a kōlam is actually forbidden to lower-caste people. It is easy to make one. Some women make them every day, with specially elaborate ones on festival days.

The word *kōlam* has many meanings, including "beauty." My host suggested that the message of the song was that a high-caste lady, though she may adorn her house with kōlams, should keep the beauty of her own body covered. Perhaps. I was struck by the references to rice flour and millet flour. The latter is never actually used for kōlams. But both kinds of flour are food. Rice is viewed as superior in every way to millet, and so once again in this song we see a decline from something better to something worse. But, could Kanyammā have been commenting on the wastefulness of high-caste ladies' using rice flour for ornamentation, while she and her family were starving and did not even have a hut to live in, therefore no doorstep on which a kōlam could be drawn? They had no ornamentation, nothing to beautify themselves with, only ragged old clothes. One high-caste woman told me that this Kanyammā had been seen running around drunk and naked. Such an accusation was as insulting and demeaning as possible. The homeless, impoverished woman must have heard such insults. The following song is a reply.

Cousin, cousin, what town is this?
Wind-like cousin, it's Chingleput.
Cousin, cousin, what do they dish out here?
Wind-like cousin, they dish out big rats.
Cousin, cousin, what town is this?
Wind-like cousin, Pukkatturai Reddiars.
Cousin, cousin, what do they dish out?
Wind-like cousin, they dish out big rats.

This song was not sung but rather screamed. Kanyammā finished in exhaustion and said to me, "Mother, stop the tape recorder," which I did. Chingleput is the name of the district in which we lived; Pukkatturai is the name of the village; Reddiars are the dominant caste in the village, the caste to which my host and his family belonged. This song was unambiguously aimed at them.

My host at first tried to deflect the song's message. He could not believe that Kanyammā had said of his family, "They dish out big rats [*peruccāḷi pōḍuvāṅga*]." He thought she must have said, "They serve nice gifts [*paricu aḷḷi pōḍuvāṅga*]." But my own ears told me that Kanyammā had definitely said the word for "big rat," not the words for "serving gifts." It was all clearly recorded on the cassette, which we listened to repeatedly. Still my host insisted that his interpretation must be right, until his wife's sister reminded him (while I looked on) that just a few days before, the Villiyars had been called to the house to capture a rat that lived there. Their pay had been the body of the rat itself, as usual.

My host flinched at this divulgence. It was a terrible insult to suggest that this purity-conscious vegetarian family "served" its visitors rats to eat. The stinging part was that it was true. Moreover the song made it clear that the Villiyars did not choose to eat rats. The fact was that they had no choice.

As times change, so do Indian castes, adjusting to new conditions. Like other forms of life, castes work with what they have, taking specializations developed for the performance of outmoded functions and using them to adapt to new times and to create new niches for themselves. Some hit upon success. Brahmans, the traditional literati, become academics, lawyers, writers, and civil servants, among many other occupations available to them. Mercantile castes ride the winds of the world economy. Leatherworkers build shoe factories; toddy tappers establish chains of liquor stores; masons unionize. I hasten to add that not all the jobs that people are niched into by caste are good. Manual scavengers must clean up and dispose of human excrement, which is everywhere. A public sewage system has not yet been constructed in this enormous country.

But in this changed world what could the Villiyars do, who once had been hunter-gatherers? Now incorporated into the village economy, their foraging skills were put to use of a sort. Instead of hunting forest animals, now they hunted vermin.

Urban and agrarian foraging is a vital activity in modern South India. For many people with little money, wild foods form an important dietary supplement. Kanyammā and her family, for instance, ate crabs and snails from the fields. The high castes, who ranked everybody minutely according to what foods they would eat, despised people who ate such things as crabs and snails, but then, crab meat is a healthy food and not really so bad tasting. Rat meat, however, is a different matter. Villiyars themselves described it as foul and tough; nobody else that I knew in the village would touch it. Further, rats carry many diseases harmful to humans. As catchers and eaters of rats, Villis had been given a niche in the agrarian environment, but they knew they were not thriving on it. If things failed to change, the one family of Villis in Pukkatturai was likely to perish bodily, as it had already perished culturally. Kanyammā's song seemed to be trying to communicate this point.

The term of address used in the song above is *macci*, which means female cross-cousin. The song is in the form of a question-and-answer dialogue. The questions all begin *macci macci*, "cousin cousin." The answers all begin *kāttām macci*, "wind-like cousin," or "cousin whose form is wind." When we listened to the tape later, I asked my host what this term "wind-like cousin" might mean. He said he did not know. A clue, however, lies in a comment that one of the Villiyar women made after Kanyammā began singing. It would be good if the singer's *macci* were here, the woman said, because that *macci* was the one who knew best how to sing. But then, she added, that *macci* was dead and gone (*cettuppōccē*).

Now in Tamil Nadu, the spirits of the dead, as well as the possessing spirits of some deities, are often said to take the form of wind. They wander about like the wind, restlessly and erratically, longing for a stable home, a flesh-and-blood body in which to find shelter, comfort, and peace. The spirit of a dead person is thought to have the form of wind because it is the breath or wind (*uyir*, *mūccu*) whose presence signals the presence of life in a body and whose absence means that life is gone. My guess, then, is that the call *kāttām macci* addresses the singer's dead cousin, whose only voice now is the voice of the wind, and the song incorporating this term is an internalized dialogue between the singer herself and the spirit of this cousin. The spirit is asking the singer where she is and what there is to eat, and the singer is answering. Perhaps there is a suggestion, in the pointed reference to rats, of a link between the "serving" of this food and the cousin's death. Perhaps, also, there is some intentional irony in Kanyammā's calling her dead cousin "wind," as though to comment upon the relation between wind and life, and the shortness of life that her own shortness of wind so acutely forebodes.

The song translated above, about the "chaste woman," was the fourth critical song that Kanyammā sang that night. The song was addressed to me. I know this because Little Boy said so, quietly but audibly, after the song was over. Kanyammā sang this one, also, after some hesitation. As before, there was a lull, and some conversation back and forth on the matter of what to sing next. Then my host, who by that time had taken on (at least externally) some of my sympathetic spirit, and who had a fairly clear idea of what I would find interesting, said to Kanyammā, "Sing some more about what goes on in this village. Sing about the people in the village. You know the way you sang about Reddiars? Sing some more of those kinds of songs." Kanyammā paused, then the song burst out of her fully armed.

On the surface, the song appears to be mostly ingratiating flattery, but in fact it embarrassed me, for the woman described in the song was definitely not me. I was neither beautiful nor bejeweled, I always tied my sari wrong, and I was usually sweaty, dusty, and tired. I was not religious and could not bring myself to pretend to be so. Although I wore no jewelry and back home was just a lowly untenured assistant professor, I was, by village standards, obscenely rich. In the song is the statement, "She empowers the cause of sin" (*pāva kāraṇam patittirāḷ*). I tried to be generous to the poor, but my relationship to "sin" and its "cause" (*pāvakkāraṇam*) was ambiguous at best. Perhaps the song was suggesting that my host was "the cause of sin" and that I was empowering him. I did not consider that this man was "the cause of sin" but I was in fact empowering him by paying him for his help with my work. He built a rice mill with the money I gave him. In my own defense, I confess that the family into which my host had married, though landowning, was in bad shape financially. The paddy fields needed water and a bore well was expensive. New clothing for the children could not be bought, so they wore their old clothes, which were ragged and too small for them. The family would not eat meat or fish and could not afford milk for all of the children, some of whom were malnourished and prone to disease and whose hair was falling out. The head of the family was beleaguered by lawsuits from the goatherds who said the family was using part of the commons for their rice fields. The other landlords of the village were manifestly wealthier than our family and put our family to shame. So I helped them with part of my research grant.[5]

Just as thunder and lightning coming from the faraway West must have been seen as fearsomely powerful and capable of boding great good or great ill, so perhaps I was perceived. Although I just wanted to be a normal person there and melt into the everyday life of the village, that was not possible. Wherever I went, children crowded around me, laughing. Perhaps these were the "forest animals leaning in crowds and crowds" to which the song referred.

The main refrain of the song was, "When they see you, desire takes hold," and this charge made me very uncomfortable indeed. Desire is a problem more than a blessing, especially if one desires the wrong things. Children in the village desired expensive goods; they desired to be like the people they saw in the movies. The parents complained about the children being consumed with desire; their larger children would beat them if the parents could not provide the goods the children wanted. Families were being destroyed because of this. My exotic presence certainly did not help.

Women in Tamil Nadu mock and criticize each other for looking too good. For a woman "to show (another woman's) beauty," *avaḷ aṛaku kāḍḍa*, means for her to shame the other woman publicly and verbally. I with my white skin was an easy target for such abuse. I tried in vain to disguise myself by dressing like a Tamil woman, even though I could not behave like one. I do not know whether Kanyammā intended to shame me, but she had just shamed my host, who was my good friend, and therefore I do not think it impossible that she decided to dish out the same thing to me.

Kanyammā sang only two songs about herself that night, both songs in the first-person singular. These songs have a number of traits in common with the traditional laments that people of that village called "crying songs" (this genre is called *oppāri* or "comparison" in formal Tamil). First, they are songs of grief and loss. Second, they contrast a happy past with an unhappy present. Third, they implicitly question the wisdom and justice of ruling powers. And fourth, they focus on the self of the singer: the words for "I" and "me" are repeated again and again. The singer's own sorrow is the topic of these songs.

Kanyammā's songs differ from formal laments in that she does not weep as she sings them; the tempo is fast and energetic rather than slow; and more importantly still, in these two songs she sings about what she does or will do rather than about what has happened to her, and the powers she challenges are not specifically the powers of gods, of senior kinsmen, but rather, the powers of politicians, landholders, and the West to which they are allied—the powers of technology and of money.

These songs are not in any way what we might call conclusive. They do not call for revolution or offer any clear answers to the problems they raise. Nor do they move from a clear beginning to a clear ending. Rather, they are cyclic, reflective, and open-ended. In my view, they are the most beautiful songs of Kanyammā's corpus.

The first song is about gifts given to the singer by her *māmā*, her mother's brother. In these songs, women sang to or about their *māmā* as a gentle, protective lover, not "higher" than the singer but equal to her. Here Kanyammā sings about modern gifts bought for cash: a "glass" (*kaṅṅāḍi*—could be a mirror or could be eyeglasses) and a bar of soap. Both of these things are luxury items and status symbols that poor people in India generally cannot afford. The singer is uncomfortable with these modern forms of beautification and contrasts them with flowers she could fetch from the forest and wear. The song is addressed to a friend called Valli, which name means "vine" and evokes the slender willowy grace of a young girl. Valli is also the name of a forest-dwelling girl of mythology who was abducted by the god Murugan after he spied her from heaven and fell in love with her.

> My *māmā* gave me a glass that
> makes my body shiver, and my
> heart pines, Valli, my heart
> goes out to him. My
> *māmā* gave me a glass that
> makes my body shiver, and my
> heart pines, Valli, my heart
> goes out to him.
> Climbing the jasmine trees, I
> brought him some jasmine flowers, and my
> heart pines, Valli, my heart
> goes out to him.
>
> Climbing the jasmine trees, I
> brought him some jasmine flowers, and my
> heart pines, Valli, my heart
> goes out to him. My
> *māmā* gave me a soap that
> makes my body shiver, and my
> heart pines, Valli, my heart
> goes out to him. My
> *māmā* gave me a soap that
> makes my body shiver, and my
> heart pines, Valli, my heart
> goes out to him.

The next song is about various methods of communicating with God. The singer prefers silent and solitary meditation, but the village is celebrating by setting off noisy fireworks, which the singer does not like and which she cannot understand. She tries to escape to the forest, but this proves of no avail. The singer's *māmā* tells her to go to a mountaintop and at that place burn camphor and break coconuts. Camphor and coconuts are "traditional" worship offerings, which get a god's attention, as it were, and establish communication with him. The singer takes her *māmā*'s advice and goes to the mountaintop, where she gets a better view of the fireworks, as well as of other distant and beckoning things. On the mountaintop she also has the opportunity to meditate in silence, and there she must choose what to do.

Fireworks, or in general any objects that explode noisily, are called *veḍi*. The word *veḍikkai* means "explosion"; it also means "show," in the sense of a loud, bright, attention-getting display; it also means "joke" in the sense of something which causes people to explode in noisy laughter, suddenly showing their bright teeth. In Batticaloa, I knew a woman who had been shot in both knees. She was called Baby. She told me people in the area called her *veḍi paḍḍa vēvi*, "Baby who got shot." The word *teriyilē* means "not see" as well as "not know" and "not understand." *Veḍikkai teriyilē* can therefore mean either "(I) can't see the show," or "(I) don't get the joke." Kanyammā's song plays on the two meanings of this phrase.

I will close my eyes myself
and I will seek the Lord, I
will close my eyes myself
and I will seek the Lord, I
want to go to the flowery forest but
bang! boom!—the rockets explode. When I
go to the flowery forest
bang! boom!—the rockets explode. When
they explode with a bang! boom!
I don't see the joke, *māmā*. When
they explode with a bang! boom!
I don't see the joke, *māmā*. If
you don't see the joke, girl,
climb to the top of the mountain, girl. If
you don't see the joke, girl,
climb to the top of the mountain, girl. When
you climb to the top of the mountain,
get some camphor and take it with you, girl. When
you climb to the top of the mountain,
get some camphor and take it with you, girl. When

you take the camphor with you,
facing forward, burn it, girl. When
you take the camphor with you,
facing forward, burn it, girl.

Look! There goes the train, but
I don't have a bit of money, *māmā*.
Look! There goes the train, but
I don't have a bit of money, *māmā*.
So what if you have no money,
I will give it—climb up, girl.
So what if you have no money,
I will give it—climb up, girl.

Bang! Boom! The rockets explode.
The rockets go far into the sky.
Bang! Boom! The rockets explode.
The rockets go far into the sky.
What if they go into the sky?
I can see the show now, *māmā*.
What if they go into the sky?
I can see the show now, *māmā*.
So what if you see the show now?
Get a coconut, little girl.
So what if you see the show now?
Get a coconut, little girl.
When you've got the coconut,
Facing forward, break it, girl.
When you've got the coconut,
Facing forward, break it, girl.

I will close my eyes myself
and I will seek the Lord, I
will close my eyes myself
and I will seek the Lord, I
want to go to the flowery forest, mother,
when I seek the Lord, I
want to go to the flowery forest, mother,

when I seek the Lord. When I
go to the flowery forest,
I can see the joke, *māmā*, when I
go to the flowery forest,
I can see the joke, *māmā*.
So what if you see the joke, girl,
go and get some camphor, girl.
So what if you see the joke, girl,
go and get some camphor, girl.
When you've gone and got the camphor,
facing forward, burn it, girl.
When you've gone and got the camphor,
facing forward, burn it, girl.

Chapter 5

The Life of Sevi

This chapter and the next address, in a small and local way, two rather large and abstract issues: the relation between art and life, and the relation between people and place. As regards art and life, the view is that an artistic performance is not an object separate from the life of the performer. Rather, the artistic act is continuous with the actor's ordinary life; it is a rendition into greater meaning of this life and is as much dependent on it as a plant is dependent on its flower.

A related view is that every person is in some way an artist, driven like a plant to produce some flower, often something of surprising beauty that can grow even under the most adverse conditions. From this perspective an ethical injunction arises, which is that when one person looks at another, even one who lives in circumstances of poverty and abjection, the one person must not define that other as equal only to her material circumstances. When you look at another person, they in turn look at you. Both people are part of the same natural environment, large or small, in which there is no fixed hierarchy of selves. One must recognize that other person to be, like oneself, not just an object in the environment but a maker, a builder of it, someone for whom creation may be even more important than survival. Siṅgammā and Sevi were cocreators of their environment, as were other people who lived in that area, as is this writer. We have all been within it, we have all been formed by it, and we have all, together with many others, contributed to the making of it around us.

As regards people and place, this chapter will make a more specific assertion: namely, that for some communities, a place is strictly identical to the people who occupy it. For such communities, place is people. On the face of it, this is probably not a very astonishing assertion. But again, it is a matter of people shaping their environment and being shaped by it. They are part of it. "It" is not distinct or separable from "them."

Here I will focus not only on the matter of untouchability but also on a closely related issue, the matter of homelessness in India. Many people of untouchable castes are without real homes and both homelessness and untouchability are states of bodily rejection. To be without a home in India is to be without people who will take you in, to be without people who will let you live with them. In a way, it is the farthest extreme of untouchability. It is no accident that the most untouchable people in South India, the Kuṟavars, are also the people most without a home.[1]

The person whose life and work will be discussed in this chapter is Sevi, a young agricultural laborer of the Paṟaiyar *jāti* living in the village of Vattippaḍḍi, near the larger village of Liṅgāvaḍi, about twenty miles north of the city of Madurai in Tamil Nadu. I must admit at the outset that I never got to know Sevi as a person, face to face, very well. She was one of over a hundred individuals around Liṅgāvaḍi who, in 1984, for a project I was working on, were asked to speak about events in their lives that had been important to them, making special reference to personal relations and to feelings. Sevi is the person who sang the song of Siṅgammā. The full lyrics of this song appear in Chapter 6.

Kuppusāmy was a twenty-year-old Paṟaiyar man from the village where I was interviewing people. His uncle, a shaman/priest of the village where I was collecting interviews, recommended him to me as a transcriber of interviews, because he had a college education. Kuppusāmy started transcribing, and when I told him the kind of interviews I was collecting and the aim of what I was doing, or trying to do, he said, "I can do this." So I sent him out with the tape recorder and in fact he did the work much better than I could have done, in part because he knew the Paṟaiyar part of the village where we were working and every individual who lived there. I showed him how to draw a kinship chart; he quickly understood and drew detailed charts of every lineage (*vakaiyarā*) in the village. Anything I asked for, he could do. When he learned that I was also interested in folk songs, he came back with the song of Siṅgammā as performed by Sevi. I was taken by the song. After I heard this song, I asked Kuppusāmy to record Sevi's own life story, and so he did. There were, then, two stories: the autobiography of Sevi, the Paṟaiyar woman, and the story of Siṅgammā, the Kuṟatti girl. And in fact, I gathered two versions of the Siṅgammā story, the first performed by Sevi, and the second recounted by Veḷḷaiccāmi, a man who told fortunes by means of a parrot and was an exorcist for people possessed by the ghost of Siṅgammā. Thus we gathered three stories in all, setting aside the many other stories that Kuppusāmy had recorded. This small but complex body of lore was left for me to interpret.

The people who spoke for us were tape-recorded and knew that their recorded messages would be taken back to the West, to be published in some form there. I conducted about half of the interviews and recording sessions. The remaining interviews were conducted by Kuppusāmy. All the people that Kuppusāmy interviewed, with the exception of two Muslim men, were Paṟaiyars of his own community. Sevi was one of these.

As Sevi sings and talks for the tape recorder, though we are her distant interlocutors, her immediate interlocutor is someone relatively close to her, and her speech is fluent and more natural than it would be if she had been trying to talk directly to me. I have gained this free flowing text, as well as a kind of objectivity toward it (having met Sevi only once) at the cost of the deeper comprehension one acquires through personal engagement with and commitment to people. I offer no other excuses or justifications for the limited nature of the material I present here, except to say that I find this material too rich and informative in itself to be discarded just because some other information that would further enrich our understanding of it is lacking.

Sevi's performance of this song is interesting not only for its beauty and its rich detail but also for the light it sheds on the unique and complex relationship that has developed between the Paṟaiyar community, to which Sevi belongs, and the Kuṟavar community, to which Siṅgammā belonged. Both Paṟaiyars and Kuṟavars belong to the group of castes called untouchable (*tīṇḍā*) in Tamil.[2]

Sevi's Story

Sevi's life history narrative is notable in that she speaks mainly of other people and says little about herself. In fact, she does not even appear as a minor character in the series of loosely connected events she recounts until near the end of the interview, when Kuppusāmy asks her about her own wedding and her subsequent married life, and even here she does not appear as an actor or speaker in the narrative but only as someone to whom or for whom things are done or not done. The major part of the narrative has to do with the injustices suffered by Sevi's older sister.

Kuppusāmy begins by asking Sevi how many brothers and sisters she has. Sevi says there are six, then mentions that one older brother is dead, murdered:

> *S:* Of the six people, an older brother, one older brother died. When he was lying down, they wrongfully and mistakenly grabbed him and beat him and killed him.
> *K:* They beat him and killed him?
> *S:* Yes. Older brother.
> *K:* In what town did they beat him and kill him?
> *C:* In this town itself, *appā* [*uḷḷūrccilē tānppā*]. They beat him and killed him. They beat him and killed him. Older brother.

Sevi says no more about this event but goes on to mention other siblings and to describe an event that happened to her parents when she was a child. I will quote her at some length here so that the reader can get a sense of her narrative style:

> They beat him and killed him. They beat him and killed him. Older brother. One older brother was married in Liṅgāvaḍi. He is alive in the house. An older sister, the place where my mother was born, in East Vaḷaccappaḍḍi, in Vaḷaccappaḍḍi, in the place where she was born, to the younger brother who was born with her they gave older sister in marriage.
>
> Father, in that place, older brother, mother, to go, to come, keeping, father was thinking very much of mother [*ammāvē romba karutuṇḍuḍḍāru*] he must not have been thinking [*kurutāmē iruntirukkiṟāru*].
>
> Then, mother, while he was spreading a chicken to split it, father split his hand. One of father's hands got split. Then, because of that, mother said she would not live with him.
>
> When she said she would not live with him, we had lots of wealth and conveniences, father, even so, they took father to Mēlūr, they took him to Madurai hospital, the people of his brothers' house itself [*paṅgāḷi vīḍu*], the people of father's younger brother's house [*cittappā vīḍu*], the people of father's older brother's house [*periyappā vīḍu*], and they had him admitted [*cēttuppiḍḍāka*]. When they admitted him like that, mother went, and she did not see him,

she did not keep him. When he was just like that, then two of the younger brothers born with mother, both of them went, the coming, the going, they went and saw and came, then one brother said to father, "Until your hand is well, send the girl to me."

So saying, the two uncles born with mother, they said that and came back to Madurai. After they said that and came, my father said, "Go, I want to go see my wife, you go tell her to come." So saying, father waited. Then mother, from there, from Madurai, the one born with mother, the one who bore mother, the grandfather, and the father, both of them father and daughter, came to Madurai to see father. Father had broken his hand, no? They came to see that. As soon as mother went and saw, mother was very troubled.

"From now on I will not live with you at all," she said to father right there. After they said that, they left the hospital and took him outside and came, they came, it is said. The people of father's brothers' house [*paṅgāḷi vīḍu*], they brought him, leaving all his belongings right there, they brought father, they brought him to Kallāntiri and they left him there, it is said. Taking him to Kallāntiri, leaving him there to be, "You stay here," so saying, taking him to Kallāntiri and leaving him there, they came here. After they came here, "These belongings, somehow we, keeping it for him, we . . . even his wife says she won't live with him, and he, from now on, this hand has gone limp [*inta kaiyi cōrammāyiruccu*]." So saying, "He will not keep his life. He will die. He will die. For this child, this girl child we must give away in marriage, no?"

There in Vaḷaccappaḍḍi they will come to an agreement [*toyappukku vantiruvāṅga*]. So saying, "We will have it all written into our name." So saying these people of father's brothers' house, no?, found a way for them to write it [i.e., sign over the father's wealth to themselves]. As soon as they found a way to write over father's belongings and wealth, then what did they do? Quickly, they took father from there in a car to the Madurai police station. Having taken him there, father's signature [*kai rēkai*], they had it written that this man had no claim [*pattivam / pattiyam*] to this wealth. Who? The people who are there now, those people. As soon as it was written and given to them, they put it in his hand. Then father had lost his belongings, no? And it is like that still; he has no claim. Afterward, we, we were four or five children. Then little children,

> how are they going to work and earn money and eat? So saying, there has to be a way to survive, no? Father, working, working with his good hand, must raise the children, bringing along his wife and also bringing along his four children, so it happened. Letting the children go, mother left. Thinking just, "We must not stay with him, he is going to take the children and raise them," mother left. Afterward, thinking, "Having left the children, what are we going to do? I must come back," she returned. Having come, when she asked what happened to the woods and fields, they wrote that there is not a thing left. Having so written, "There is just a little bit, in an old field there is just a little space," said [the people of] father's brother's house, "Only what is in that, you may take only from that mango grove, you may not take from the other mango grove," they said it to mother and father. "Then if you harvest it, only one bag of paddy will come," they said. "If you plant cotton, ten or twenty rupees of cotton will come. That is all that will come."
>
> Keeping that, raising the children, father and mother were living. While they were like that, they performed a wedding for my older brother in Liṅgāvaḍi. Then, between Liṅgāvaḍi and our people there was a quarrel from past time, between father's house and two people. Then three months after the wedding, older brother went blind. . . .

The story told here may be paraphrased. The narrator's father, thinking of his wife and not thinking of what he was doing, while cutting a chicken, accidentally splits his own hand. When this occurs, his wife, the narrator's mother, fearing that the father has been so handicapped that he will be unable to work anymore, deserts him and the children. The father's brothers take him to the hospital, where his wife's brothers also come to visit him. He asks them to bring his wife to him, but they say they cannot convince her to come if her will is against it. The wife's father then brings the wife to the hospital to see her husband. When she sees him, she repeats her decision that she will not live with him.

Afterward, the father's brothers move him to another hospital, where they abandon him. Deciding that with his wounded hand he will not be able to work and support himself and will die, the father's brothers make plans for the future. One of the things they think of is that they will soon have to marry off his oldest daughter and this will take money. They consider that a marriage alliance with the people of Vaḷaccappaḍḍi will be advantageous. With these future plans in mind, before the father has even died, his brothers seek to legally appropriate his property. They do this by taking him to the police station and having him sign away all his possessions to them. The father recovers, however, and manages for a while to support his children by working with his good hand. The mother returns to live with them, and the father's brothers give him permission to cultivate a small portion of his former property and so support his family. The brothers do not give back to him the property they forced him to sign over to them in anticipation of his death. Though later in the narrative we learn that Sevi's father did not survive long, but died before she came of age and married, Sevi says, "Still he has no claim" to his former property. The dead father's having no claim means that his children have no claim to his land and must live at the mercy of the father's brothers.

If we look at the narrative style of this portion of Sevi's story, we find a number of textural patterns, patterns that recur again and again throughout the narrative, and that, I will try to show later, link up with the Siṅgammā story in interesting ways.[3]

First I should note that Sevi's speech style is liltingly musical. Like most Tamil villagers, she speaks very rapidly; every two or three seconds her voice rises to a high pitch or drops to a sentence-final low, and she pauses, evoking an "mm" from her yes-sayer, Kuppusāmy. About half of her sentences repeat in participial form the predicate of the previous sentence, so that the end of the last sentence becomes the beginning of the next. This, combined with the falling and rising intonation, creates a rocking effect, which seems almost to lull Kuppusāmy to sleep. Occasional tag questions wake him again, forcing him to respond. Important phrases are bracketed in pauses, murmured in low whispers, or conversely spat out in tense staccato syllables, reinforced by intonational parallelisms and much internal rhyme.

But when deprived of its music and put down on paper, Sevi's narrative (like many oral narratives) becomes choppy and hard to follow. Grammatically, it is fragmented and chaotic, or so it would be judged by Tamil pundits. Syntactic and lexical organizing and clarifying devices, present in written Tamil, are largely absent here. There is quite a bit of repetition, of stopping and starting over again, of self-correction, which comes out in the form of saying one thing and then immediately afterward saying something else parallel but contradictory to it.

There is also in Sevi's speech a kind of topic "forefronting" in which the narrator says the name of a person somewhat in advance of when she actually starts talking about that person, sometimes several sentences in advance, so that the name seems for a while to be dangling there, unconnected to anything until the narrator picks up the thread to which the name belongs.

Often, several topics are forefronted simultaneously, that is, a series of keywords is listed, before they are joined together into a sentence, as though the speaker were audibly laying the pieces of her thought before her before uniting them in a single construction. Different people and different voices become commingled. The boundary between quoted speech and Sevi's own voice is often unclear. The speech and actions of several people are sometimes treated as though they were the speech and action of one person.

Many of these features of Sevi's narrative can easily be attributed to the fact that Sevi is not a literate person. Her talk is not in any way modeled upon writing. What she says is heavily dependent for its meaning on many features of sound and context that do not come through in the transcribed text. Although an objective anthropologist would not evaluate Sevi's personality negatively for her way of speaking, in the Tamil world it is nonetheless true that Sevi's way of talking is inseparable from her moral and social status. For the speaker, too, what she says must be part of what she is.[4]

The action of the story told by Sevi is dominated by coming and going, bringing and sending, keeping and leaving; the verbs "come" and "go" appear as fillers in many places. This incessant coming and going is one indication of what seems to be a strong preoccupation with place and placelessness in Sevi's narrative. People are always moving or being moved around; the moving is always a matter of what people are in what places; and the questions of who belongs where, what place belongs to whom, and who belongs with whom, are constantly being examined and reexamined.

The close identification of people with place is expressed in several distinct ways. First, Sevi has a habit of saying, "so-and-so's house" when she really means "the people of so-and-so's house." So, for instance, in this section of her narrative, she mentions *periyappā vīḍu* (father's older brother's house), *cittappā vīḍu* (father's younger brother's house), *paṅgāḷi vīḍu* (brother's house), when in all these cases she is actually referring to the people having rights to a particular piece of property and not to a physical house at all.

Second, when a marriage is mentioned, the common way that Sevi refers to it is to say that so-and-so was married in such-and-such a place, as in: "An older sister, the place where my mother was born, in East Vaḷaccappaḍḍi, in the place where she was born, to the younger brother who was born with her [i.e., to the mother's younger brother] they gave older sister [i.e., a young woman older than the speaker] in marriage." Or again, she says that her brother was married "in Liṅgāvaḍi" and then, "between Liṅgāvaḍi and our people there was a quarrel from past time, between father's house and two people."

Third, from time to time in the narrative, certain people are referred to as being "in the house." For instance, "One older brother was married in Liṅgāvaḍi. He is alive in the house." Elsewhere, the convalescing father is said to be "in the house." Similarly, later in the narrative, an aged parent, a boy who has finished the tenth standard and is waiting for work, and a girl who has come of age and is waiting to be married are all said to be "in the house." But none of these people is actually confined to the house. The boy who has finished tenth standard travels around quite a lot, and the girl, the mother, the brother, and the father all go out to work every day. Considering all these cases, one surmises that to be "in the house" means to be okay, to be taken care of by others.

Given this identification of place with people, we now may begin to understand why, at the beginning of the interview, Kuppusāmy, upon learning that Sevi's older brother was beaten and killed by someone, does not ask what to us would be the obvious question, "Who did it?" but instead asks, "Where was it done?" It seems that, for people of Sevi's community, to ask "Where?" is to ask "Who?"

A certain characteristic of the world in which Sevi lives recurs six or seven times in the story she tells and gives us a hint, or a partial answer, to the question as to why people and place are so closely identified by Sevi and those around her. This real-world fact is the frequent co-occurrence of bodily destruction (illness or injury), fragmentation of the kindred group, uprooting or expulsion of someone from their home, and loss of property, especially land. Violence of kinsman against kinsman almost always has some or all of these consequences, and in Sevi's narrative, such violence is abhorred but not unheard of. Indeed, all of the events that Sevi describes in her narrative are composed of some combination of these four different kinds of breakage (body, kin group, land, land-body connection). It is no wonder then that her speech seems also to be, on one level, broken.

After describing how her father lost his land to his brothers, Sevi tells of the following events: An older brother becomes ill and is taken to the hospital. For the hospital expenses, money is needed. Sevi's father and her first older brother are unable to earn enough, so they sell, to the father's older brothers, the final tiny patch of land that has been left them, for one hundred rupees. "You know those who are there today? The people of father's brother's house [*paṅgāḷi vīḍu*].They wrote it over to them [*eṛutikkuḍuttiḍḍāka*]. As soon as they wrote it away, then between them and us there was no kinship [*urimai*]. Belongings, affection, in none of that was there any kinship. It had all gone."[5] The bond of affection and belonging between brothers is carried in the land and lost when the land is lost.

In the next and longest episode, Sevi's older sister comes of age and is married into Liṅgāvaḍi.

> They brought her well, majestically, with all the proper rituals. But sister's husband kept her in a very countrified, uncivilized way [*romba nāḍoḍinḍu vaccukkoṅgo*]. Then, when they are very countrified, from day to day it will be just like this. Once a month they will beat her, keep her, and being like this watch over her in violence. And when they were watching her like this, sister became three months' pregnant. And when he became angry, in murderous violence beating her [*uḍankolaile aḍiccu*], breaking her skull, making the blood flow, he told her to go and sent her away. Sister, throbbing and burning, did not go to Komanampaḍḍi, her parents' home, but came here to Vattippaḍḍi.

In Vattippaḍḍi, where Sevi herself subsequently married, the sister stays with the family of a medical practitioner named Bambaiyan. "Bambaiyan's house are very kind to us, no? [*Bambaiyan vīḍu namāḷukku romba urimaiyānavakuḷḷo*]." But the husband comes there, beats her again and tells her she must not stay in Vattippaḍḍi but must go to Komanampaḍḍi, and he "puts her on the road."

At this point in the story, Sevi exclaims in outrage to her young male kinsman Kuppusāmy: "To beat her when she was three months pregnant—see the madness of it, boy! [*pittunatē pārappā!*]" The sister goes to Komanampaḍḍi, where she finds that her brother's wife has just died. She stays there for the funeral. She continues to stay there, thinking her husband will come and fetch her, but he never comes.

Her child, a son, is born. Her husband takes another wife and lives with this other wife. Then one day he gets into a fight with his second wife's family, "A hitting and grabbing fight. In the place where he married, the people of the house of that younger wife cut my sister's husband, they cut him on the hand, and sent him off with his blood." On his way out of town, bleeding, he passes through Komanāmpaḍḍi, where his first wife is living.

> Then all the people gathered there said, "Oh no, how sad, your husband is cut and is going along bleeding." So they spoke. Then between sister and her husband the agreement [*toyappu*] had ceased. To clash is not agreement, is it? Then, in that place he married us, our husband, our child has been born, whenever it may be, we will join with that husband.
>
> We have written that between us as husband and wife there are no claims [*pattivam illai*]. We have written that our kinship [*urimai*] is to the child. Tomorrow, if good or bad comes to the child, our husband must come, he can only come. However our husband is, older and younger brothers, opposing them all, I must go and see my husband in the stronghold of Madurai [*marutākkōḍḍaiyilē*].
>
> So saying, older sister, bewildered and weary, taking a hundred rupees in her hand, started out, to see who? To see her husband.

The sister finds her husband in a bed (*poḍḍiyilē*) in the Madurai hospital. When the two see each other, they both weep. Daily she visits him there, bringing him food and money and protecting his life. The son, now ten years of age, comes too, affectionately calling, "Father, father." Then the husband vows that he no longer wants the other wife. "You alone are my wife," he says. "When he spoke, a woman's heart, in that place it causes it to be truly affected [*anta iḍattilē pātikka tānē ceyyutu*]. Aha, our husband has come this distance, has spoken this far, for ten years our life has been ruined, but having been this way, from now on every day we will be together with our husband. In that place will be true kinship [*anta iḍattil urimai tānē irukkum*]. So spoke the heart of a woman, and older sister's thoughts were of belonging [*urimaiyā nenacciruccu*]."

But when the husband is healed and returns back home, he changes his mind and sends his first wife, Sevi's sister, away, telling her to leave him and the second wife alone. Still, while she lives with her parents in Komanāmpaḍḍi, she continues to visit her husband in Liṅgāvaḍi, borrowing hundreds of rupees and spending it on him: "Out of kinship [*urimaiyāve*] she spent it."

Then one night the son also runs away from his mother: "Feeling kinship with his father [*appā mēlē urimai paḍḍu*], the son went off to Liṅgāvaḍi."

There he stays with his father's sister, who keeps him "in great *urimai*." When the mother comes searching for him, her husband and his family send her away, saying, "What *urimai* is there between you and him? You go back and stay in your own house."

But Sevi's sister stays the night at her husband's house and in the morning gets up, washes his clothes and his body, and ponders how she has spent so much on her husband to no avail, thus angering her natal family, "the people who are there," with her stubborn wifeliness. She thinks about how it is wrong (*urimai illai*) for her son to heed the father who deserted him rather than the mother who cared for him for ten years.

There follows a kind of tug-of-war concerning where she is to live. Her husband's sister tells her to stay. Her husband's brother tells her to go. Finally she tells herself, "You must not go there. We must not come. We must not think of him as our husband."

But she cannot maintain that frame of mind for long. She decides to have an ear-piercing ceremony for her son, now twelve, and says to herself, "I will come and go and ask my husband."

But when she arrives at Liṅgāvaḍi, her husband's kin tell her that he has left, and they ask her to stay. She answers angrily, "You say, 'Stay, stay, on the morning my husband has gone.' So saying, sister's mind was troubled," Sevi narrates. Then the husband's family tell her, "'If you come and have the ear-piercing ceremony here, all the people of the *jāti* who would come and give you things, they will take all those things they have come to give you and will keep them, they will not give them to you. In a former time, they would lovingly accept you. At this time, not desiring acceptance, you depart and go and stay. Wherever you are in your house, have the ear-piercing ceremony there.' So saying, they sent her off." The sister has the ear-piercing ceremony performed for her son in her own home. At that time, a relative convinces her that the boy should be sent to Bombay to learn masonry work.

"Then sister signed him up [*eṛuti poḍḍu vaccu*] for that masonry work. This one boy, our life, he must make it a good life—so saying, she sent him to study there. Here, he did not know how to read, so what did she do, she sent him to Bombay. . . . " "'He may work for a mason's wages,' they said, and, 'We must send him to Bombay,' they said, and 'We will ask him,' they said, and they wrote a letter on the very morning of that ceremony, and they took sister's son. Now sister is alone, and does some kind of work, just enough to eat, and for her part she sits in the house, while that boy is in Bombay."

Kuppusāmy asks, "Does he send any of his wages to her?"

Sevi replies, "He has not sent any yet."

Kuppusāmy asks, "How long has it been since he left?"

Sevi replies, "Now since he left—that ceremony was done, no? Three months have passed since that boy left, three months. Since he went, he has sent five or six letters, saying, 'Mother, I am alive, I am holding on, I am in good shape, you stay there, mother. Don't you worry.' In the letter he just sent, he told me to come. 'Mother, you must come quickly,' the boy wrote in his letter."

In the remainder of Sevi's narrative, at Kuppusāmy's urging, she tells something about her own married life. She explains how the people of her father's younger brother's house took on the job of arranging and paying for her marriage. "The four people who were living there said, 'For this girl, I am responsible. If any mistake comes to this girl [i.e., if she is found to have any flaw], it is our responsibility.' So the people of our father's younger brother's house spoke."

Sevi complains that when her father's brothers married her, they promised her a field and a garden, a set of cattle and a well, but after twelve years none of these things has been given her. "So far, they have not given anything, saying 'This ten cents is just for this girl.'"

Sevi and her husband have a minute patch of land by the roadside (three-quarter *kuri* or 108 square feet) and they also plant some things on the borders (*vārattilē*) between other people's fields. Yet Sevi and her family have gotten along adequately. Her three oldest sons are in school. In the interview, she stresses the importance of education above all things in making a better life for her children.

When Sevi married, she and her husband were sent to live in a Muslim house (*rāvutta vīḍu*), apparently a house that had been owned and abandoned by a Muslim family and then taken over by Sevi's father's brothers. At the end of the interview, Kuppusāmy asks Sevi if she has a family god (*kula teyvam*).

Sevi answers with two names: Siṅgamputukāri, Sevukapperumān.

Kuppusāmy asks if this deity has been any help to her. Sevi answers,

> The help he has given us is that we, husband and wife, have kept in good order. We have worked hard for our meals. Now for two years' time, for two years, that deity, we, in a polluted person's house [*oru tuśḍakkāravuka vīḍḍulē*], a Muslim house [*oru rāvutta vīḍu*] in the house of people of no particular caste [*entaccātikkāravuka vīḍḍulēyum*], without making an error of hot or cold water, in a good way, our arms and legs must be well.
>
> Sevapperumān, you alone are our help. You alone must give health to our arms and legs. So saying, we pray only to that god. Now for these two years . . . since this small little boy [her

youngest son] was born, well, a little well off, without debt or falsehood, we have been able somehow to eat. . . .

Somehow, a bowl and a pot, what is needed for a house to survive—what way to buy them?

For that, before, our husband worked very hard. Only if he labored very hard, only if he took up a shovel. . . . We were without rice. There was no rice. Now for two years, since this little brother was born, since then, because he took on the burden of going north and south a little bit, somehow a little cash has come into our hands. We are a little well off. We are able to eat a little to cool our hunger.

Kuppusāmy asks, "Has the god helped you in any other way?"

Sevi replies, "He has not helped in any other way."

Let us return now to a consideration of the other text Sevi has given us in conjunction with this one, her song about Siṅgammā.[6] At the beginning of this chapter, I suggested that an artistic performance might be understood as a rendition into greater meaning of the performer's experienced life. One takes the substance of one's own life, whatever that substance may be, and one tries to make something better, truer, and more beautiful out of it—something, at least, that makes more sense, something more worth keeping as memory, as part of self. Here we may consider Sevi's two texts, the one representing her life's raw material, the other representing the more perfect thing she would make out of this material, as illustrating this process of rendition-into-meaning of life, the artistic transformation of experience into knowledge.

Some of the more obvious similarities between the two texts may also be noted, before we consider the subtler, as it were subliminal, links between them. First, the key figure in both song and narrative is a battered woman; and second, this woman is not the singer/narrator herself but someone worse off than the singer, with whom the singer evidently sympathizes. Third, in both texts, an evil collectivity of brothers, more or less undistinguished from one another as individuals, plays a prominent role. Fourth, both texts dwell upon the linked themes of bodily destruction, fragmentation of the kin group, and loss of place. In both, the central events entail violence of kin against kin, uprooting, and confused wandering from one location to another. A fifth similarity is that in both texts there is a strong sense of moral outrage. People are not behaving toward each other as they should, and in

Siṅgammā's case, the painful loss of the girl's innocence results from this immorality. Hence the copious weeping on the part of Siṅgammā and her brother. But under the circumstances, she has no choice but to allow herself to be killed. One imagines her to be a girl seeking independence and suffering the consequences, through no fault of her own. She is vindicated only after her death, when she returns as a spirit wanting only to stand up straight, on her own, outside the confines of the house.

The song manifests the same basic preoccupations as are apparent in the narrative but in more extreme form and with sharper resolution. For instance, in the narrative, the heroine is merely beaten; in the song she is killed and dismembered. In the narrative, the integrity of the heroine's womanhood is violated by her husband's beating her during her pregnancy. In the song the violation is stronger; Siṅgammā has done something, or something has been done to her, that causes her to be expelled from caste, so that she will be without home or family, forever. The song makes it clear that she is loved by her mother and by her lame older brother. But they are powerless to protect her. They can only save her from the ultimate pain by putting her to sleep.

In the narrative, the heroine into whose consciousness the narrator enters is only slightly removed from the narrator—she is her sister. In the song the heroine, with whose feelings the singer's feelings merge, is of a whole different caste, as well as of a different time and place from the singer—the embrace is wider, the message of solidarity stronger. One transformation that occurs, then, between life and song, is a clarification and strengthening of the meaning of certain kinds of relations and certain kinds of events.

Now we may begin to reconsider the identity of place and people and the close link between caste exclusion, or untouchability, and homelessness or landlessness that this identification of place with people implies. We have already seen how important and complex the notion of "house" (*vīḍu*) is in Sevi's narrative. *Vīḍu* means not only a physical structure but a group of people related by sometimes tenuous ties to each other. When a person moves from *vīḍu* to *vīḍu*, she not only changes location, she also changes the people with whom she lives, and her right to live in a certain place is determined by the nature of the ties she has with the people who already occupy that place. So when Sevi sings of Siṅgammā being trapped in or escaping from the house, one must remember and understand that Kuṟavars rarely have actual physical houses with doors and locks. Instead what they have are other people, embracing them or driving them away, locking them in or locking them out. The demand, at the end of Sevi's song, that Siṅgammā finally, after her death, be given a real physical house of her own, is worthy of emphasis.

Closely related to the concept of *vīḍu* is the concept of *urimai*, a term that also appears frequently in Sevi's narrative. In legalistic Tamil, *urimai* means "entitlement," "privilege," "right," "genealogy," and so forth, but clearly to Sevi, *urimai* has more complex and personal meanings. I have translated *urimai* as "kinship," but as Sevi uses the term it seems to mean something other than just a genealogical link between persons. It means kindness, affection, emotional closeness, belonging, commitment between human beings that has nothing to do with law or signatures. One may behave in a fashion characterized more or less by *urimai*, at one's will. *Urimai* between uterine brothers may be broken completely, as may *urimai* between parent and child or between wife and husband. All this we learn from Sevi's narrative. If *urimai* has a core meaning for Sevi, it would seem to be the feeling of rightness of people living together in the same place, taking care of each other materially, and sharing the same property. In a given context, the moral, or the affective, or the physical component of *urimai* may be stressed. They are all bound together.

A sense of wholeness is suggested by both *vīḍu* and *urimai*. But in Sevi's narrative, she dwells upon these two terms perhaps because in her life the wholeness they offer is precarious. For Sevi and her people, no home is reliably home, no kin can be counted on to recognize kinship forever.

Anomalies of Inclusion and Exclusion

In the song about Siṅgammā, as in Sevi's life history narrative, there occur a number of contradictions and anomalies having to do with confinement in or exclusion from houses. These contradictions and anomalies are not of the singer's making. They belong to the story and the language themselves. Sevi introduces her performance of the song by stating that Siṅgammā is "a child of the house of Kuṟavars" (*orukuṟava vīḍḍuppiḷḷai*). Kuṟavars have no physical houses but they do have families, they have *urimai*. But in the song, *urimai* between brother and sister is shattered. A second reference to houses consists in Siṅgammā's being interred in the floor of one, in violation of all local convention. There she is told to "stay and be happy," in somewhat the same way as Sevi's sister is told to stay alone in a house where she does not want to be. A third strange episode involving houses consists in the erection of one upon the remains of another. This also is a violation of traditional Tamil building code, about which more will be said presently.

Images of confinement and exclusion, wandering and bondage, are similarly interwoven. The song begins with Siṅgammā being confined within a house and fleeing from it. The place where she stays after she flees is excluded, discarded ground—"the rocky wasteland of Mēlūr" (*Mēlūr kallānkuttu, kallānkuttu kāḍu*) it is called. On this rocky wasteland there occurs a wedding (the act of inclusion par excellence), where Siṅgammā finds and gathers rice that has been discarded (excluded, remaindered). She is punished by being locked in a house that is outside the village—"yonder, in the forest," says the song. Finally, she demands that a house be built for her alone, and then she demands to be taken outside of it, so that she may stand up straight. Her brothers are ordered to build this house, and then they are told, "Even if you build palaces, you may not stay."

Even on the level of grammatical categories, states of exclusion and inclusion are repeatedly stressed, and then overturned, in this song. The key example of this scrambling of categories of inclusion and exclusion appears in the section describing the reason for the caste exclusion of Kuṟavars. At the beginning of this section, the song tells how Siṅgammā is punished by her brothers for leaving the house and going to the market. They lock her in the house alone in the forest:

> Leaving you within the house, Siṅgammā
> All four doors they closed and locked and came, Siṅgammā.
> All four men went inside the house, Siṅgammā.
> And as they went inside the house, Siṅgammā,
> the mortar stone pounds, doesn't it, Siṅgammā.
> And as the mortar stone pounds, Siṅgammā,
> all four doors they pulled shut and locked, Siṅgammā.

This passage, though indirect, strongly implies rape of Siṅgammā by her four brothers. The image of incestuous multiple rape is linked to ambiguities concerning who is in what house with whom: have the brothers locked Siṅgammā in the house and left her alone there, or have they locked themselves in the house with her?

The questions of incest and caste expulsion, like the question of who is in what house, are, of course, themselves questions of inclusion versus exclusion. The dilemma that is suggested here is simple: to stay within the caste (as well as to abide by the rules of the caste system as a whole) we must marry within our group. But if we marry too closely within our group—that is, if we stress inclusion too heavily—we will be radically excluded: either we will be driven from our caste, or our caste will be driven from among the body of castes. The song proceeds:

> To them, to all four of them, Siṅgammā,
> Siṅgammā could give an answer, Siṅgammā,
> On our [excl.] good *jāti*, Siṅgammā,
> the sun has fallen and gone, Siṅgammā, we [excl.]
> From the *tāli* . . . from the *jāti* are excluded, Siṅgammā.

In this passage, it is notable that the first person plural forms, "our good *jāti*" and "we are excluded" are both grammatically exclusive rather than inclusive. In Tamil, the exclusive "we" (*nāṅgaḷ*) and "our" (*eṅgaḷ*) does not include the listener. But here, if the sister is addressing her brothers regarding "our" good caste, it would only make sense for her to use the inclusive form. If she is talking about her own exclusion from the caste, she should use the singular, not the plural form: "I am excluded," not "We are excluded." Whoever is speaking, though the topic of the passage is exclusion, the pronoun "we" should be inclusive.

Sevi's slip, saying *tāli* when she means *jāti* (and so correcting herself) is also telling. The *tāli* is the marriage necklace that a husband ties around his wife's neck on their wedding day. It is a powerful symbol for Tamils of the bound and confined state of married womanhood. The term *jāti* means caste. By accidentally substituting one word for the other, Sevi indicates how closely associated are the notions of confinement within marriage and confinement within caste. "we are excluded from the *tāli* . . . from the *jāti*" (*tālilēyum . . . jātilēyum taḷḷuvaḍi*), she is striking at the heart of marriage and caste all in one.[7]

Fragmentation of Body, Place, and Kin Group

One would be hard pressed to find the life story of a spirit or deity in India that was not rife with all sorts of rule breaking. Still, it is not unreasonable to think that people whose lives are especially damaged by adherence to the rules of Indian society might be especially inclined to break those rules in fantasy. So, as I have argued in a previous chapter, the most oppressed in

India might very well be in some ways the most creative. I have tried to show here how broken into pieces is the world of Sevi's everyday life. Perhaps this is another reason why the song she sings is characterized by various kinds of normally whole things being broken into pieces.

I will only mention briefly at this point the various overt violations of Tamil social convention that take place in the story of Siṅgammā: how she breaks out of the house against the will of her brothers; how she "wears different clothes"; how she sells herself in the market; how she gathers up polluted rice to take back home; how her sisters-in-law lie about where she has gone and drive her out of her natal home by ordering her to catch a poisonous worm; how her brothers rape, murder, and dismember her; how they bury her in the floor of the house; how they build one house upon the remains of another. I will only mention in passing also that the notion of code violation is itself a difficult one in a society where there are, from the beginning, multiple codes. The appropriation and legitimation of a multiplicity of codes for conduct and their subsumption into a hierarchical order can thus be seen as a crafty defensive maneuver on the part of the code makers.

Just as, in this song, there is on the grammatical level a scrambling of the categories of exclusion and inclusion, reflecting perhaps a preoccupation with problems of belonging versus not belonging, so there is a scrambling of the categories of singular and plural, perhaps reflecting a related preoccupation with problems of wholeness versus brokenness. Thus, many of the things that in the ordinary Tamil world are decreed to be singular come up plural in this song. For instance, when Sevi sings, "On our good caste the sun has fallen and gone" (*porutu viruntu poyiddaka*), the verb is given a plural personal marker. But even if the sun is personified, it should be singular, like any other deity. In Tamil, deities are invariably *avan* ("he," familiar, sg.) or *aval* ("she," familiar, sg.). Consider the distant, all-encompassing unity that the fiery eye of the sun represents. Consider, in Tamil as in English, its powerful masculinity. In the song of Siṅgammā, it is by the sun's authority that she is outcast(e), and again, that rice pots will not boil for her. By calling the sun plural, could Sevi be quietly shattering this authority?

But Siṅgammā's own unity is also broken in the same way. Shortly before her death, she takes a louse comb in her hands and takes the form of louse eggs (plural). Lice, with the eggs they lay, are small, inconsequential, and undesirable creatures that one seeks to exclude from one's hair. The instrument of their exclusion is the louse comb, which Siṅgammā takes in her hand. Lice, besides being annoying, are also defiling, because they drink blood. High-caste people will not admit to having lice. So it is appropriate, if apparently bizarre, that a girl of the Kuṟavars—a defiled, excluded, and for many, inconsequential caste—should choose as her animal form louse eggs.

The fragmentation of Siṅgammā's living self into louse eggs is followed by the fragmentation of her dead body and its burial, not in one hole but several. Both the louse eggs and the holes are specified as plural in the song.

Another plural presence in the song is the set of Siṅgammā's brothers. Needless to say, it is not unusual or illegal for a woman to have several brothers. But the rape of Siṅgammā by her several brothers contrasts sharply with the normal and, for Tamils morally most legitimate, sexual arrangement, marriage of one woman to one man (*ōr āṇ, oru peṇ*—an oft-cited formula). And of course the one man should not be the woman's brother.

The plurality of the several brothers as against the one sister is further highlighted and made strange by Sevi's habit throughout the song of changing the number of brothers that Siṅgammā has. The first stanza of the song begins, "There were five brothers, Siṅgammā." In the fourth stanza, we learn that the five brothers have five wives. In the fifth stanza, it is down to four wives. In the tenth stanza there are five brothers again, in the thirteenth stanza only four. In the forty-ninth stanza, the number of brothers becomes seven, in the sixty-ninth stanza, six. In the eighty-fifth stanza, there are again seven brothers and they have four wives. All these changes in numbers go unexplained. It is as though the singer must defy even the pattern of expectations that she herself has set up. Or else, it may seem as though precision as regards numbers, adherence to the notion of fixed boundaries between entities, is not especially important. Yet another possible explanation is that as the number of brothers with their wives mysteriously increases, so too does their power against Siṅgammā, who has no protection or support at all. The whole family acts against its youngest member, a single girl.

Two other pluralities stand out in the song. When the brothers mix lime for Siṅgammā's palace, not one building but buildings (plural) grow up on that spot. And finally, when Siṅgammā emerges, glorious and triumphant, from the buildings that have been built for her, she speaks out, and the song says, not "She spoke the truth," but "She spoke the truths" (*uṇmaikaḷai colliḍuccu*, plural).

Partial Attachment to Places and Partial Connection with People

I have tried to show that, in Sevi's life history narrative, the sense of belonging to a certain place and the sense of belonging to a certain people are one, so that place and people are in many contexts spoken of interchangeably. I have also tried to show that in Sevi's world, attachments to places and people are tenuous, so that wandering lost, coming and going continuously with no clear sense of where or with whom one is really supposed to be, seem to be the main activities that people engage in.

The text of Sevi's narrative manifests one other related property, and this is a near total merger in many places of Sevi's voice and consciousness with the voice and consciousness of her beleaguered older sister. It is a common characteristic of much informal Tamil narrative, as well as of many Tamil songs, that the distinction between reported speech and the speech of the narrator or singer is often very hazy. There tends to be no cue until the end of the reported speech that it is in fact not the narrator but someone else talking. This is a property of Sevi's narrative overall. But the older sister is treated in a different way from the other characters in Sevi's story, in that Sevi often seems to be inside this sister's mind. She does not report what the sister said in particular situations but what the sister thought, very much as though she were describing her own thoughts. One imagines that Sevi must have had many conversations with this sister, given her advice, shelter, and so forth, but as far as the narrative is concerned, Sevi does not represent herself as a character distinct from the sister at all. There is no "I said" and "she said." There is only "she thought." This perfect unification of the voices and consciousnesses of the two women reminds me of the unification of the voices and consciousnesses of the *talaivi* and *tōṛi* (heroine and heroine's close friend or foster sister) in early Tamil poetry, where the *tōṛi* sometimes speaks the thoughts of the *talaivi* as though they were her own.

In other words, just as the characters in Sevi's narrative are not firmly grounded in one place, so Sevi the narrator is not firmly grounded in one voice but dwells sometimes as much in her sister's mind as in her own.

The wanderings of the older sister, and the frequent entry of her thoughts into the mind of the narrator Sevi, find expression in the song to Siṅgammā in a sharp and powerful way. Let us say that Sevi's feelings for

Siṅgammā are much the same as her feelings for her sister. Perhaps in some way to Sevi, Siṅgammā is her sister, and both the Kuṟavar girl and sister are also in some way Sevi herself. The wanderings of the sister in the narrative are echoed in the song in the wanderings of Siṅgammā. As the sister wanders, her social identity and her attachments to others also shift. So, in the song to Siṅgammā, just as Siṅgammā the person physically wanders about, we find the name of Siṅgammā wandering, its grammatical place shifting, its identification with various voices constantly changing.

The name Siṅgammā is the refrain of this song. It is cried out repeatedly at the end of every line, regardless of the content of what is being said, as in, "They looked inside the house, Siṅgammā, and they cried with tears, 'Younger sister is missing,' Siṅgammā." Thus the name Siṅgammā plays the role that some chains of nonsense syllables play in other songs, grammatically superfluous, a filler between stanzas, which gives the performer time to think about what she is going to say next.

But "Siṅgammā" is also a term of address in the song. Thus, near the beginning of it Sevi sings, "I am going to tell the story of your birth, Siṅgammā, I am going to tell the story of your growth, Siṅgammā."

Siṅgammā is first outside the story in the sense of being a refrain, just a word tacked on at the end to keep time. Then she is outside the story in a different way: she is the person to whom the story is told. She is its audience. But she is also inside the story as its heroine, so as the story goes on, Sevi sings, Siṅgammā you did this, Siṅgammā you did that—"You put on different clothes, Siṅgammā. . . . You went to the market to sell beads, Siṅgammā," and so forth.

And finally, the name Siṅgammā becomes even more deeply embedded in the story when in some stanzas it appears as ambiguously incorporated into the speech of one of the characters of the story, as when the brothers send Siṅgammā into exile:

"Where have you been?" they ask you, Siṅgammā.
They stand there asking, don't they, Siṅgammā?
"In the forest, ammā, Siṅgammā,
See that house, go there and stay, ammā, Siṅgammā.
You will be pounding with the mortar, Siṅgammā."

In some stanzas, Siṅgammā speaks to herself, and then she seems to be saying her own name, divided from herself and reflecting upon herself:

Six o'clock has come, Siṅgammā, Siṅgammā.
If my honor is destroyed, Siṅgammā, I, too
Must stay inside the house, Siṅgammā, I am
A woman of perfect honor, Siṅgammā, these
Four doors must open up, Siṅgammā, Siṅgammā.

Here, the words "I, too" (*nānum*) suggest that some "I" is identifying with some other "I," perhaps that the singer is telling Siṅgammā, "I, too, Siṅgammā (like you), am a woman of perfect honor." But the implied identification between singer and addressee remains always partial and ambiguous.

A similar partial and ambiguous identification is set up between Siṅgammā and her mother:

In the lap of the mother who bore Siṅgammā,
Being laid to sleep, Siṅgammā, Siṅgammā
Sleep won't come at all, mother, Siṅgammā, Siṅgammā
Must tell the order to the mother, Siṅgammā.
The mother says, Siṅgammā, Siṅgammā,
Excluded from our caste, mother, Siṅgammā,
The rice pot will not boil, mother, Siṅgammā
Your brothers are going to kill you, Siṅgammā, Siṅgammā

In Tamil, *ammā* means "mother," but it can also be used as a term of address for any female human being. It would not be strange for a brother to call his sister *ammā* or for a mother to call her daughter *ammā*. So Siṅgammā is addressed by her brothers and by her mother in the lines above as "*ammā*, Siṅgammā," but the same "*ammā*, Siṅgammā" is echoed when Siṅgammā speaks to her own mother (saying to her, "Sleep won't come at all, *ammā*, Siṅgammā") as though she is calling her mother by her own name.

Near the end of the song, Siṅgammā addresses her elder brother and accuses him, saying,

You are the one who killed me, Siṅgammā
The one who saw my sin, Siṅgammā Siṅgammā
The one who undid me, Siṅgammā . . .

And here again, it is as though she is calling one of her kinsmen by her own name.

There are also stanzas in which the name Siṅgammā becomes split into two or three forms; one form a free-floating refrain, one form a term of address loosely bound to the content of the narrative, and one form an integral part of the narrative, tightly bound into the particular context and syntax of that stanza. For instance,

> To them, to all four of them, Siṅgammā,
> Siṅgammā could give an answer, couldn't she, Siṅgammā?
> And in Siṅgammā's grave, Siṅgammā,
> And in Siṅgammā's grave, Siṅgammā, for you,
> A red oleander blossomed, didn't it, Siṅgammā?

In this way the song expresses, more clearly than any analysis could, the fragmentation of the heroine; her lack of any one firm and unambiguous personal identity; her sometimes inside, sometimes outside status; her search for a place to be.

The Power of Death and Remainders

Kuṟavars and Paṟaiyars are said to be polluted and dangerous because they deal with remainders: human corpses and feces, leftover food, dead animals, shells abandoned by the animal that inhabited them.

Remainders are reminders. Reminders of what? Of the unwholeness, the incompleteness of existence. No matter how much you try to sweep up, there is always some bit of dirt in a corner somewhere. Nothing can ever be perfect. Nothing is ever totally finished, past, and forgotten.

Reminders are remainders. "Backward castes," supposedly still carrying habits that others have left behind, are themselves reminders living in leftover time, and, pushed to the edge of the village, they are themselves remainders living in leftover space. If things were perfect and without remainders, though, things would never change; there would be no growth, no life. Indians know this very well. "Upon remainder the name and form are founded, upon remainder the world is founded. . . . Being and nonbeing, both are in the remainder, death, vigor." So speaks a certain Sanskrit remainder.[8]

In modern Tamil there is a whole body of folklore concerning the power and the importance of remainders, of leaving things imperfect.[9] The image of a god should not be made perfect or terrible chaos will result. A house should not be perfectly finished, a brick should be left out. A transaction should not be perfectly finished, a rupee extra should be given. Something more should be left to the future, something should be left as seed.

Just as in the building of material works of art, so in the building of verbal works, the remainder is important in Tamil. One stylistic device which frequently occurs in all varieties of verbal art, and which Sevi employs very heavily in the song to Siṅgammā, is enjambment. Enjambment appears when a metric line (or musical phrase, or set of words uttered in a breath) does not correspond with a grammatical sentence or phrase, so that the first word of a new sentence appears at the end of a metric line, and the sentence is completed on the next line. What results is a kind of verbal "remaindering." In the song to Siṅgammā, the word that is most frequently so remaindered is *nī*, "you," so that many lines end, "Siṅgammā, you." What is predicated of "Siṅgammā, you" is left to the next line. Meanwhile this "you," like the spirit herself, hangs in limbo.

A related device, which might be called "predicate chaining," is also very common both in Tamil spoken prose (including Sevi's autobiography) and in Tamil oral poetry (including the song to Siṅgammā). Here the speaker or singer picks up the last part of the previous stanza or sentence or paragraph, and begins the new stanza or sentence with that same phrase. For instance:

> The wives of your five brothers, Siṅgammā,
> Kept you inside the house, Siṅgammā . . .
> And while you were kept inside the house, Siṅgammā,
> The four women came, Siṅgammā . . .
> And when the four women came, Siṅgammā,
> You put on different clothes, Siṅgammā . . .
> Putting on different clothes, Siṅgammā,
> you went to sell beads and needles, Siṅgammā . . .

In Tamil predicate-chaining, what is picked up to begin a new sentence is generally a participial phrase. If it was a finite verb phrase in the preceding stanza, it is converted to a participial phrase in the new one. These participles are themselves inherently dangling forms. Unlike finite verbs, they need something more to complete them. Their frequent use as a poetic device in both song and conversation bespeaks, like enjambment, a detotalizing vision of the world, a stress on the incomplete, the ongoing.[10]

Sevi's song to Siṅgammā stresses the theme of death and remainders strongly. The entire song, indeed—though Sevi says, "I am going to tell the story of your birth, of your growth, Siṅgammā"—is really devoted to the story of Siṅgammā's death.[11]

The story of Siṅgammā is one of a great many Indian tales about women who become deities by dying. In this song, however, the identification of the deity with death, especially its physical aspects, seems more prominent than usual. For example, at several points in the song, Siṅgammā's activity is associated with the loss of light, the setting of the sun, or the failure of the sun to exert its power. In other ways, also, it is suggested that Siṅgammā's power is the power of death. The plant that grows from her grave, for instance, the red oleander (*Nerium odorum carnea*), is a deathly poisonous plant. To consume even a tiny amount of it can be lethal.

Finally, Siṅgammā is identified with the earthworm or "flower snake" (*pūnākam*) that emerges from the plant growing from her grave. This consumer and transformer of death's remains becomes, in the song, Siṅgammā's only spokesperson.

The other direct references to remainders in the song to Siṅgammā have already been spoken of: the leftover rice Siṅgammā gathers, and the new house for Siṅgammā built over the remains of the old. A new house must never be built over the remains of an old house, Tamil villagers say firmly, because there might be the bones of some dead animal there. Here the bones of Siṅgammā herself are buried, and the place where her ending, her grave, was dug becomes the place where they dig her beginning.

> Crumbling the hut, Siṅgammā, for you
> A foundation they dig, Siṅgammā, Siṅgammā,
> And as they dig a foundation, Siṅgammā, for you,
> A bud comes and blossoms, mother, Siṅgammā.

I will end this still incomplete essay by comparing the denouement of the Siṅgammā story with the end of Sevi's own life story, in which she tells how she and her husband have been forced to live in a Muslim house, a "polluted house," a "house of people of no caste"; and yet in this house, with the marginal land they cultivate near it, they have found some peace and some hope. It is as though, by placing their faith in remainders, they may perhaps see something new and good rise from the wreckage of their lives.

What are these remainders in which they place such faith? One is tradition: the family god, the set of values, the knowledge, the songs of their own past. Another is writing (what some people now call our human spoor, our calling card, the dried ink on the page): this quasi-magical thing which, as Sevi shows us, has exerted a terrible destructive power in the life of her family, is that which she now seeks, through the education of her sons and through the present inscription of her thoughts and words, to turn to her own advantage. The third, finally, is Siṅgammā herself, this deity of cast-out people, whom Sevi has chosen to address rather than to despise. Rather like her most famous compatriot, who became great of heart the day he realized he was not above blacks but was black himself, Sevi, I think, becomes great when she sings this song, recognizing her kinship with others poor even beyond her own poverty, filthy even beyond her own filth. Performing this difficult act, she makes something beautiful out of her life.

Chapter 6

The Song of Siṅgammā

> Every being is instantiated in this world as the line of its own movement and activity; not a movement from point to point, as though the life course were already laid out as the route between them, but a continual "moving around," or coming and going. Significant moments—births, deaths, encounters with animals or spirits, coming out of the ground or going back in—are constituted *within* this movement, where the life-lines of different beings cross, interpenetrate, appear or disappear (only, perhaps, to reappear at some other moment).
>
> —Timothy Ingold, *The Perception of the Environment* (2000)

Kuṟavars

The Kuṟavars are by tradition hunters, an honored profession. The word Kuṟavar in Tamil means hunter. In earlier times, Kuṟavars are said to have lived by hunting wild animals in the mountain forests, where they also cultivated millet, and where the young women drove away the birds that came to eat the millet. Mention of Kuṟavars is found in Tamil poetry of the Sangam period nearly two thousand years ago. One Sangam poem about Kuṟavars is translated thus:

O Lord of the country
where the clouds
will pour down
many dense, stinging drops

if the hill man so much as raises a cry,
if she so much as sees
the swiftly flowing waterfall
of your town
with its fields and small mountains,
she will weep.

This is the first of a decad of poems in the *Aiṅkuṟunūru*, "The Five Hundred Short Poems" (Selby 2011, 104–7). The full decad tells the story of a young girl and a Kuṟavar lord of the hill country. The Kuṟavar lord is the hill man, Kuṉṟa-k-kuṟavan. It is up to the reader to ascertain why the young girl is weeping. One interpretation is that the young girl is weeping because she is to be married and leave her father and the home she loves. In this interpretation, the hill man is the girl's father. An alternative interpretation is that the young girl is weeping because her family disapproves of her planned marriage with the hill man, and she therefore elopes with him. Here, the hill man is not the father but the lover of the young girl. Eloping is a common theme in old Tamil poetry, which is capable of multiple interpretations (Trawick 1988b).

Kuṟavars appear again as prominent characters in Tamil dramas of the eighteenth and nineteenth centuries. By then the Kuṟavañji, or Kuṟavar woman, was portrayed as a multilingual fortune-teller of formidable skill (Peterson 2008).[1]

During British rule, Kuṟavars were designated a "criminal tribe." This was because, in times long past, they had been warriors. The British Raj considered that every caste and every tribe was as it had always been and as it would always be.

In present-day Tamil Nadu, the most numerous Kuṟavars, perhaps the only ones, are Narikuṟavars. *Nari* means jackal, and Narikuṟavars are Jackal Hunters. Kuṟavars from the Madurai area state that Narikuṟavaṅga (Jackal Hunters), Kuruvikkāraṅga (small fowl catchers), and Kuṟava *jāti* (hunter caste) are all legitimate names for themselves. As with Villiyars, whose job is to hunt rats and snakes, so with Kuṟavars, whatever they hunt they also eat. Narikuṟavars are expected to hunt and eat jackals, scavenging wild animals that are more despised even than feral dogs in Tamil Nadu. But they do not do much of that anymore. Their best source of protein is the pigs they raise. Normally, neither Muslims nor Hindus will eat pig meat, therefore eating pig meat is a social handicap but a nutritional asset.

In Mēlūr, where in the twentieth century the tragic life and death of the Kuṟatti girl Siṅgammā is believed to have happened, is a temple to Draupadi, in which the famous goddess appears in festivals disguised as a Kuṟatti (Muthukumaraswamy 2006).[2] Even now, despite their small numbers and absence of rank, Kuṟavars have the special privilege of riding in trains without tickets, though they must wear special Kuṟavar clothing to do so. Some of the men are allowed by special law to carry rifles in public places, so that they can kill crows or cats or other pests. The women sell beads and pretty beaded jewelry. They still are known for fortune-telling. The men sell teeth and oils of wild animals. In general, Kuṟavars are associated with birds, because of their role in driving birds away from fields of grain, shooting crows, catching small birds in nets, and using parrots in fortune-telling.

In particular, however, Kuṟavars are famous for hunting and eating crows. In modern times, Kuṟavars may still be seen wandering with their rifles through cities, fields, and wastelands, with crows their principal quarry. While members of middle castes are not ashamed to hunt and eat wild fowl such as doves and herons, only Kuṟavars will eat crows, for crows are, above all others, the birds of death. Crows, like some other birds, eat carrion. In ancient times, human corpses used to be offered by Tamil Jains to crows, and crows are still treated as the embodiment of dead ancestors and given offerings of rice on the festival day of Poṅgal, which marks the end of winter, the season of the crow, and the return of the life-giving sun. Paṟaiyars are despised by other castes for eating the meat of cattle, the purest, most life-giving of animals, whose destruction, therefore, is the gravest of sins. But as eaters of crows, Kuṟavars eat the eaters of death.

Eaters of wandering animals, Kuṟavars are themselves wanderers. While most Paṟaiyars are landless, hence impoverished and symbolically disembodied, Kuṟavars are even more conspicuously without a place. They have no fixed homes, no mud huts, but only rag tents and a territory through which they roam, a territory which in no sense belongs to them. Their regular haunts are train stations, bus stops, markets, and festivals—crossroads of every kind. There they sell trinkets and are reputed also to survive by petty thievery and prostitution. The notion that Kuṟavar women sell their bodies together with their trinkets is helped along by their different style of dress—they wear a kind of skirt and blouse instead of the supposedly modest and respectable sari. The term *siṅgi* in Tamil means both Kuṟavar woman and whore.

It is impossible for anyone to live in India by hunting anymore. Wild animals are scarce there, except for monkeys, which are dangerous thieves but are considered sacred by Hindus, tigers which are protected in a refuge in Tamil Nadu, and perhaps some other protected and therefore unhuntable species. Kuṟavars now are scavengers of garbage in the towns and cities. They camp out in vacant lots, where they sometimes keep pigs, and their children beg for coins, along with countless other beggar children in Indian towns and cities. They are said by some to be gypsies, to hail from Maharashtra, and to be related to the Roma people of Europe and the United Kingdom. They are said by others to come from the hilly areas around southern India, where the men hunted and the women protected the millet fields from marauding birds. The god Murugan married such a girl. She was romantic, attractive to him because she came from the wild mountain area, where elephants and tigers roamed. In the lore of the Sangam age, this was the place where young lovers, at risk to their own lives, met.

During British rule, Kuṟavars came to be classified as "tribal" people, who were outside the caste system, and when they were incorporated into it, were incorporated at the bottom. Their role as scavengers consolidates their low status. They are beneath the more numerous castes of Paṟaiyars and Pallars, who are farm laborers and who have, or had, certain inherited rights to work on certain land belonging to certain higher-caste people. All the untouchable castes were also slaves to the landowners. There were, however, Kuṟavars who did not belong to any owned land or landowner. Siṅgammā and her family were among those unowned.

Currently, as cultivable land becomes scarcer, as more people move into the cities, and as people of the lower castes see better options for themselves, the education and jobs available to the children born to agricultural laborers are changing. Kuṟavars see these same options but, probably because there are fewer of them, it is harder for them to fight, collectively and politically, for their rights. Some of them are well educated, and some of them advance because of this. Others are left jobless.

The Kuṟavars are said to be strict in their regulation of sexuality. They are praised for this by people of upper castes who admire this aspect of their way of life. But there is another side to their proud strictness, and this other side is told in the song sung by Sevi of Liṅgāvaḍi near Mēlūr north of Madurai. The song is about a Kuṟavar girl, Siṅgammā, who was gang-raped when she went out to the market, then murdered by her brothers to protect the honor of their caste. Her body was cut into pieces and buried in the floor of the hut where the brothers lived with their wives and their one younger sister, Siṅgammā. This might have been the end of her story, as it is of unnumbered other girls who are killed to save the honor of their family. But Siṅgammā returned as a ghost, demanding honor for herself as well. A shrine was built for her near the place where she was killed. Still she comes back from time to time to possess girls who pass by the shrine. An exorcist must then be called to give the possessing spirit the clothing and food that it demands, and to convince it to leave the body of the girl.[3]

"Poisonous" might be the most apt translation of the term *tīṇḍā*, which comes from the verb *tīṇḍu*, meaning not only "defile by touch" but also "poison, as with a snake's bite." People around Mēlūr, where I was working in 1984, use the term in both senses. Paṟaiyars are considered untouchable, defiling, or poisonous because their traditional occupation is to handle and process human and animal wastes and corpses, a set of tasks that the members of the Paṟaiyar community in that area still perform conscientiously and among themselves, like funeral Brahmans in Benares (Parry 1982). Paṟaiyars are defiling also because they eat beef, though they revere living cattle, attributing protective spiritual powers to them and in general treating them more kindly as animals. Cattle are not always treated kindly in India, despite the stereotype. Most Paṟaiyars nowadays earn their living as agricultural laborers and are rooted by kin and property ties to particular locations. By training and in values they are farmers. What they know best is how to work the soil. Land they hold dear, the more so in that most of them are landless.

The name Siṅgammā would be synonymous in Tamil with "Kuṟavar woman." Kuṟavars are said to hail from north India, where "singh," meaning "lion," is a common surname. In Tamil also, *siṅgam* means "lion." In Tamil cities, Kuṟavar women are highly visible as they move through their daily rounds of urban food gathering picking through garbage bins and gathering rice off the polluted *eccilai*, the "spittle leaves," thrown away by others after meals and feasts. To scavenge, to eat remainders, and to be themselves cast to the margins, left to drift with no permanent home—this is the fate of Kuṟavars.

The Paṟaiyars who spoke to me on this topic seemed to have an ambivalent view of the people below them, the Kuṟavars. On the one hand, some Paṟaiyars romanticized the Kuṟavars, seemingly admiring their evident freedom, resourcefulness, and creativity, and occasionally singing for me, with evident enjoyment, rather raunchy songs which they said they had heard from Kuṟavars. On the other hand, they avoided contact with Kuṟavars, despised them for their dirtiness, and sang songs mocking them for lawlessness and brother-sister incest.

However, Sevi's rendition of the song to Siṅgammā, the Kuṟavar girl, does not fit this pattern. It is not sung in fun but is straight and serious, and Sevi pours her heart into it, singing beautifully and with a high degree of control, yet almost weeping as she sings. Her rendition of the Siṅgammā song, in fact, has several salient properties in common with Paṟaiyar "crying songs" (*ayiṟa pāḍḍu*) or laments. Each line is marked by a rapid rise to a peak in pitch, followed by a gradual descent to the original pitch level. Each line ends in the cry "*ammā*" (mother), with the final syllable "*mā*" drawn out into a descending glissando wail. Each line is sung in a single breath, reeling the breath out to its end, so that a deep and audible inhalation occurs at the completion of the line. Finally, the topic of this song, like the topic of all Paṟaiyar laments, is not just death but the injustice of this particular death, with many comments as well upon the injustices suffered by low-caste women in life. Sevi speaks of her own life in Chapter 5.

The Siṅgammā song differs from Paṟaiyar laments in that its protagonist is able to come back from death and right the wrongs done to her. As Sevi performs it, the Siṅgammā story, like other Indian tales of apotheosis, moves through tragedy to triumph and ends with a powerful woman renouncing dependency; rising from defilement, death, and corrosion; and standing at last as a deity, defiantly alone.

One question that may be asked of the moving performance Sevi offers us is this: Why does she do it? Why does she choose a girl of this most despised people to sing to, and why does she sing this particular song for us? As an untouchable singing to and about a being untouchable even to herself, is she perhaps saying something about the state of untouchability, about the state of being classified together with poison and corpses? Is she perhaps trying to move beyond the pecking-order mentality of caste, to create a more enlightened response to her own abjection? Out of the stench of pollution, to produce something not conditioned by that stench?

The Story of Siṅgammā

The story of Siṅgammā, as recounted in Sevi's song, is stark and elliptical. As it opens, we learn that Siṅgammā is kept confined in the house by her brothers' wives. Note that in this song, Siṅgammā and her brothers live in a house. They would not have had an actual, physical house when the event recounted in this song took place. But later in this chapter, it will be clear that "house" (*vīḍu*) does not necessarily mean a physical structure.

One day, as she sees her brothers' wives coming, Siṅgammā changes her clothes and slips off to the market to sell trinkets. Her brothers weep when they come home and find her missing. They go to the market, where Siṅgammā is singing and playing cymbals (*siṅgi poḍḍu*), selling songs for coins at the dried fish store. Siṅgammā is seen singing and playing cymbals next to the dried fish store by her brothers. One brother, "the lame older brother" (*nōṇḍi aṇṇan*), sees her there but does not recognize her, or pretends he does not, and again weeps when he returns home and cannot find her.

Siṅgammā, still in town at dusk, goes to a wedding feast, gathers up the leftover rice from discarded leaves there, and brings it back home in jars. Questions suggest that while she was at the market, Siṅgammā was doing more than just selling beads and singing, getting coins for her songs. As punishment for going out alone, she is sent to a house in the forest and made to stay there, grinding and pounding with a mortar stone. Four brothers go into the house, pull the doors shut and lock them, and the mortar stone pounds. Then Siṅgammā says to them, or they say to her: "The sun has set on our good caste; we are excluded from caste [*jātilēyum taḷḷuvaḍi*]."

The lame older brother's wedding day arrives. Siṅgammā is to cook and serve at the wedding feast, but the pots of rice and milk won't boil for her—the sun will not allow it. (The Tamil festival of the sun, celebrated around winter solstice time, is marked by the boiling of a rice and milk dish called *poṅgal*. If the pot boils over, it means that the sun will bless the family with abundance in the coming year. If the pot fails to boil over, it is a bad sign.)

Siṅgammā is again locked in the house, "weeping in her heart." But at dusk she declares, "If my honor [*patti*] is destroyed, let the doors of the house stay shut, but if my honor is undestroyed, let them open."

The doors open, and Siṅgammā flees. Her brothers come home and ask where Siṅgammā is, and their wives say, "A husband has married her and taken her away." (This is a lie. But it is the third strike against Siṅgammā. First, she went to the market alone. Then the pots did not boil for her. And now this.)

The brothers then dig holes in the floor inside the house. The holes are to be Siṅgammā's grave. Siṅgammā is now with her mother. She lies down to sleep with her head on her mother's lap. Her mother tells her that because she is excluded from the caste and pots will not boil for her, her brothers are going to kill her. As she lies with her head in her mother's lap, she takes a louse comb in her hand and assumes the form of louse eggs. While she is in this form, her brothers pound rice for her mouth (rice is put in the mouth of corpses before burial) and drop chicken and crow meat in the holes in which she is to be entombed. The lame older brother weeps yet again, and then Siṅgammā is killed and dismembered (*kulaicukum*). Only the heart of the mother (*āttā*) is not made happy by this act, says the song.

Siṅgammā is interred in the holes dug for her, and from them a beautiful poisonous red oleander (*sevvaraḷi*) springs up. The lame older brother comes to the places where the oleander has grown. A poisonous snake (*pu nākam*, "flower snake") emerges from the oleander and tells the brother to build a palace there for Siṅgammā. They crumble the house and build a foundation on that site; when they do so, an oleander bud blossoms for Siṅgammā. Then the elder brother touches (*tīṇḍu*) the snake, which, in return, tells him a story. It says it once lived in the house. It says that Siṅgammā's brother's wives saw it and told Siṅgammā to catch it and take it away; both it and Siṅgammā left the house, "weeping and sobbing." The snake concludes its story by saying, "Even if you build palaces, you may not stay. Only the lame older brother may stay."

All the brothers and their wives then come to that place to burn lime for mortar. As soon as they have burned and moistened the lime, buildings grow up in that spot. A woman comes to live there, and when she does so, the building in which she lives "leans over with its foundation." Siṅgammā then appears to the woman. The woman asks her where she comes from. Siṅgammā replies, "I came from within the house itself." Then, as the song goes, Siṅgammā, having emerged from within the house, "rising up high, speaking with unsheathed energy, wearing pearls," addresses her lame older brother, telling him, "You are the one who killed me, who saw my sin, who undid me. That which entered the house truly was. Tell me to rise up outside. Now I will stand up straight and show you." She leaves the house, she goes outside, they raise her up. And the final stanza of the song says, "As soon as they raised you up, Siṅgammā, your building, too, stood up tall."

Siṅgammā Song by Sevi

Brothers there are five, Siṅgammā, brothers there are five, Siṅgammā, Siṅgammā, of you,
the story of your birth I will tell, Siṅgammā, Siṅgammā.
The story of your birth I will tell, Siṅgammā, of you,
the story of your growth I will tell, Siṅgammā, Siṅgammā.

The story of your birth I will tell, Siṅgammā.
Brothers there are five, Siṅgammā.
Brothers there are five, Siṅgammā, Siṅgammā, for you,
the high court is a servant, Siṅgammā, Siṅgammā.
And the five wives of your brothers, Siṅgammā, you,
they kept you in the house, Siṅgammā, Siṅgammā, Siṅgammā.
They kept you in the house, Siṅgammā.
And while you were in the house, Siṅgammā, while you
were in the house, Siṅgammā, all four women came there, Siṅgammā, Siṅgammā,
all four women came there, Siṅgammā, Siṅgammā.
And when you saw the women, Siṅgammā, you
put on different clothing Siṅgammā, Siṅgammā, you
put on different clothing Siṅgammā, Siṅgammā.
Having put on different clothing, Siṅgammā,
to sell beads and needles, Siṅgammā, Siṅgammā,
to sell beads and needles, Siṅgammā, Siṅgammā, you
departing on your way, Siṅgammā,
tears and weeping on the way, Siṅgammā, Siṅgammā,
tears and weeping on the way, Siṅgammā, Siṅgammā.
To the market of Mēlūr, Siṅgammā,
to the market of Mēlūr, Siṅgammā, Siṅgammā, you,
are you going just to sell beads, Siṅgammā, Siṅgammā?
And when the five brothers go looking, Siṅgammā,
saying, "Our young sister is missing," Siṅgammā, Siṅgammā,
they come into the house, Siṅgammā, Siṅgammā, Siṅgammā.
And when they look inside the house, Siṅgammā,
when they look inside the house, Siṅgammā,
"Younger sister is missing," they cry weeping tears, Siṅgammā, Siṅgammā.
In the market of Mēlūr, Siṅgammā,
in the market of Mēlūr, Siṅgammā, Siṅgammā,
inside the dried fish store, Siṅgammā, Siṅgammā,
when they saw little sister, Siṅgammā, you
all four of them left and went away, Siṅgammā, Siṅgammā, left you
and went away, Siṅgammā, Siṅgammā.
And when they left and went away, Siṅgammā, you,
next to the dried fish store, Siṅgammā, Siṅgammā, you

were singing songs, weren't you, Siṅgammā, Siṅgammā?
And while you were singing songs, Siṅgammā,
did they give you ten paisa, Siṅgammā, Siṅgammā?
Did they give you ten paisa, Siṅgammā, Siṅgammā? Having gotten ten paisa, Siṅgammā, you
went into the market, Siṅgammā, Siṅgammā, you
went into the market, Siṅgammā, Siṅgammā.
When you went into the market, Siṅgammā, you
played cymbals and got coins, Siṅgammā, Siṅgammā, you
played cymbals and got coins, Siṅgammā, Siṅgammā.
Having gotten the coins, Siṅgammā,
having gotten the coins, Siṅgammā, Siṅgammā, you
came again outside, Siṅgammā, Siṅgammā.
And when you came to the outside, Siṅgammā, you,
your lame older brother saw you, Siṅgammā, Siṅgammā.
Your lame older brother saw you, Siṅgammā, Siṅgammā.
When your older brother saw you, Siṅgammā,
when your older brother saw you, Siṅgammā, ammā
because you were his sister he knew you not in any way, Siṅgammā, Siṅgammā
Having seen and forgotten, Siṅgammā,
the older brother came to the house, Siṅgammā, Siṅgammā,
came to the house, Siṅgammā, Siṅgammā.
Having come into the house, Siṅgammā,
"Our younger sister is missing," he says, Siṅgammā, Siṅgammā,
and he asks and looks around, Siṅgammā, Siṅgammā.
When he asks and looks around, Siṅgammā,
when he asks and looks around, Siṅgammā, Siṅgammā,
he weeps and he grieves, Siṅgammā, Siṅgammā.
When you go into the market, Siṅgammā,
on the Sharp Stone Hill of Mēlūr, Siṅgammā, Siṅgammā,
a wedding is happening, isn't it, Siṅgammā, Siṅgammā?
In the house of the wedding, Siṅgammā,
there is rice here on the way, Siṅgammā, Siṅgammā,
there is rice here on the way, Siṅgammā, Siṅgammā.
And when they saw the women, Siṅgammā,
the spittle leaves were piled up, Siṅgammā, Siṅgammā,
the leaves of leftovers were piled up, Siṅgammā, Siṅgammā.

And when the spittle leaves piled up, Siṅgammā,
gathering the rice grains in a bottle, Siṅgammā, Siṅgammā,
southward turning your head, Siṅgammā,
you're coming home, Siṅgammā,
you have set out, Siṅgammā, on the way weeping and grieving,
Siṅgammā.
Four people are waiting, Siṅgammā, Siṅgammā.
A grinding stone for grinding, Siṅgammā, Siṅgammā,
a grinding stone for pounding, Siṅgammā, Siṅgammā,
they call you and they ask you, Siṅgammā, Siṅgammā,
saying, "Where were you?" Siṅgammā,
saying, "In what place?" Siṅgammā, Siṅgammā,
they stand asking, don't they, Siṅgammā, Siṅgammā?
"In the forest itself, ammā, Siṅgammā,
seeing that house, go stay there, ammā, Siṅgammā,
grinding with the grinding stone you will be, Siṅgammā,
Siṅgammā."
All four people saying this, Siṅgammā,
they said to Siṅgammā and sent her off, Siṅgammā, Siṅgammā.
In the house, locking the house, Siṅgammā,
all four doors indeed, Siṅgammā, Siṅgammā,
they closed and they came, Siṅgammā, Siṅgammā.
And all four of the men, Siṅgammā,
and all four of the men, Siṅgammā, Siṅgammā,
went inside the house, Siṅgammā, Siṅgammā.
And when they go inside the house, Siṅgammā,
the grinding stone pounds, doesn't it, Siṅgammā, Siṅgammā?
The grinding stone pounds, doesn't it, Siṅgammā, Siṅgammā?
And when the grinding stone was pounding, Siṅgammā,
all four of the doors, Siṅgammā, Siṅgammā,
they pulled shut and locked, Siṅgammā, Siṅgammā.
And to them, to all four of them, Siṅgammā,
Siṅgammā gives a final answer, doesn't she, Siṅgammā, Siṅgammā?
"In our good *jāti*," Siṅgammā, "in our good *jāti*," Siṅgammā,
Siṅgammā,
"the sun has set and gone," Siṅgammā, Siṅgammā,
"We are expelled from caste," Siṅgammā, Siṅgammā.
"We are expelled from caste," Siṅgammā, Siṅgammā.

For our older brother, for the lame older brother,
for our older brother, there is a wedding.
For the lame older brother, older brother, a wedding.
For the lame older brother, older brother, a wedding.
To cook and to serve, there is Siṅgammā.
To cook and to serve, there is Siṅgammā, Siṅgammā.
Over the seven pots, the boiling pots must boil over, Siṅgammā,
  Siṅgammā.
The boiling pots must boil over, Siṅgammā, Siṅgammā.
Because you acted wrongly, Siṅgammā,
excluded from our caste, Siṅgammā, Siṅgammā,
excluded from caste, Siṅgammā, Siṅgammā.
The seven pots will not boil over, will they, Siṅgammā?
The seven pots will not boil over, will they, Siṅgammā, Siṅgammā?
Even if it dawns, he will not let them, Siṅgammā, Siṅgammā.
Even if it dawns, he will not let them, Siṅgammā, Siṅgammā.
All four doors indeed, Siṅgammā,
they pulled shut and locked, Siṅgammā, Siṅgammā.
There are tears and weeping inside, aren't there, Siṅgammā,
  Siṅgammā?
Six o'clock has struck, Siṅgammā.
Six o'clock has struck, Siṅgammā, Siṅgammā.
"If my faith [*patti*] is destroyed," Siṅgammā,
"If I have my faith destroyed," Siṅgammā, Siṅgammā,
"then I must stay within the house," Siṅgammā, Siṅgammā,
"must stay within the house," Siṅgammā, Siṅgammā.
"If I am a woman of undestroyed faith," Siṅgammā,
"a woman of undestroyed faith," Siṅgammā, Siṅgammā,
"These four doors must open up," Siṅgammā.
When this was said and finished, Siṅgammā,
when this was said and finished, Siṅgammā, Siṅgammā,
all four doors parted, Siṅgammā, Siṅgammā, Siṅgammā.
From within the house, Siṅgammā, Siṅgammā,
running, running fast, Siṅgammā, Siṅgammā,
on the Sharp Stone wasteland, Siṅgammā,
darkness gathers, Siṅgammā, Siṅgammā.
Darkness gathers, Siṅgammā, Siṅgammā.
On the way coming to the house, Siṅgammā,

on the way coming to the house, Siṅgammā, Siṅgammā,
six o'clock strikes, Siṅgammā, Siṅgammā,
six o'clock strikes, Siṅgammā, Siṅgammā.
And when six o'clock strikes, Siṅgammā,
and when six o'clock strikes, Siṅgammā, Siṅgammā,
all seven brothers ask, Siṅgammā, Siṅgammā
ask of their wives, Siṅgammā, Siṅgammā, "Where is our sister?
Where? Where?"
thus they ask, Siṅgammā, Siṅgammā.
And when they thus ask, Siṅgammā,
"Your sister a husband married and took away," Siṅgammā,
Siṅgammā,
"a husband married and took away," Siṅgammā, Siṅgammā.
"Tell what is the news, girl, Siṅgammā. Tell what is the news, girl,
Siṅgammā, you
What is the news about your going, Siṅgammā, Siṅgammā?"
All seven of the brothers, Siṅgammā,
call their sister, but not with their mouths, Siṅgammā, Siṅgammā,
when they call, Siṅgammā,
seven times, seven times beating cymbals, Siṅgammā, Siṅgammā,
they perform the cymbal art, Siṅgammā, Siṅgammā.
"We will not eat chicken meat, Siṅgammā,
we will not go to the temple, Siṅgammā, Siṅgammā,"
telling you to eat the chicken, Siṅgammā, Siṅgammā,
they give it with kindness, Siṅgammā, Siṅgammā.
Having made you eat the chicken, Siṅgammā,
within the house they dig holes, Siṅgammā, Siṅgammā,
they dig holes, Siṅgammā, Siṅgammā.
In the lap of the mother who bore you, Siṅgammā,
in the lap of the mother who bore you, Siṅgammā,
they put you to sleep, Siṅgammā, Siṅgammā.
"Sleep will not come, mother," Siṅgammā,
"Sleep will not come, mother," Siṅgammā, Siṅgammā,
to the mother who bore you the order must be given, Siṅgammā,
Siṅgammā.
When you are put to sleep, Siṅgammā, ammā
when you are put to sleep, Siṅgammā, Siṅgammā,
younger sister's story they ask, Siṅgammā, Siṅgammā.

And when they put you to sleep, Siṅgammā,
and when they ask the story, Siṅgammā, Siṅgammāḷē,
they say to play the cymbals, Siṅgammā, Siṅgammā.
And all four brothers, Siṅgammā, Siṅgammā
play the cymbals, don't they, Siṅgammā, Siṅgammā.
The mother who bore you says, Siṅgammā, Siṅgammā, ammā,
"Excluded from the caste, ammā, Siṅgammā, Siṅgammā,
the boiling pot will not boil over, Siṅgammā, Siṅgammā,
you are to be killed by your brothers, Siṅgammā, Siṅgammā."
Saying to lie down in her lap, Siṅgammā,
saying to lie down in her lap, Siṅgammā, Siṅgammā,
you took a louse comb in your hand, Siṅgammā, Siṅgammā,
you took a louse comb in your hand, Siṅgammā, Siṅgammā.
When you took it in your hand, Siṅgammā,
when you took it in your hand, Siṅgammā, Siṅgammā,
you took the form of louse nits, Siṅgammā, Siṅgammā,
you took the form of louse nits, Siṅgammā, Siṅgammā.
And when you were in the form of louse nits, Siṅgammā,
and when you were in the form of louse nits, Siṅgammā, Siṅgammā, for you,
for your mouth they pounded rice, Siṅgammā, Siṅgammā.
Bringing the meat of crow, Siṅgammā, Siṅgammā,
bringing the meat of chicken, Siṅgammā, Siṅgammā, for you,
they dig holes in the ground, Siṅgammā, Siṅgammā.
Your six brothers are going to cut you up, Siṅgammā, Siṅgammā,
They are going to cut you up, Siṅgammā, Siṅgammā.
When the lame older brother sees, Siṅgammā,
when the lame older brother sees, Siṅgammā, Siṅgammā,
he weeps and he sobs, Siṅgammā, Siṅgammā,
he weeps and he sobs, Siṅgammā, Siṅgammā.
And because of the weeping, because of the weeping, you,
Siṅgammā, Siṅgammā, because of the weeping, you,
Siṅgammā, Siṅgammā, you,
he does not want to cut up, Siṅgammā, Siṅgammā.
And when they cut you up, Siṅgammā, Siṅgammā,
they put Siṅgammā in the holes, Siṅgammā, Siṅgammā,
they put her in the holes, Siṅgammā, Siṅgammā.
Only the mother's heart, Siṅgammā, Siṅgammā,

did not feel happy, Siṅgammā, Siṅgammā.
Being covered in the holes, Siṅgammā, Siṅgammā,
you stay there and be content, Siṅgammā, Siṅgammā,
stay there and be content, Siṅgammā, Siṅgammā.
Siṅgammā, from the hole, Siṅgammā,
Siṅgammā, from the hole, Siṅgammā, Siṅgammā, for you,
a red oleander blossomed, didn't it, Siṅgammā, Siṅgammā?
In the spots where the oleander bloomed, Siṅgammā, Siṅgammā,
the lame older brother went, didn't he, Siṅgammā, Siṅgammā?
The lame older brother went, didn't he, Siṅgammā, Siṅgammā?
A flower-snake [earthworm] was waiting, Siṅgammā,
a flower-snake was waiting, Siṅgammā, Siṅgammā, for ammā,
it said to build a palace, Siṅgammā, Siṅgammā.
And the hut they crumble up, Siṅgammā, for you,
and they dig a foundation, Siṅgammā, and they dig a foundation, Siṅgammā, Siṅgammā.
And when they dig a foundation, Siṅgammā,
and when they dig a foundation, Siṅgammā, Siṅgammā, for you,
a bud blossoms, ammā, Siṅgammā, Siṅgammā.
And when the snake bites, Siṅgammā,
to the older brother it tells a story, Siṅgammā, Siṅgammā.
"In the house I was sitting and waiting,
in the house I was sitting and waiting, and four women came, for me,
and four women came, Siṅgammā,
and told her to catch me and carry me away
they told and sent Siṅgammā,
Siṅgammā, the four wives of the brothers, Siṅgammā, Siṅgammā.
And when they told and sent Siṅgammā,
then I weeping and grieving went away, I went away, ammā, didn't I, Siṅgammā, Siṅgammā?"
And even if they build houses, Siṅgammā,
you all must not stay here, must you, Siṅgammā, Siṅgammā?
Must not stay here, must you, Siṅgammā, Siṅgammā?
The lame older brother only, Siṅgammā, the lame older brother only, Siṅgammā, Siṅgammā,
here he must stay, mustn't he, Siṅgammā, Siṅgammā?
He must stay, mustn't he, Siṅgammā, Siṅgammā?

And all seven of the brothers, Siṅgammā,
all seven of the brothers, Siṅgammā, and their four wives, Siṅgammā, Siṅgammā,
came seeking a place to burn lime for mortar, Siṅgammā,
Siṅgammā, came seeking a place to burn lime for mortar, Siṅgammā, Siṅgammā.
At one o'clock in the afternoon, Siṅgammā,
at one o'clock in the afternoon, Siṅgammā,
they finished moistening the lime, Siṅgammā,
Siṅgammā, they finished moistening it, Siṅgammā, Siṅgammā.
And as they finish moistening it, Siṅgammā, Siṅgammā, here,
buildings grow up, don't they, Siṅgammā, Siṅgammā?
Buildings grow up, don't they, Siṅgammā, Siṅgammā?
And as soon as buildings grow up, Siṅgammā,
as soon as buildings grow up, Siṅgammā, Siṅgammā,
a woman went to live there, Siṅgammā, Siṅgammā.
And when she went to live there, Siṅgammā, Siṅgammā,
it leaned with its foundation, did it not, Siṅgammā, Siṅgammā?
And saying "Siṅgammā," when it came,
and saying "Siṅgammā," when it came, Siṅgammā,
truths it told, Siṅgammā, Siṅgammā.
"Where have you come from, ammā?" Siṅgammā.
"Where have you come from, ammā?" Siṅgammā, Siṅgammā.
"I come from within the house itself, ammā," Siṅgammā, Siṅgammā.
When you came from within the house, Siṅgammā, Siṅgammā,
you rising up to your full height, saying energetically, wearing pearls of divination,
"What is the story? Tell," Siṅgammā,
of you the lame older brother asks, Siṅgammā, Siṅgammā.
"O, you who murdered me," Siṅgammā, Siṅgammā,
"You who saw my sin," Siṅgammā, Siṅgammā,
"You who caused my cutting up," Siṅgammā, Siṅgammā,
"Having entered the house. It was true and it happened," Siṅgammā, Siṅgammā.
"Tell me to rise up outside," Siṅgammā,
"I say, tell me to rise up outside," Siṅgammā, Siṅgammā, "I now stand straight and show myself, Siṅgammā, Siṅgammā."

Leaving the house and coming outside, Siṅgammā, Siṅgammā,
they raised you up completely, Siṅgammā, Siṅgammā.
They raised you up completely, Siṅgammā, Siṅgammā.
And when they raised you up completely, Siṅgammā,
your building, building also stood up straight, amma, Siṅgammā.
Your building also stood up straight, Siṅgammā, Siṅgammā.

Conclusion

The South Asian subcontinent is like a net: it holds what it catches. Much of what it catches and holds is beneficial, such as writings in magazines and newspapers, now all online, free to express a wide range of views in half a dozen or more different languages; delicious food of countless varieties; gorgeous saris; superb poetry ancient and new; classical music. But over time, damaging elements have accumulated that cannot easily be tossed out—harmful beliefs, misogyny, and the cruel *jāti* (caste) system, which ranks human beings by family of birth, by occupation, by food eaten, by religion, and by political persuasion, which often is aligned with religious ideology. All of these rankings are packed into one bundle, with different jātis pitted against each other in struggles for rank and status. If you are born into one jāti, you must marry a person of that same jāti, so that you are forced to participate in a massive eugenic experiment that cannot easily be undone.

The current prime minister, Narendra Modi, is trying to bring Dalits, Adivasis, Muslims, and Christians "back" into the Hindu fold. Many people of the lowest, and a few of the highest-ranked jātis, oppose the systemic injustices of India and sometimes fight against them, in a range of different ways. No matter how they fight, with words or with actions, if they are not well protected, extreme violence threatens them. Arundhati Roy writes in the *Indian Express* of November 5, 2015, "'Intolerance' is the wrong word to use for the lynching, shooting, burning, and mass murder of fellow human beings. . . . Whole populations—millions of Dalits, Adivasis, Muslims and Christians—are being forced to live in terror, unsure of when and from where the assault will come." The beneficent juxtaposed with the maleficent, the new juxtaposed with the old, the known juxtaposed with the imagined, these and other ironies and contradictions are part of the Indian world.

The introduction to this book briefly describes how the first human settlers in South Asia entered through the south, with the first coastal migrations of people from Africa, some fifty to seventy thousand years ago. Those were among the ancestors of South Indian peoples, those called Adivasis, the aboriginal people of South Asia. They stayed in warmer climates, fishing from the coasts, hunting in the forests, settling in places they chose along the way. At the beginning of their presence on the subcontinent, they spoke languages that came from long ago, when people had languages that were known then but cannot be known now. Every living language changes over time, as does every living culture. There are several language families in South Asia. Members of the Dravidian language family are spoken primarily by people in the southern part of India and parts of Sri Lanka. Today they live also in the United Kingdom, France, Switzerland, Norway, Canada, Malaysia and Singapore, the United States, Australia, New Zealand, and probably other countries. In all these countries, they are a minority. The oldest member of the present Dravidian language family is Tamil. Written forms of the Dravidian family date back to the second to fourth centuries CE. By the time written Tamil appeared, fine poetry was already there.

For a person trained in linguistic anthropology, as I was, the connection between language and culture is essential. Each shapes the other. A person whose first language is American English, then as an adult learns to read and write Tamil, goes to Tamil Nadu and eastern Sri Lanka to learn more about spoken and written Tamil cultures, follows a profession that has been, for me, both challenging and rewarding. People who from birth speak Tamil sometimes criticize my efforts to speak their language, but mostly they appreciate the fact that I even try.

In high school, I read a book about the world's great religions, and decided that I liked Hinduism best, because of its beautiful, weird mythology. And in college, I learned more about Hinduism, read more, and wrote my senior thesis about the Lingayats, who started off as an egalitarian movement. In graduate school at the University of Chicago, I learned more, and was happy not to be involved in politics. Slowly, I learned that there were some not-so-good things about India, but I thought that was just the Third World, which was what young anthropologists of the day liked to study. To get the kind of grant I got, we were required to learn a non-Indo-European language, as well as to know a European one. We were encouraged to do our fieldwork outside of the United States and outside of Europe. I had already learned French in primary and secondary school, and at Chicago I learned the Tamil language, became entranced by it, and kept on learning. I went to do research in Tamil Nadu several times, went to Sri Lanka during the war there, and saw that Theravada Buddhism was not necessarily benign. At some time I started writing a book, this book, about women of the lowest-ranked jātis in Tamil Nadu, did more reading, and came to see that Hinduism and jāti were bound together in India, and that the jāti system was harmful to human beings, as well as to Indian civilization as a whole. Unlike China for all its flaws, India has no nationwide public health system, and it shows. Maybe there would be some way to let Hindus in India have their gods and their mythologies without having to bend under the weight of social, political, religious, and familial hierarchies. People labeled untouchable would have to be freed. B. R. Ambedkar wrote the same thing, better than I ever could. He argued also that the Hindu religion should be abolished together with jāti. What he said was convincing to many, including Arundhati Roy.

People who live in the wild do not live long. Nevertheless, they are adapted to conditions of hardship, and they pass on to others nearby, including children, all that they have learned about how to survive. As time goes on and cultures develop and diversify, knowledge and memory grow wide and deep. Knowledge about fishing in a particular place, hunting in another, gathering in another, growing a particular crop, or raising a particular group of animals in yet another environment, each kind of place and form of activity develops in human beings certain diverse ways of thinking about the world. For example, a young child who loves the goats she herds, and yet is not at all distressed at learning that her favorite goat's throat has been cut, is a perfectly normal child. And another child who grows up reading and writing and can do little else remains within the bounds of normalcy. Knowledge and memories grow, and meanwhile, slowly or suddenly, everything changes. Rivers flood, volcanoes erupt, new people appear and take over, new diseases strike and kill. Such events may cause many deaths. The survivors may have to start life all over again.

Like music, death is what it is. People may believe in an afterlife, create elaborate tombs, leave flowers, but all of this activity is to comfort the living. Death is what the living, after having said their prayers, sung their songs, or poured water over their heads, perforce must turn their backs to. I learned this from the Tamil text *Tirumantiram*, in a chapter called "The Impermanence of the Body" (*yākkai nilaiyāmai*) even before anyone close to me had died. Death is not a thing or being, it is a process. When you are dying, other people generally participate in the process, just to be with the loved one in their last moments of life. But some dying people are simply abandoned on the street or in the wild.

The first word in the title of this book is "death" because untouchables are meant to manage the bodies of the dead, and because the work they have to do—preparing dead animal and human bodies for whatever fate awaits them, cleaning sewers, removing fecal matter wherever it falls—often leads to an early death. There and here, the rich live long while the poor die young. The Dalit women I knew spoke and sang of the process of dying, of being themselves caught within that process. They wept for themselves and not for the dead, but the loss of the one for whom they did not weep might still leave them bereft. Even, as in some of the Paṟaiyar women's songs, the lost one was not really lost, they mourned and wept. With the rise of the Internet, people around the world may learn that mass murders of more lowly ranked people by people of higher ranks are not uncommon. Meena Kandasamy and many others have brought such events to light. An organization called Dalit Camera has formed. Ethnic minorities, no matter how they are ranked or not ranked, no matter what country they live in, are too often subject to genocide. We may mourn in our hearts for those who have been killed, far away in a distant place, even when the ones we mourn are strangers.

Kanyammā and her family were required to kill poisonous snakes and to eat "big rats" (Asian bandicoot rats, *peruccāli*) and other vermin such as "white ants" (termites). Those big rats carry disease. Termites eat anything organic. When I met her, Kanyammā was dying of tuberculosis. She and her family lived in an orchard or on a village road, one or the other, without any shelter. In the same village were laborers of the Paṟaiyar jāti who were better off than Kanyammā and her family but who, like members of other jātis deemed untouchable, were not allowed into the village school. Instead they sang remarkable songs that nobody listened to but the occasional curious anthropologist.

When one writes about local knowledge, one must understand that such knowledge is not all carried in writing, or even necessarily in words. Writing is a recent development, used and deployed by a narrow range of specialists. None of the Dalit women I knew could read or write, but their memories were long and their knowledge deep.

By the time I came along, Dalit women knew basically the kind of person I was—female, Western, wanting to listen to what people like them might say. They knew about the world—as much as, though differently from, what I had learned by reading from early childhood on—and they learned a bit more from me just by observing me. Sarasvati knew me better than I knew myself. Pushpam, Kanyammā, Sevi, and Jagathambā knew me before I knew them. Though I just wanted to be treated like a normal person, my reputation, fortunately or unfortunately, preceded me, attributing traits to me that I never had. But what I learned from each of the women whose words I heard changed me, and makes this book what it is now as I write it.

Jagathambā, a Narikuravar woman, does not appear in previous chapters of this book. She is prominent in an article I wrote (Trawick 1995) where she shows her understanding of what may be called the modern world. She knows the story of Siṅgammā, of whom she says, "That poor girl. She died twenty years ago," and then continues to describe one educated Narikuravar woman who is married to a progressive Reḍḍiyar man. "Wherever she casts her eyes, there she buys land." Jagathambā and the people with her, all sitting together by a railroad track, tell me exactly what they want. An educated man among the group tells me that he has an MA but no job, housing but no water. "Tell the president of your country that I want a bore well," he says.

Two autobiographies appear in this book, comprising Chapters 1 and 5. Each of these was given to me in spoken or sung Tamil. A remarkable biography of one person was given to me, and the story of this person is sung in Chapter 6. Elsewhere, the biography of this same person is spoken, chanted, and extended. The person about whom the singing and chanting was performed, Siṅgammā, had been a girl of a nomadic tribe called Narikuṟavars, "Jackal Hunters." Through the chant of a man of a higher jāti, she was apotheosized. To change a ghost into a deity is not an easy task. One needs considerable knowledge, skill, and experience to accomplish such a task. A man named Veḷḷaiccāmi accomplished it. He was not alone in his efforts, but he was alone in his recorded performance, gazing intently into the dancing lights of the recording machine.

Hindu temples are built as concentric structures. The human body has been imagined by Hindu savants in the same way. According to Ayurveda, a set of Sanskrit medical texts, there are seven substances (*dhatu*) composing this body. They are juice (*rasa*), blood (*rakta*), flesh (*mamsa*), fat (*meda*), bone (*ashli*), marrow (*majja*), and semen (*shukra*). These substances go from the least digested to the most refined. I learned all this from different sources including my friend and teacher Mahadev Aiyar, and my other teacher and field assistant, S. R. Themozhiyar. The latter considered the body to consist of layers, from the hardest and most external, to the finest and most internal. He spoke of the temple at Chidambaram where the concentric model is most apparent, and he taught that women are more soft and fine and therefore more subtle than men. This is a far cry from what Sarasvati was telling me.

But at the time, I was taken by the vision of the savants, even while I knew that the worldview of Sarasvati was more congruent with my own.

The theoretical purpose of the concentric model is to protect the innermost place by means of impenetrable walls. The innermost place in the body is the womb, although the womb is in reality all too penetrable. The innermost place in the temple is the same. It is called *garbha graham*, "womb room." But there is an even more innermost place in the temple of Chidambaram, and that is where the lord Siva dances. He is so fine as to be invisible, the purest of the pure. On the outside walls of some temples are scary masculine figures. These are guardians, to keep demons and demonic people out. I never asked who the demons and demonic people might be.

The innermost place in the jāti system is imagined to hold the purest of beings, who are thought of as gods. These are Brahmans. They are protected not by walls of stone but by walls of people, people of different jātis, from closest to the center, to least close. Each jāti, each category of people, has its own job to do. Those who live outside all the walls are untouchable. Their job is to take on impurity. Mohandas Gandhi spoke of untouchables as sacred precisely because they and they alone could accept the impurities excreted by the more protected. Gandhi called them Harijans, "children of God." Some Harijans believed in this idea. This is the jāti system, prettily imagined. The unpretty part is the life that people of the lowest jātis experience. Within most jātis, women are considered to be, by nature, lower than men.

People at any level of the system seek to raise the status of their jāti, or keep the existing status of their jāti respectable. This is what Sevi sings and talks about in Chapters 5 and 6. For Siṅgammā, the worst fate was to be excluded from jāti, to be pushed out. For this reason, because a shadow of doubt was cast upon her chastity, she allowed herself to be murdered by her brothers, and, as a ghost, sought vengeance against her rapist, and not against the men who killed her. This is one reason why to abolish jāti altogether, as Ambedkar insisted must be done, is going to be difficult. Even people of the lowest jātis cannot abandon jāti itself. To do so would be worse than suicide. Where else could they go? What else could they do? They had no options. More privileged people may experiment more.

In the foreword to this book, Ann Grodzins Gold writes about filaments, threads of shining light that glint here and there from my earliest work until now. She chooses some of the best parts that a reader may enjoy and learn from, and four persistent themes that she finds in what I have written. These are gender and social justice, intertwined emotions and ecologies, interpenetration of divine and mortal biographies, and unrepentant anthropology. I acknowledge that the first three themes are present in this book. But for the fourth, I never thought of anthropology as a profession from which one might have to repent. I just did it, in the only way I knew how.

I cannot do justice to what Ann has written. Here I develop some other threads, shining or not, that weave through this book. In no particular order, these threads are time and change, place and movement, environment and ecology, song and creation, separation and untouchability, and womanhood.

Time and Change

Every good thing I have discovered came to me serendipitously. I was keeping an eye out, but did not know what I would find until I found it. Events I experienced became memories. Everything is tangled together now: personal memories, memories of things read and said, images, thoughts. Finally, this book has been about, among other things, time and change—how the lives of Dalit women in India have changed over time and how my perceptions have changed along with theirs. One important change in their perception is that they are not made by God to be untouchable. They are not inherently poisonous. But learning some reality is one thing. Convincing others is another.

Time (Kāli) means death. It is a necessity, but not a good thing. For people in traditional Tamil Nadu, south means death. Where there is a village, the south end of the village was where the untouchable people lived.

As a person from the West, I never believed that people called untouchable were poisonous, or more dirty than higher-caste people. Though I did not believe, I was still tested. For the women who sang, my listening to their songs critical of privileged people may have been enough. One old man wanted more solid proof. Munusāmy came to the place I was staying to tell me his feet were damaged by the concrete that had been laid near there. I offered him a pair of my socks. He asked me to put the socks on his feet with my own hands. So I did.

When Kanyammā sang, she sang of the south, for she knew that death was coming. She also sang of the west, as a place bearing thunder and lightning. And she knew without a doubt that her life and environment were changing for the worse. She knew this because she sang it, not melodiously but harshly, with an angry, hoarse scream. She wanted to sing those songs, like that, to me. When Sevi sang about Siṅgammā, her song was a lament for a girl who had died, who knew she must die, and laid her head on her mother's lap, waiting to be killed. The song was melodious and beautiful to listen to, but it was a horrible event that the victim may or may not have earned. The story that Sevi told of her sister's life was a story of many things that should not have happened, bad things that people had done to others. Pushpam and Muttammāḷ sang of the south in ambiguous terms. For them, when they were unmarried, rain fell in both the south and the north. Afterward, they had to ask for a pot from their husband's sister in which they could carry water. For them, as for most people in southern India, rain is a good thing. But as Pushpam and Muttammāḷ sang, rain was a thing of the past. The change they experienced in their lives may have been, among other things, the shortage of rain.

The India of today has its beauties, but it also has its horrors. Most of the beauties are old and the horrors new. But not all. An old and enduring horror is the jāti system, bringing with it hunger, disease, contempt, and deprivation of many kinds. People belonging to the highest jātis are, with some exceptions, happy with the way things are. Some landlords and people of middle jātis showed anger that the laborers of untouchable jātis expected more for their labor—more *dosais* on holidays, more respect, more money. It was reported that Munusāmy wanted not cash but a larger share of rice. In retrospect, I think his decision may have been wise. All the people in the village experienced changes. Some considered some changes to be good. Climatic changes, most of all the absence of rain, affected everybody in this agrarian society, and not in a happy way.

For many of us in the West, our lives improve with age and accomplishment, then level off, then drop. Perhaps some higher-jāti Indians experience a similar trajectory. But in the songs of Paṟaiyar women, their lives grew persistently worse from early childhood on. Marriage was a kind of death. Death of a girl's mother is death of self. The discovery that you are untouchable, though never explicitly mentioned in these songs, is a strong and lasting blow.

Place and Movement

Veḷḷaiccāmi was the only man whose voice was raised in full, undiluted praise of Siṅgammā. There is not room to include the full text of his performance in this book. Though Veḷḷaiccāmi was not himself a Kuṟavar, he was the one ritual specialist in regular contact with the spirit of Siṅgammā. He lived and plied his trade as fortune-teller in the town of Mēlūr.

After her death, Siṅgammā became known when the daughter of one of the men who raped her became possessed by her ghost. Veḷḷaiccāmi spoke, sang, and chanted the story of Siṅgammā before the Mēlūr crowd. In this song, the girl danced for days, singing incomprehensibly. The words of the song were the cries of a Kuṟavar girl, selling her wares in the marketplace. She chanted the names of the small birds with whom Kuṟavars were associated. She sang of a sparrow caught and trapped, a sparrow alighting within a virgin, a virgin caught and trapped like a sparrow. Thus she provided clues as to the possessing ghost's identity and history. But still the surrounding crowd was mystified, and the elders kept asking, "Who are you?"

Through Veḷḷaiccāmi, the ghost of Siṅgammā made her identity known to the townspeople who, impressed by the beauty of the girl's dance and fearful of the dead Siṅgammā's power, initiated a fine festival for her, celebrating her "like a god." Through the medium, she told the crowd that she wished to return to Sharp Rock Hill, the site of her old home, her death, and her burial. And so she was returned there. The thorny wasteland on which she was buried was razed, and a government spinning mill was built on the site. The spinning mill became Siṅgammā's temple, and she reigns there still, satisfied. Veḷḷaiccāmi at the end of the song asks her to bless all those who sing of her, all those who hear, and all those who read her story.

In Veḷḷaiccāmi's song and chant to Siṅgammā, many places through which she traveled are named. Following Tim Ingold, one might say that every place her bare feet touched was affected by her presence, and she was affected by every place she walked. For Ingold, bare feet and walking are important. Our ancestors traveled like that for countless thousands of years, after all. Siṅgammā was a Narikuṟavar, and traveling is what Narikuṟavars do. While studying the transcript of Veḷḷaiccāmi's words, I wished I could draw a map of the places that Siṅgammā traveled through, but most of the places named by Veḷḷaiccāmi were not on any map that I could find. I hope a Tamil scholar who lives near Mēlūr will draw a detailed map of the area around Mēlūr for students to see. Place names are important. Siṅgammā slept and died in a place called Sharp Stone Hill (*kallānkuttu mēḍu*). The name is important. Plant names are also given in her story. People who move through those places should know those places, what the places mean, who the people are. Just as important are gods and their shrines. A shrine marks a place where something happened, sometimes just a place where a woman died in childbirth or in some other horrible way. Thus a shrine is erected and maintained near the place where Siṅgammā died.

Veḷḷaiccāmi is the only person who speaks, chants, and sings for, through, and about Siṅgammā, beseeching her for what Christians would call forgiveness. He may have been hired by one of the men who raped Siṅgammā, whose daughter was possessed by her. As it happens, in the town of Mēlūr, near where Siṅgammā was killed and where Veḷḷaiccāmi performs, there is a Draupadi temple. Draupadi is the heroine of the Mahabharata, a very long epic that is one of the two most famous in India. Draupadi is angry because of the way her husband's enemy attempted to strip her. She vows to wash her hair in the blood of this enemy. There are countless Draupadi temples, and the attempted stripping episode is performed in countless towns and villages throughout the countryside. What Draupadi has in common with Siṅgammā is that she is justifiably angry and incomparably beautiful. In this book the reader meets Siṅgammā and Māriamman, both of whom started as mortal women and both of whom were killed by men to whom they belonged as sister or wife.

Many interpretations of Draupadi and Māriamman are out there. Siṅgammā could be added as another, except that her own people, the Narikkuṟavars, want to move past her into a future, where they can have paid employment, houses, and, hopefully, water.

Environment and Ecology

As the farmland expands and water grows scarce, forests dwindle away, and the story of forest dwellers is one of almost irretrievable loss. Iruḷars (people of the dark) and Villiyars (bow people) are forest dwellers or former forest dwellers. Veḷḷaiccāmi referred to Siṅgammā, a Kuṟavar, as a forest dweller (*āranaṅgāḷ*). This term was one of admiration, not a term of abuse. Iruḷars, Villiyars, and Kuṟavars all were classified as "scheduled tribes" by the British, and the classification remains. It is difficult to imagine what South Asia would have been like ten or twenty thousand years ago, when everybody, or nearly everybody, was a hunter, a gatherer, a fisherman, possibly a herder of animals, possibly a grower of plants.

Better off but still lower-jāti people in the village where we lived in 1980 ate wild greens that the higher jātis would not touch. Some were returning to cultivation of millet, which had been the staple crop until rice, which demanded large amounts of water to cultivate, took over as an everyday food. Higher-jāti people grew many kinds of greens and vegetables to supplement their diets, but the higher-jāti people with whom I lived eschewed meat, to the detriment of their own children. For milk, they had only one buffalo. In all cases, what could be grown by whom, and what could be eaten by whom, were fundamental political issues. Political concerns also determined what land could be used for mining and logging.

Paṟaiyar singers named many kinds of flowers, vegetables, and fruits in their songs. They are all found in Chapter 2 of this volume. In Chapter 3 the same singers described aspects of their human environment. In Chapter 4, Kanyammā sang of her lost forest environment. I wonder now where those singers are, where their children are, what kind of work they do. The village of Pukkatturai is no longer on the map, if it ever was. Members of the family that I lived with have all either died or moved into cities, where they either live by the generosity of their children or work at white-collar jobs. The one with whom I am still in contact says he has forgotten Tamil. Now he speaks only Hindi and English. He was sent to private schools from childhood and has worked hard to get where he is. The fact that he is a Reḍḍiyar and not a Paṟaiyar must have helped.

Back in the villages and fields, global climate change has been cruel to South India where, in addition to the ravages of deforestation, heat waves, drought, and shortage of water have weakened and sometimes killed field laborers.

Song and Creation

Sarasvati in Chapter 1, though surrounded by family and clients, was effectively solitary and jāti-less. She served and touched the high and the low, but her only real companion was the spirit of Māriamman. The Paṟaiyar singers were collective and the name of their jāti was well known. The Paṟaiyar singers learned from each other, although their songs were ignored by men and by people of higher jātis. Perhaps this very hiddenness gave the singers more freedom to sing as and what they pleased. I learned only later that the singers' crying songs were of a universal genre of which the singers themselves were unaware. The singers were generally despised, and it was easy for them to keep their songs hidden from those who despised them. But for those open to the singers and their songs, the Paṟaiyar women singers were perfectly open and generous with their songs. Their weeping poured out their unabated sorrow. They were not afraid to look in the eyes of the listener as they sang. One of the bolder and younger of the singers was not afraid to sing against her husband. Music, including song, is what it is. It can be heard and felt, but it cannot be translated. Words can be translated but not music. Weeping can be heard and seen, tears can be seen and tasted, but the sorrow of another can only be felt, or not. The music, song, and tears of Paṟaiyar singers were ignored by all but the singers themselves. But although the singers will die, their music will continue, their words will be remembered.

Each of the Paṟaiyar singers made her song herself, out of experience and memory. The song was not about the singer or people she knew. But it evoked sorrow and weeping nonetheless. All the Paṟaiyar women knew each other, but each song was unique. A Brahman man that I knew in the United States could not believe that so many unique songs were made and sung by people in one village, laboring women of an untouchable jātis. I had to remind him of Emeneau's *Toda Songs*, where everybody created songs about everything.

Separation and Untouchability

Some break away from others, whether by accident, by force, by choice, or by a combination of the three. By the time human beings started exploring by moving along the sea coasts, the motive of choice must have been present. Curiosity, which other animals also have, may have been an additional mover. Breakaway by whatever cause or for whatever reason assisted evolution, both biological and cultural. Cultural difference among human beings is a central feature of humanity. When we became human beings, all one species and all one subspecies, human cultures multiplied and flourished. We had the capacity for language, and many different languages developed. We had goals beyond the present place and time. We created teleologies. Then something contrary to life emerged. Not death, but obstacles to growth. Walls, lines, boundaries that did not always exist. The concepts of purity and pollution may or may not be related to the concepts of health and disease. To keep themselves "pure," high-caste people avoided the touch or even proximity of low-caste people, whom they considered to be bearers of "pollution." A conceptual wall was built between the high and the low. The consequences of that wall have been endemic pollution and disease. Untreated sewage and garbage, accumulating over centuries, infect water, soil, and air.

Untouchability is itself a radical separation from life. "Even the crow will not touch the food I cook" is a line in one of the Paṟaiyar singer's songs. Untouchability is expulsion. An untouchable child, given that status by dint of birth alone, is not allowed to attend school with other children. An untouchable person may not take water from the same well as other people. In Tamil, an untouchable is *tīṇḍā*, poisonous. Even if she knows for a fact that she is neither dirty nor poisonous, that in fact she is beautiful and good, other people around her will not agree. If she is beautiful she will be suspected of being unchaste and impure. If she is ugly, she will be called a ghost or a demon, *pēy*.

Womanhood

If this series of excursions, movements, and changes of place and time have shown me anything, it is the obvious fact that not all women of Tamil Dalit jātis are the same.

Sevi and Siṅgammā were in a sense closely bonded, as the former sang of the latter. Sevi did all in her power to represent both in a good light, while showing the shadows cast on the lives of both. Sevi's life, or more precisely her sister's life, is fraught with tragedies and betrayals, the worst of which happens when her father accidentally cuts his hand, is taken to the hospital, and is forced to sign away all his property to his brothers. Sevi ends with herself and her husband living in an apparently abandoned house of "dirty people." The house has some gods living there, but Sevi acknowledges that they have not helped her at all. Siṅgammā is, in Sevi's song, more dramatically betrayed, in that she is raped by men who offer her food, and then killed by her brothers to save the family honor.

Kanyammā, who lived on the edge of the wilderness and the edge of death, insisted on singing the best songs she knew, and they were good songs. Remarkable songs. The last of them is most compelling. In this song, the unnamed protagonist, who might as well have been Kanyammā herself, has a friend named only Māmā. This would be a male cousin or uncle or maybe just a friend, who takes her on a train to see the fireworks, which at last she sees. He teaches her also to perform simple religious rites, which I guess will put her in the Hindu fold, but she is unlikely to know what that might mean to people in Mumbai writing about the machinations of Modi aimed to make everyone in the country either Hindu or dead.

The Paṟaiyar singers were as though one. They did not sing together, though, but rather one at a time. Their songs all followed a similar pattern. Maybe they were sung at funerals, for this was the purpose this genre of songs was made for. They were called crying songs because they were meant to cry for the recently deceased, although, as Isabelle Clark-Decès pointed out, "No one cries for the dead." These singers, however, did weep real tears as they sang these songs. They were weeping not just for themselves, but for all that had been lost over time.

Sarasvati and her spirit partner Māriamman lived in a modern urban environment, but their story is centuries old. Sarasvati opened my eyes to the fact that women are not equivalent to men. We are not identical to men. We can do the same work as men, but not if we have multiple pregnancies and children to look after. Women must make their own paths. We must not depend on men for anything. Sarasvati and Māriamman are solitary creatures, bonded to no one but each other, embodied and bodiless, successful but not wealthy. Avoidance of wealth beyond need was necessary for women with this vocation to continue their chosen way of life, and for them to help others. They flourish where they are, whether in Chennai or in Tiruvērkāḍu. The city may grow to bursting, the forest may dwindle to nothing, but the names and the places will be remembered for as long as memory lives.

Notes

FOREWORD

1. Adiga's morally reprehensible narrator tells us, "I was born and raised in Darkness. . . . I am talking of a place in India, at least a third of the country, a fertile place, full of rice fields and wheat fields and ponds in the middle of those fields choked with lotuses and water lilies, and water buffaloes wading through the ponds and chewing on the lotuses and lilies. Those who live in this place call it the Darkness. . . . India is two countries in one: an India of Light, and an India of Darkness" (Adiga 2008, 11–12).

2. For the ramified significance of improvisation see Jeffrey (2010) on *jugar*.

3. Journalistic reports on Delhi Braveheart—the gang rape and its aftermath—are legion; see for example Biswas (2012); Rediff.com (2013). On rape and revenge in North Indian Dalit literature in Hindi, see also Brueck's chapter "Rescripting Rape" (2014, 154–77).

4. See, for example, one early collection in English (Joshi 1986).

5. See Allocco (2013) for a surprisingly similar contemporary case study of an urban priestess in Chennai.

6. On South Indian Hindu practices around menstruation see Nagarajan (2007) and Narasimhan (2011).

7. Of course Trawick was not the only one to speak of emotion, to acknowledge intimacy, and to practice reflexivity in the late seventies and early eighties. But she was writing about India, she was female, and her particular voice is the one that inspired me.

8. Besides Cohen and Pandian, others who contributed papers and comments honoring Trawick's anthropology of love and war included Isabelle Clark-Decès, E. V. Daniel, Sarah Lamb, Diane Mines, Kirin Narayan, Kalpana Ram, Martha Selby, Susan S. Wadley, and Mark Whitaker.

INTRODUCTION

1. Such views are not new to anthropologists, and they did not stop with Boas. They continued through "Boasian" anthropologists such as Paul Radin's 1927 book *Primitive Man as Philosopher* (where "primitive" was not a term of abuse); Gerald Berreman's 1960 article, "Caste in India and the United States"; Marcel Griaule's 1967 book *Conversations*

with Ogotemmeli; and the works of many anthropologists of the present day, who are radically egalitarian and antiracist in their views and fieldwork methods.

2. Mukherji (2014): "'Ch . . . ch . . . chamaar' was a taunt that followed Manish Kumar through the corridors of IIT Roorkee, a constant reminder of his caste tag. The young man's body was found on campus in 2011, his death shrouded in mystery. The case bears an uncanny resemblance to that of Aniket Ambhore, a young Dalit student who died under, what his parents call, 'fishy' circumstances at IIT Bombay last week. They now talk of the barbs he faced in college for having taken admission under the SCST quota. . . . Ilaiah believes that much of the caste discrimination on campuses has to do with the attitudes of faculty members towards reservations (affirmative action programmes), which percolates down to a section of students."

3. The South Asian subcontinent is the area south of the Himalayas, which are the highest mountains in the world and difficult to cross. This geographical fact has made a big difference in the history of peoples in the subcontinent. Boundaries between countries did not always exist. In some places, walls were built; in others, not.

In recent times the subcontinent has been divided into several countries, the largest and most populous of which is India. Pakistan was formed in 1947. It was divided off from India so that it could be a separate Muslim nation. In the process of partition, fourteen million Hindus, Muslims, and Sikhs were displaced, and hundreds of thousands of people on both sides of the new border were killed. The horrors of this division severely exacerbated tensions between Hindus and Muslims on the subcontinent. Multiple wars between India and Pakistan have since taken place. Other countries in South Asia are Nepal, Bhutan, Sri Lanka, and Bangladesh. Bangladesh fought for and achieved independence from Pakistan in 1974 and now is a sovereign country, adjacent to the state of Bengal. Sri Lanka is easily reached from South India. It is a separate country. Nepal and Bhutan are high on the southeast side of the Himalayas. Travel through the mountains generally happens on the southwest side.

4. People living before the formation of large civilizations, and living in widespread areas where there was nothing to fight over, had no reason to engage in warfare. Some have argued that human beings have an "instinct" for aggression that will cause them to fight each other no matter what. But that instinct has no basis in biological fact. People before the Neolithic hunted to eat. That is different from killing just for the sake of killing. During the Neolithic, people developed the cultivation of plants and animals, so that they could feed more people without having to forage or starve.

5. Encyclopaedia Britannica (2014), "Indus Civilization": "How and when the civilization came to an end remains uncertain. In fact, no uniform ending need be postulated for a culture so widely distributed. But the end of Mohenjo-daro is known and was dramatic and sudden. Mohenjo-daro was attacked toward the middle of the second millennium BCE by raiders who swept over the city and then passed on, leaving the dead lying where they fell. Who the attackers were is matter for conjecture. The episode would appear to be consistent in time and place with the earlier Vedic people's entry to the Indus region as reflected in the older books of the Rigveda, in which the newcomers are represented

as attacking the 'walled cities' or 'citadels' of the aboriginal peoples and the Vedic war-god Indra as rending forts 'as age consumes a garment.' However, one thing is clear: the city was already in an advanced stage of economic and social decline before it received the coup de grâce. Deep floods had more than once submerged large tracts of it. Houses had become increasingly shoddy in construction and showed signs of overcrowding. The final blow seems to have been sudden, but the city was already dying. As the evidence stands, the civilization was succeeded in the Indus valley by poverty-stricken cultures, deriving a little from a sub-Indus heritage but also drawing elements from the direction of Iran and the Caucasus—from the general direction, in fact, of the Vedic people's arrival. For many centuries urban civilization was dead in the northwest of the Indian subcontinent."

6. *The Hindu* (2013), "Love in the Time of Caste": "Even as Tamil Nadu reacts violently to inter-caste marriages, Lakshmi Krupa finds three couples who dared to break the unwritten law. . . . In 1967, Tamil Nadu chief minister C. N. Annadurai created history by amending the Hindu Marriage Act, 1955. To this day, it's the only state in India that recognises what's called a 'self-respect' marriage (*suyamariyaathai* or *seethiruththa* marriage) rejecting priests and dowry and encouraging inter-caste matrimony. Garlands, mangalsutras, even rings are optional. Tamil leader Periyar called this 'daring not just for Tamil Nadu but also the entire world.'"

7. "Can't Change Caste, SC to College Student," *Times of India,* 2007.

8. Dirks (2001) shows that the British played a major role in the hardening of caste boundaries, which previously may have been more flexible.

9. Kakar (1978) wrote that in India, childhood is considered the golden age of human life, because from there it is all downhill. Likewise, former ages in human history are considered to have been better than now, whenever now is. There are, however, other points of view among Indian villagers. Gold and Gujar (2002) wrote that the elderly Rajasthani workers with whom they spoke consider that they are unequivocally better off in postindependence Rajasthan than they were when they were ruled by despotic monarchs, despite the fact that the forest with its beautiful trees and diverse vegetation is no longer. And yet, for these same people, the past was also a time of "less dense population, less intensive land use, more cattle and milk, organic fertilizer, coarser but more nourishing and tasty grains, stronger digestion, greater compassion, more leisure to tell stories, and many fewer consumer goods to crave and to arouse envy."

10. Since about 1995, when access to the Internet became widely available, new organizations have arisen and information and opinion about what is happening in India, among other countries, has become accessible to billions. Dalits in India who are educated and are able to collect facts on the ground have availed themselves of this facility to report events of concern, and newspapers and magazines in Western countries have picked up some of this information and passed it on. Non-Dalits sympathetic with the Dalit cause publish in prominent newspapers. The Internet also has room for those politely and not so politely opposed to Dalits.

11. Srinivasan et al. (2015) demonstrate that caste attitudes are linked to intuitive theories about intellect. They write, "Intuitive theories affect how we interpret and

respond to our experiences from early in life. For example, children's beliefs about the nature of intellectual ability affect their motivation and achievement in school. . . . Children who believe that intellectual abilities are malleable ('incremental theorists') are more likely to attribute academic failures to changeable contextual factors. . . . In contrast, children who believe that success is determined by natural ability ('entity theorists') are likely to attribute failures to fixed attributes of the self." The caste system is likely to support "entity theories" because the caste system as it stands and has stood for centuries renders individual change nearly impossible. One is what one was born to be.

Venkatanarayanan (2014) describes school situations in which children are subject to discrimination based on caste. For example, "As a private-aided school teacher (FC) told her students who were SC/ST and BC/MBC: 'Buffalo, you people will never change, and will never be able to learn. Rather than coming to school, you should go and work somewhere. You are coming here and troubling me.'" FC means "Forward Caste." SC and ST mean "Scheduled Caste" and "Scheduled Tribe." The latter two are hereditary groups that were formerly deemed "untouchable" and sometimes "criminal" and are still considered to be intrinsically low and stupid by many people belonging to Forward Castes. OBC and MBC mean "Other Backward Class" and "Most Backward Class."

According to Downey and Lende (2012, chapter 2): "The developmental dependency of infants and children means that our complex hierarchies, even our societies' errors, cruelties and injustices, end up shaping our neurological inheritance. The worlds we have built as families, cultures, societies, and civilizations affect the nervous system that each of our bodies build during development. and this distinctive neurological potential is only possible because generations upon generations of humans have constructed worlds to support, protect, and teach each other."

Seung (2012) shows that a child begins learning at birth, and learns very fast. Connections between neurons, which encode learning, grow stronger if the same lesson is learned repeatedly. Learning gradually slows with time, but never stops.

If a child learns early and continuously certain practices and the feelings that go with them, then those feelings will remain even if the child learns later that the beliefs and practices he or she accepted earlier were wrong. Thus if a person develops throughout early life a sense of revulsion toward certain kinds of people, that sense of revulsion, like a fear of heights, may hobble that person forever. Not only Dalits must be educated. Children of higher castes must also be educated; they must be taught that all human beings are of equal value, that the highborn can learn more from the lowborn, the mighty can learn more from the humble than the reverse.

12. Hardgrave (1969a) argues that the Nadars did not oppose the caste system but raised the status of their caste through education, caste solidarity, political, and economic means.

Christianity and Islam have been offered as alternative ways to escape the Hindu caste system. Before and after the arrival in India of those two religions, there have been other religious movements, such as Lingayatism, arising from what would now be called Hinduism, that were strongly opposed to caste and gender hierarchy. Caste hierarchy is said to have affected all of these movements. But egalitarianism remains a popular alternative. In the process of organizing under an egalitarian policy, the Lingayats grew not only in numbers but in status (Trawick 1970).

13. Nur Yalman (1963) did not necessarily like the system he was writing about, viz., the subjugation of women for the sake of family and caste prestige. Nambudiri Brahman women and girls were kept in the homes of their high-caste fathers, brothers, or husbands to protect their chastity. They were kept behind screens at weddings. Any lapse, or perceived lapse, in sexual purity on the part of a woman was considered a major sin. This viewpoint has trickled down all the way to the lowest castes in India. A low-caste woman is at least as subject to domestic abuse as a high-caste woman would be for any real or perceived misstep. Chapter 5 of this book provides examples.

Berreman (1960, 123) discussed this issue more broadly, pointing out that high-caste men in India, like white men in the southern United States, benefited from the social systems to which they belonged in that they had access to women of their own caste as well as to women of lower castes. In India, Berreman wrote, high-caste women and low-caste men are restricted in their choices. If a lower-caste man or a higher-caste woman crossed the line, he or she would be severely punished or killed. It may be argued that a low-caste woman may benefit from being the mistress of a higher-caste man. More often, though, she is simply raped.

14. Berreman (1960) argued that African Americans in the United States occupied a position comparable to that of untouchables in India. "In a study of caste functioning in Sirkanda, a hill village in northern Uttar Pradesh, India, I was struck by the similarity of relations between the twice-born and untouchable castes to race relations in the southern United States. In both situations there is a genuine caste division according to the definition above (a hierarchy of endogamous divisions in which membership is hereditary and permanent). In the two systems there are rigid rules of avoidance between castes, and certain types of contact are defined as contaminating, while others are non-contaminating. . . . Enforced deference, for example, is a prominent feature of both systems. . . . The crucial fact is that caste status is determined, and therefore the systems are perpetuated, by birth: membership in them is ascribed and unalterable. Individuals in low castes are considered inherently inferior and are relegated to a disadvantaged position, regardless of their behavior." (Berreman 1960, 122). Berreman was respected and admired as an anthropologist writing and speaking passionately against inequality in the United States as well as in India. He did field research in both countries. He died in December 2013.

Pandey (2015), like Berreman, compares inequalities in the United States with those of India, also focusing on the situation of untouchables in India and African Americans in the United States. He too has lived in both countries. Unlike Berreman, who writes from an American anthropological view, Pandey writes from an Indian sociohistorical point of view. Both men write about northern India, which is noticeably different from the south of that country. For instance, in northern India, more people are classified as twice-born. But treatment of Dalits throughout India is bad.

As Berreman offered an American view of untouchability in India, so Pandey offers an Indian view of blackness in America. "Prejudice—the already known," Pandey begins, "has often been reserved for the spat-out, half suppressed, word-of-mouth and, one might add, for the gesture of disdain, contempt and recoil, the refusal to touch, what in India is called untouchability."

Setting aside issues of untouchability, American schoolgirls will be familiar with this kind of behavior, as will low-status university men and women in both countries. In both countries such words and gestures of disdain have led to suicide, while the perpetrator remains innocent of legal wrongdoing. Outside of school, such behavior is seen as normal by both sides, although clearly the ones treated despicably are not happy with this behavior on the part of twice-borns, arrogant schoolboys, or white boys who consider that their whiteness entitles them to treat black women or men with contempt. All too often, both in America and in India, there is little or nothing that low status badly treated women or men can do. Black people are killed by white people, and nothing can be done. Dalits are killed by higher-caste people, and nothing can be done. Women are raped and beaten by men, and nothing can be done.

Pandey also discusses prejudices in both India and America against people who do not speak using what is considered the proper dialect.

Race-based murder still happens in the United States, as does caste-based murder in India, and sex-based murder in both countries. Murder comes under the purview of the law in both countries, inadequately enforced as such laws can sometimes be.

15. Leena Chandran (2014) interviewed Arundhati Roy on different responses and reactions to Roy's "The Doctor and the Saint." See Visvanathan (2005) on the denial of panchayat office-holding rights to Dalits and intimidation of Dalits by caste Hindus.

16. See Wikipedia, "Caste-Related Violence in India." This list is continually changing. When I first downloaded it, it contained the following: 1996 Bathani Tola massacre, Bihar; 1968 Kilvenmani massacre, Tamil Nadu; 1997 Laxmanpur Bathe carnage, Bihar; 1997 Melavalavu massacre, Tamil Nadu; 2003 Muthanga incident, Kerala; 1999 Bant Singh case, Punjab; 2006 Kherlanji massacre, Maharashtra; 2006 Dalit protests in Maharashtra; 2008 caste violence in Rajasthan; 2011 killings of Dalits in Mirchpur (Haryana); 2012 Dharmapuri violence; 2013 Marakkanam violence, Tamil Nadu. All but the last of the massacres and incidents reported above involved higher-caste people versus Dalits. Several of them involved higher-caste landlords versus Dalit laborers. More information is available at the Wikipedia website. See also *The Gypsy Goddess* by Meena Kandasamy (2014). This book is based on the massacre that took place in the village of Kilvenmani on Christmas Day, 1968.

17. William Labov (1966 and 1972) was the founder of sociolinguistics. He showed how language and dialect variation were not just the result of random drift, as Edward Sapir argued, but were pushed by political and social factors. This is why Black English has grown so far away from standard (white) English as to be almost a second language. African Americans, subject to serious racial discrimination, need their own language in order to survive.

Still more relevant to this book is Labov's recent discussion (2013) of narrative and death. The women in this book narrate the story of their lives, and in the case of Siṅgammā, her death. In Labov's terms, they transform life into narrative. Without narrative, the reality of their experiences, of their life

In India more than twenty-two major languages and countless dialects are spoken. Dialects are differentiated by educational status, region, city, occupation, gender, and caste, among other factors. Officially in India, in addition to major languages and dialects, there are "mother tongues" (Tamil *tāy moṛi*). Not only Dalits, but high-caste Tamils moving up the ladder of professional success, may forget their *tāy moṛi* in favor of English and perhaps Hindi. Meanwhile, nonliterate Dalits may protect themselves and their thoughts by speaking or singing in such a way that they will not heard or understood by higher-caste men or women.

However, these protective boundaries are falling, most of all for and against Paṟaiyars, who are numerous and organized in Tamil Nadu. Because they have become powerful, they are a threat to higher-caste landowners, with often violent consequences.

In this book, all of the singers and speakers are women, most are rural, all of the women are nonliterate, and all of the women are of very low caste. The few men who speak in this book are, as it were, supporting actors. Even within the group of nonliterate Tamil women of low caste, the speech and song of a rural Paṟaiyar woman from north of Madurai will be noticeably different from the speech and song of a rural Paṟaiyar woman from a village south of Chennai.

18. Gumperz (1962) wrote about code-switching. This is another political mechanism separating those who know from those who don't. If a person code-switches between two or more languages, another person who does not know all those languages will not be able to follow what is being said.

19. Geertz (1983) raised the topic of "local knowledge," which has only later been defined. Briefly, one may that that local knowledge is based on experience, adapted to the local culture and environment. It takes time to develop local knowledge. If a person moves from place to place all her life, she may feel like a stranger everywhere. If a place that has been long inhabited by a community is abandoned, then all the local knowledge developed by the people who lived there is lost. One may say, so what? But people who are forced to leave their homes lose most or all of what they had, material, cultural, spiritual, personal, and interpersonal. And places that are abandoned are like the dead who can never be brought back.

20. Lévi-Strauss says in *The Savage Mind* (1966, 17), "Like bricolage on the technical plane, mythical reflection can reach brilliant results on the intellectual plane." He says in *The Raw and The Cooked* (1969, 12), "I therefore claim to show, not how men think in myths, but how myths operate in a person's mind without their being aware of the fact." In *Myth and Meaning* (1978, 15–16) he says, "I have the feeling that my books get written through me, and once they have got across me I feel empty and there is nothing left. . . . You may remember that I have written that myths get thought in man unbeknownst to him . . . but for me it describes a lived experience . . . that is, my work gets thought in me unbeknown to me. . . . Each of us is a kind of crossroads where things happen. The

crossroads is purely passive; something happens there. A different thing, equally valid, happens elsewhere. There is no choice, it is just a matter of chance. . . . The way of thinking among people we call, usually and wrongly, 'primitive'—let's call them rather 'without writing.' . . . People who are without writing have a fantastically precise knowledge of their environment and all their resources. All these things we have lost, but we did not lose them for nothing." In "Race, History and Culture" (1996) he writes, "The one real calamity, the one fatal flaw which can afflict a human group and prevent it from achieving fulfilment is to be alone."

In these books, Lévi-Strauss argues that myth is an attempt to establish a sense of order within the world, in other words, a structure. At the same time, he argues that myth, and the thought of nonliterate people in particular, while fully structured and cognizant of every detail of the experienced world, is not chained to the practical necessities of life. Mythic thought is free but for the constraints placed on it by the structures of the human mind, which, as has now been shown, vary.

Literate people, in my view, are also capable of wild thought (translated from French *la pensée sauvage* to English as "the savage mind," but "wild thought" is a more accurate translation). In any of these books, change the word "myth" to the word "song," such as the songs appearing in this book, and Lévi-Strauss's views on myth become more plausible.

21. Ingold (2009) says that each organism, including each human being, is less a discrete entity than a node in a field of relationships. Less of a human being is inherited than is developed ecologically. One makes oneself more than one is made, but always one makes oneself through contact with one's environment, and never in isolation. Thus in a sense Ingold has grown out of Lévi-Strauss and beyond him. Keller (2010) shows that so-called "nature" and so-called "nurture" are not separate things, the first inherited genetically and the second acquired through learning. Rather they are a single process. Doolittle (2000) shows that connections between life forms are not so much vertical as lateral. Woese (1998) argues that there was not one universal ancestor, but from the beginning, life was a community of organisms. Seung (2012) argues that a human being is not so much a product of genetics as a process of learning, managed through what he calls the "connectome," the vast network of connections between neurons. Here, too, then, the creation of one's self is a matter of lateral connections within the central nervous system and beyond it, all of these connections developing together.

22. Viswanath (2014) provides an historical account of the political situation and living conditions of Paṟaiyars—then called pariahs—from 1890 to 1920. At that time, all members of what are now called scheduled castes—Paṟaiyars, Pallars, and Chakkiliyars—were called pariahs. Viswanath writes, "Pariahs in Madras, throughout the nineteenth century, were kept in miserable conditions, subject to violent physical discipline, often tied to particular plots of land, and actively prevented from absconding or obtaining land of their own" (loc. 286).

Viswanath writes that pariahs were slaves. "The entire agrarian political-economic system depended on unfree pariah labor." But where there are slaves, there are slave revolts, violently, sometimes murderously, put down by the slave owners and their allies. Such events were rarely recorded, except in memory.

CHAPTER 1. MĀRIAMMAN

1. Adages women cited—such as "Marriage shackles the hands and children shackle the feet," "Women are born as mud," and more simply, "We [women] are slaves"—summed up this view.

2. De Beauvoir ([1949] 2011). "What a misfortune to be a woman! And yet the misfortune, when one is a woman, is at bottom not to comprehend that it is one," says Simone de Beauvoir, citing Kierkegaard. "On ne naît pas femme; on le devient" (one is not born, but rather becomes, a woman) (bk. 1, pt. 2, ch. 8). However, the women with whom I spoke in Tamil Nadu comprehended this fact and more.

3. Of Chakkiliyars in the late nineteenth century, Thurston (1909) wrote: "In social position the Chakkiliyans occupy the lowest rank, though there is much dispute on this point between them and the Paraiyans." He also observed, "It was noted by Sonnerat, in the eighteenth century, that the Chakkiliyans are in more contempt than the Pariahs, because they use cow leather in making shoes. 'The Chucklers or cobblers,' the Abbe Dubois writes, 'are considered inferiors to the Pariahs all over the peninsula.' . . . The very Pariahs refuse to have anything to do with the Chucklers, and do not admit them to any of their feasts." Thurston quotes the Madura Manual of 1868 as saying, "They are men of drunken and filthy habits, and their morals are very bad. Curiously enough, their women are held to be of the Padmani kind, i.e., of peculiar beauty of face and form, and are also said to be very virtuous. . . . Their gods include Madurai Viran, Mariamma, Muneswara, Draupadi and Gangamma."

Of Chakkiliyars of the present, Gorringe (2015) writes: "In the last decades of the 20th century, Dalits—who constitute 18 percent of the population—have organized politically in Tamil Nadu, but this mobilization has often been on caste lines representing the three main Tamil SC groups; Pallars, Paraiyars and Chakkiliyars. Pallars are the most developed and organized Dalit group, partly due to their higher social status. . . . . Paraiyars are the most populous and portray themselves as the most radical. They are concentrated in the central and northern districts. Chakkiliyars, the lowest of the three, are traditionally landless and are least active politically. All three are increasingly mobilizing on caste lines for representation and resources, which brings them into competition with each other and with 'Backward' and 'Most Backward' Classes (BC, MBC). BC is the official term for low (but touchable) castes who suffer from educational and economic backwardness and are entitled to affirmative action. In Tamil Nadu, however, BC groups are often politically influential or landowners and may be jealous of their power."

4. The central part of this chapter was first presented in 1978 at the annual meetings of the American Anthropological Association, Houston, Texas. The paper was then entitled "A Tamil Priestess." The paper was never published until now, in this book. The

interviews which form the body of this paper were conducted during the period of my dissertation research in Tamil Nadu, from January 1975 to August 1976. I revisited Sarasvati in 1980, 1984, and 1990. Since my first visit to India, anthropological theories have moved on, and the chapters in this book reflect that movement, but the ethnography in these chapters remains intact, and the theories remain as valid now as when they first appeared. New information has emerged about the situations of women in India. Some women classified as Dalits have escaped and have attained positions of prominence. But the information I have seen indicates that the situations of Dalit women in general have not improved.

5. Shortly after I first met Sarasvati, I observed her training a young woman in this way. But it was only twelve years later that I learned that one of her Brahman trainees had become a successful priestess and healer in her own right.

6. Babb (1970: 144) reports that in Chattisgarh also the smallpox deity "hates the sight of married couples and pregnant women." This view would accord with the smallpox deity's demand of her followers that they leave their families and live alone. It would also accord with Māriamman's life history, in which she is murdered by her husband and her son and even after she is resurrected is forced to live in the forest alone.

7. Mylapore is an old, well-to-do Brahman neighborhood in Madras.

8. The oldest child in Tamil families is often accorded higher status and is given more responsibilities than younger siblings. The oldest daughter is generally most closely identified with the mother and takes over many of the child-rearing tasks, while younger daughters have more freedom. This priestess seems proud of being the oldest.

9. Sarasvati is a distinctly Brahman name. Brahmans are the highest caste in India. Lower caste people are generally not given high caste names. Māriamman/Sarasvati is a split woman in several ways. She is both very high and very low. As a woman, she is torn between bring a good Tamil wife and living alone, free of any husband. She became a goddess when her head was cut off.

10. Only lower-ranked castes trade in liquor, which is regarded by Brahmans as an impure substance. The trade in alcoholic beverages, especially during British rule, was one route of advancement for such castes.

11. *The Hindu* was one of two English-language newspapers with a wide circulation in southern India. Working for this newspaper was clearly not a "traditional occupation"; at the time, it would have been a highly prized job for a person of any caste. The English word "retired" has been borrowed into Madras Tamil, as the concept has been borrowed into the culture. In Madras, however, only luckiest of men would be able to retire with a pension.

One surmises from all the information she gives at the beginning of the interview that Sarasvati's natal family was considerably wealthier, more "Westernized," and better educated than most low-caste people; indeed, they were probably better off than most Brahmans.

12. Attention to the exact time and date of nonritual events is another result of Western influence. Sarasvati is accustomed to referring to the Western calendar rather than the Tamil one, and, if asked what Tamil month it is, does not always know. Most villagers I

spoke with, on the other hand, still thought in terms of the Tamil calendar, upon which the agricultural and ritual cycle is based, and were only vaguely aware of the Western calendar. Few village people kept track of their age.

13. "Amman pērile enakku rōmba ācai." An easier translation would read "I liked the mother very much." The word *pēr* means "person" or "name." As Sarasvati uses it, it emphasizes the distinctiveness of the individual referred to. The word ācai means "desire or attraction." It is an emotional response rather than a moral decision, and implies a longing for physical intimacy. Subsequently in the interview, Sarasvati will attribute this same personal response to Māriamman. Just as human beings place "desire" in the "person" of Māriamman, longing to have her with them, so Māriamman places desire in the person of certain human individuals, wanting to enter their bodies.

Murugan is a popular young boy god, son of the mother deity. Tamil Hindus, including children, choose Māriamman or deities they like the best to worship. The choice is an entirely personal and emotional one. Children keep images of their favorite deities and play with them almost like dolls, treating them as though they were alive. These feelings toward the images in which the spirits of the gods are lodged are carried over into adult worship ceremonies, in which the image of the god is bathed, fed, dressed, taken to visit its friends, given away in marriage, and (frequently afterward) destroyed.

14. Another nontraditional but highly coveted occupation.

15. "Following one's desire and marrying," i.e., marrying for love rather than by arrangement of the parents, is a defiance of convention, but this kind of daring is romanticized by some groups. Sarasvati implies that sixteen is early for a girl to get married, saying this happened "as soon as I came of age," which would mean immediately after her first menstruation. In fact sixteen is a little late for a Tamil girl to marry, just as it is a little late for her to come of age. Nowadays the norm for most villagers is to start looking for a husband for a girl shortly after her first menstruation ceremony. Meanwhile Brahmans and other high-caste groups have changed to the custom of educating their daughters through college if possible and then marrying them at around the age of twenty. Thus there is some mixture of norms and ideals as regards the best time for marriage. Marrying for love is still off-limits to most people, however.

16. Questioning the reality of particular deities is common among South Indians, villagers as well as city dwellers.

17. As an act of devotion, children's heads are shaved and the hair offered to a deity, usually Murugan. Adults may also grow their hair long and then shave it off for this purpose.

18. At temple consecrations and at certain festivals, Māriamman is invoked to possess a member of the crowd, as a sign of Māriamman's presence.

19. There is a fine line between possession by a demon and possession by a deity. The external manifestations of both kinds of possession are very much the same. When a person becomes possessed, it is up to the people around to find out who the possessing spirit is. It is a sign of grace (*aruḷ*) to be possessed by a deity, but it is a sign of weakness to be possessed by a demon. Demons are said to seek out impure places, deities to seek out

pure ones. Māriamman is ambivalently pure and impure. When one of her diseases besets a community, some people (the unafflicted) will say that she enters only the impure, to punish them. Others (the afflicted) will say she enters only the pure.

20. Possession by a deity makes one resistant to physical injury, so successful fire walking, hook swinging, and the like are considered proof of the presence of Māriamman's grace. Murugan may also be named. When speaking of her relationship with Māriamman, Sarasvati often interchanges the pronouns "she" and "I."

21. Here she denies identification with Brahmanical Hinduism.

22. Māriamman is identified by some Tamils with feeling (*uṇarcci*). The heart is the container of feeling, and Māriamman also dwells within the heart. Part of the meaning of Māriamman's having a body of wind is that, like wind, her presence is known only by the feeling she gives when she possesses a person. When one perceives things, only the feeling of them enters the heart, as when one eats food, only the essence of the food reaches the innermost part of the body. Feeling is the core of devotional religion or *bhakti*, perhaps the strongest element of Tamil religious life, in opposition, or at least in complementarity, to the formalism of Brahmanical ritualism.

23. Protection is the boon most often asked of Māriamman.

24. She seems to be saying that no matter how much it receives, the heart is never satisfied. Later that day Sarasvati spoke to me jokingly about all the trouble that people go to fill their small bellies (*oru jān vayiṟu*), and yet no matter how much you pour into it, that small belly is never satisfied.

25. The priestess supports her family by means of donations from devotees she has helped. In that way, Māriamman indirectly provides for her. The donations are Māriamman's *śakti*. (In modern Tamil Nadu, the word *śakti* has come to be used as a synonym or euphemism for money.)

26. Sarasvati's first six children are daughters. The birth of a string of daughters to a Tamil family is a great hardship because of the expenses of marriage, which today are borne entirely by the girl's family. The marriage of one daughter, including dowry expense, may cost more than five times a family's annual income. Until this generation, low-caste people in South India did not give dowry. Often bride-price was given instead, or there was no significant exchange of goods at the time of a wedding. Presently people celebrate weddings they cannot afford largely for the sake of respectability and "advancement" of the family. The combined effects of Brahmanical ritualism and Western-style consumerism in this case have been devastating to family economies as well as to the status of women. Māriamman, being a representative of "traditional" values and being concerned as well with the fate of women, of the poor, and of low-caste people, responds strongly to these developments.

27. "No one of my heart" means no man that she loved, no husband. Her husband was living elsewhere and not supporting her.

28. Note the concern with educating her daughters. She is gambling on their getting ahead by earning an independent income as something other than wage laborers. Many

low-caste Tamils see the education of their children as the one strongest hope for the children's having a better life and will make considerable sacrifices to pay for their schooling.

29. Her second daughter, Vasanti, worked briefly as a domestic servant for a German woman living in Madras, who provided for Vasanti's education during that time.

30. Construction work, in which the workers' bodies are the only earth-moving equipment, is one of the more grueling types of day labor.

31. The trident is a sign of Māriamman. It is her weapon.

32. *Māṅgalayam* is the Sanskritic word for *tāli*, a pendant worn around the neck of married women, signifying their auspicious state.

33. These are all "Western diseases" associated with a wealthy cosmopolitan way of life.

34. In this way, she reconciles her own system of healing, healing through belief (*nambikkai*) with positivistic modern medicine. But the doctor is subordinate to Māriamman.

35. All of these practices confirm with Brahmanical standards for the maintenance of purity.

36. The poḍḍu is the spot of red kumkum worn on the forehead by adult unwidowed women, another sign of their auspicious state.

37. Matted locks are a mark of asceticism and devotion to a deity. They are also dirty and unpleasant, which is why ascetics adopt them. Cf. Obeyesekere (1981) for more on the significance of matted locks to female ascetics.

38. A woman's chastity (*kaṯpu*) is a source of spiritual power, and this power can be lost by as small a failure as her smiling at, or being admired by, a man other than her husband. In general, Tamils believe that if one looks with desire upon a beautiful person or thing, harm will come to that person or thing, through a light emitted from the eye (*kaṇ drishti*). All beautiful and desirable things must therefore be protected against this light in some way.

39. The fruit is symbolic of an offer of sexual pleasure, which the priestess/deity turns down.

40. A strong act, for ordinarily a woman only removes her tāli when her husband dies, and then she tears it off, as the priestess does here. Good women are supposed to fast and pray for their husbands' well-being and fervently hope to die before their husbands do. But by tearing off her tāli Sarasvati in effect says to her husband, "I wish you were dead."

41. These are more Brahmanical restrictions.

42. These are the names of three great deities with major temples in Tamil Nadu.

43. One nāṟi is equal to twenty-four minutes.

44. The Sanskrit loanword, *āvēcam*, means rage or fury and also the state of spirit possession.

45. The rage seems to be a power which comes into her against her will, and the voice she hears seems to condone it.

46. The word *kuṟi*, "sign, mark," here means healing session, when Māriamman enters her medium at a scheduled time and divines the problems that people have brought

to her and their future outcome, promising a cure for them. The healing session is called *kuṟi*, say worshippers, because Māriamman's divinations are always on the mark.

47. For all those to whom she speaks, Māriamman uses familiar and diminutive (disrespectful) grammatical forms, *-ḍīmmā* and *-ḍāppā*, which I have translated into vocative "girl" and "boy" respectively. Reciprocally, only familiar forms are used by people when addressing or referring to deities. Māriamman even refers to her husband, the god Siva, by the disrespectful masculine singular, *avan*, and at one point even utters his name, calling him "my Sivan," though women are not supposed to say their husband's names. When telling the story of her life as a human woman, however, she refuses to utter the name of her human husband, calling him simply "my *muni*" (*muni* means holy man or ascetic), at which point a bystander at the interview interjects that the name of the husband in the story is Jatharagni.

48. The same origin story for Māriamman is found in Whitehead (1921). A similar story is also told for Kanykumāri, the Virgin of Cape Comorin, who, to avoid marriage, trades bodies with a fisherwoman and casts all the auspicious substances laid out for her wedding into the sea, where they turn into multicolored sand.

49. The tāṛam flower is a large, heavily fragrant blossom which grows singly on a spiky plant beneath which snakes are said to make their homes. It is sacred to Māriamman, and it is never supposed to be used at weddings. It symbolizes a woman who is difficult to access, dangerous, and alone.

50. Only women can understand her nature, she seems to be saying, and of these, Tamil women will understand her best and benefit most from her, because they are most like her.

51. Married Tamil women wear silver rings on their toes.

52. Much has changed since I first wrote and spoke about Māriamman. Fine analyses have been written about spirit possession by Nabokov 2000, later Clark-Decès 2005, and by Ram 2013. Many of my students have not agreed with the idea that release of useful energy may arise from a cessation of warfare between different aspects of the self. On the Internet I came across a bit of advice to men: "Choose a woman for her personality. We have so many of them."

CHAPTER 2. SORROW AND PROTEST

Note to epigraph: Bertolt Brecht, "Motto to the 'Svendborg Poems'" (1939), trans. John Willett, in *Poems, 1913–1956* (New York: Methuen, 1976), 320.

1. The songs presented in this chapter and the next were collected from June to November 1980 in the village of Pukkatturai, Chingleput district, Tamil Nadu. The project of which the collection of these songs was a part was made possible by a Senior Research Fellowship granted by the American Institute of Indian Studies. This chapter is a revised and updated version of Trawick (1986).

2. In the dialect of Paṟaiyar women in the region where these songs were recorded,

retroflex /ṛ/ becomes the retroflex /ḷ/. The same retroflex /ṛ/ becomes palatal /y/ in some words. The term *ayiṟa* is thus equivalent to *aṛukiṟa* in literary Tamil. This is one tiny piece of what could be a detailed study of language change and variation in Tamil. Such change and variation are pushed in assorted directions by the politics of caste, gender, and region. This study might be similar to the ones conducted by William Labov (1966, 1972, 2014) in New York City.

3. Until the 1930s, no one understood how Homer, the blind poet, was able to perform the Iliad and the Odyssey, two epic poems composed in Greece around 800 bce. After all, Homer was blind and could not read or write. A solution to this enigma was discovered in the early 1930s, when Milman Parry and Albert Lord found and documented a tradition of oral performance of epic poems in southern Yugoslavia. Each epic took days to perform, and no written text accompanied them. (In 1968 I was a student of Albert Lord at Harvard, where he taught folklore and mythology.)

The study of oral literature is a mainstay of anthropology. It is verbal art that is not written down. Writing is recent in human history. Even after writing developed, most people did not know how to read or write, and there were no recording devices. But people did not need writing, because they had songs, stories, epics, jokes, ritual texts, curative chants, epic poems, creation tales, myths, legends, word games, life histories, and other genres of verbal education and entertainment that they performed for each other and passed down through the generations. None of these were memorized, but they were remembered, and memory works its creative changes within every mind, and in the process of transmission through many minds over many generations.

4. Dué (2003) writes, "In two trips to the former Yugoslavia in 1933–35, Parry and Lord collected 12,544 songs, stories, and conversations from 169 singers of the South Slavic epic song tradition. . . . The singers whom Parry and Lord recorded composed extremely long epic poems in performance. In order to do this, they drew on a vast storehouse of traditional themes and phrases that worked within the meter or rhythm of the poetry. They used these formulaic phrases, instead of what we know as words, to build each verse as they went along. Each song was a new composition, and no two songs that they recorded were ever exactly the same."

With rare exceptions, only songs and heroic epics performed by men were studied. "In fact, the vast majority of the songs in the Parry Collection are women's songs—of the 12,544 texts contained in the collection, approximately 11,250 are women's songs" (Dué 2003).

Recently, new attention has been given to these women's songs (Vidan 2003). "Richard Martin (1989) . . . has shown that the Iliad and Odyssey include within the overall epic frame the conventions and allusive power of a number of other pre-existing verbal art forms, including prayer, supplication, boasting, and insulting, as well as lament."

"Vidan's work gives further support to the thesis that women's lament traditions have not only been incorporated into Greek epic; they are in fact the very backbone of it. It is very likely that the laments of Greek epic, although performed by a male aoidos, would have evoked for ancient audiences the songs of their mothers and grandmothers, performed at funerals upon the death of family members and extended relatives" (Dué 2003).

In short, structured laments, with formulae and emotional expression of the kind performed by Paṟaiyar women today, have been in existence for more than two millennia. And laments, like other forms of verbal art, have traveled outward to distant communities and upward to the powerful, the elite, and the literate.

5. Ingold (2011a): "Langer contends that the meaning of art should be found in the art object itself, as it is *presented* to our awareness, rather than in what it might be supposed to *represent* or signify. . . . (T)he ways in which we respond to objects or performances themselves are forever getting confused with our responses to whatever they are supposed to stand for. One way around this difficulty, Langer suggests, is to concentrate on the kind of art that—at least for Westerners—is apparently *least* representational, namely music. Music, surely, can stand for nothing but itself, so that an investigation of musical meaning should show how meaning can reside in art as such. 'If the meaning of art belongs to the sensuous percept itself apart from what it ostensibly represents,' writes Langer, 'then such purely artistic meaning should be most accessible through musical works' (1957: 209). Pursuing this line of argument, Langer suggests that, 'what music can actually reflect is . . . the morphology of feeling' (p. 238).

"In song, both music and words are present. The music in crying songs reflects what Langer calls 'the morphology of feeling'—the music of the songs. The words of the songs represent objects and events not necessarily present in space and time. Texted lament is a marriage of feeling and thought."

Moreover, "Speech, for Janacek, was a kind of song, and so we're all the other sounds that resonate through our consciousness. . . . We should cease thinking of the sounds of speech merely as vehicles of symbolic communication. . . . For sound, as Janacek wrote, 'grows out of our entire being. . . . *There is no sound that is broken away from the tree of life*' (1989: 88, 99, original emphasis)."

". . . When you yell in anger, the yell *is* your anger, it is not a vehicle that *carries* your anger. . . . Your yell '*does not make me think of anger*, it is anger itself' (Merleau-Ponty 1962: 184, original emphasis)" (Ingold 2011a:22–24).

Ingold (2011a, 2011b) argues that for hunters, and in general for non-Western, nonliterate peoples, equivalences are not even metaphors. They are realities. Every living being, including a living plant, is sentient, and perceives and acts on its world in different ways. A human perceives things that a buffalo, for instance, cannot perceive, and vice versa.

6. Hierarchy within the family is not defined in terms of a single parameter or a single quality which individuals in different positions possess more or less of. For instance, according to Kakar (1978), those in senior positions in a Hindu family have the right to greater authority, those in junior positions the right to greater protection. Among siblings, the one to whom greatest protection rightfully accrues is the younger sister; though most junior, she is also in one sense the most privileged.

7. The organization of a family and kin group anywhere is vastly more complex than

any simple typology can hold. Every family and kin group anywhere is different from every other. To reduce the realities to some common denominator, like a score in an IQ test, is to blind oneself to both the forest and the trees. There may exist some ideal image of "the American family" or "the Dravidian family." In fact, I have drawn kinship charts; but as soon as one looks at particular families in any group of people who supposedly fit the same kinship mold, the ideal bends, changes, adopts some practices while abandoning others, and may break entirely if it is too rigid. Political pressures and emotional pressures inevitably affect what choices are made within a family.

It may be better to look at particular practices, their distribution over time and space, the relation of one practice to another, the political and emotional forces that come into play, and what resources are available to whom, to understand what enables a living family to endure.

8. In Batticaloa, both Tamils and Muslims speak Tamil as their mother tongue. A non-Muslim man would address a Muslim man as *maccān*, which means male cross-cousin or brother-in-law in Batticaloa. This was an expression of solidarity between Muslims and non-Muslims during a war when Muslims were being killed by non-Muslims and vice-versa (D. S. Sivaram, personal communication). Women in the town of Mahiladittivu, where I lived, expressed the same sentiment (Trawick 2007). The women that I lived with were Christians. Before the war, there was no animosity between Muslims and non-Muslims in this region. Muslims and Hindus in that area even shared the same matrilineal kinship organization, though there was no intermarriage between them that I know of. That kinship system survived the war in Sri Lanka and still flourishes there (Dennis McGilvray, personal communication).

Also in Batticaloa, female cadres of the LTTE (Tamil Tigers) were called *akkā* (older sister) and male cadres were called *aṇṇan* (older brother), regardless of age difference. "We call them *aṇṇan* and they call us *akkā*," an eighteen-year-old girl said to me, smiling.

9. The analogy between caste and kin is culturally recognized in terms of address and reference. Yalman (1963), for instance, mentions that the Sinhalese washer man is addressed as "mother's brother." At the other end of the scale, Manavadharmaśāstra calls the Brahman the "first-born" among varṇas; and certain subcaste divisions as reported by Dumont (1957) trace their beginnings to "senior" and "junior" branches of single families. The hierarchy appears more solid in some times and places than in others.

But here is where the little-used term "classificatory kinship" comes alive again, after the whole concept of kinship, including Dravidian kinship, has been hammered, torn, and soundly denounced from multiple quarters (Sahlins 2013; Schneider 1980; Clark-Decès 2014).

In the Batticaloa Tamil systems of kinship that I knew, each person in a community was kin to everybody, including people whom that person had never met and with whom no genealogical relationship existed. In Batticaloa I was Auntie. In Tamil Nadu I was *ammā* by default, or Peggy Ammā. In fact any female, including a female child, could be called *ammā*. A junior man could be called *ammā* by a senior man, if there was a bond of affection between them. A man could call a woman *-ḍā* (boy) and a woman could call a young man *-ḍi* (girl). I asked my host what was going on here, and he said that confusion of categories was a sign of love (Trawick 1990).

The term *māmā* meant mother's brother, but it had other meanings as well, in particular, a man with whom a woman shared affection. And an old woman could call her dead mother "mother that I bore" and "mother that I raised" without being considered senile. In this as in the other examples cited here, the feeling involved in the relationship was more important than birth or marriage ties.

Speakers of white American English are in some areas less creative in their use of language than they might be, because for some of us, creative use of language is deemed a lie. See, for instance, Shirley Brice Heath's *Ways with Words* (1983), and Mark Twain's *Huckleberry Finn* (1884). The latter work was translated into Tamil by K. Paramasivam.

10. Fall from a higher to a lower state does not seem to fit here, but it may. Many lower castes have attempted to raise their status, and some have succeeded by developing an origin myth for themselves in which their present low status is described as the result of a slipping from an older original high status (see, for example, Hardgrave 1969b). O'Flaherty (1980a, 65–76) points out that this is a general theme in Hindu mythology where it is used for political purposes: since a movement from low to high is not considered possible, those who wish to acquire or legitimize a new high position of status and power for themselves must define it mythologically as primordial.

11. For a discussion of the immediacy of folk poetry, as opposed to classical poetry, through reference to the feelings, relations, and experiences of embodied beings, see Ramanujan (1986).

12. This idea is frequently expounded in the literature and in the lore of higher castes, and it is certainly not absent from the thought of middle-caste people. A mother angry with her child, for instance, will lash out at him with the epithet *nāṉ ceñca pāvam* (the sin I did), implying that the child is her punishment for past wrongs, including the "sin" that resulted in the conception of the child. The same phrase occurs as a general explanation for present suffering.

13. Michael Moffatt (personal communication), in interviews with Harijans living in the city of Madras, has found the same interpretation of karma expressed there: it is not one's own past sin, but the sin of one's ancestors, that causes one's present suffering. Kolenda (1964) also finds that Harijans reject the conventional definition of karma, the better to preserve their self-esteem. O'Flaherty (1980b) points out that the association between personal karma and the deeds of one's ancestors has ancient literary precedents. See also Keyes and Daniel (1983).

In the present song, although the source of sin has shifted from suffering junior self to senior other, the nature of the sin (killing a cow, killing a Brahman) remains conventional. Thus there is expressed both consensus to the rules of hierarchy and departure from these rules; or, to put it another way, the singer avoids either total submission to the existing symbol system or total rejection of it, either of which course of action would leave her with no possibility of communication.

In his study of Tulu folk heroines, Peter Claus finds that undeserved suffering, or righteousness, in the midst of unrighteously inflicted suffering, is an important component in the mythological creation of heroines and goddesses (personal communication; see also Claus 1975).

14. South Indian culture abounds with expressions of esteem for children. The much-quoted *Thirukkuṟaḷ* contains adages such as "He who has never heard the voices of children thinks the lute sounds sweet" and "There is no greater joy than to have a child more learned than oneself." Small children are exempt from many rules of pollution, and, more to the point, children are said to be like gods because both are "innocent"—they do or should not suffer the consequences of their actions. Many of the most beloved deities—Krishna, Murugaṉ, Ayyappaṉ, Piḷḷaiyār, Māriammaṉ—are worshiped all or part of the time as children. Hence there is much reason to seek identity as a child. Paṟaiyars who are servants of landowning households are already classified in certain respects as "children" (*iḷaiyōr*) of those households. In many contexts, the distinction between a lower-caste household servant and a poor or junior relative resident in the household is hard to see.

15. The idea that marginal members of a society are among the most creative is not new, especially in studies of religion. Somewhat more rare are assertions that this creativity on the margins ultimately transforms the mainstream, and more rarely still are people on the bottom edge of a society portrayed as sources of mainstream cultural transformations. In the present essay I am concerned with the creativity that emerges from an area of social darkness, though the experience of such an area surely has psychic effects as well. "He who speaks a private language understood by no one else does not speak at all. But he who speaks only a language in which conventionality has become total forfeits the power of address" (Gadamer 1976, 85–86).

CHAPTER 3. WORK AND LOVE

1. This chapter is a revised and updated version of Trawick (1988a).

2. Berreman (1971), Mencher (1974), Gough (1973), and others have argued that untouchables in India are at a kind of cognitive advantage with respect to members of higher castes. Being forcibly excluded from the center of authority, untouchables (like ethnographers and other outsiders) can see the social structure more clearly "for what it is." These authors claim that untouchables have a more egalitarian, materialistic, body-affirming, agonistic, system-subversive viewpoint than do members of higher castes. Consequently, untouchables form a potentially revolutionary force in India—they are not far from being Marxists already.

In opposition to this position, Moffatt (1979) points out that untouchables of Tamil Nadu demonstrate in many ways that they subscribe to the validity of caste hierarchy, hence they independently replicate this hierarchy among themselves. There are many more continuities than discontinuities between untouchable and high-caste world views, Moffatt says. Untouchables deal with the problem of being at the bottom of the social hierarchy not by subverting it but by creating another bottom beneath themselves.

My own view is that untouchables have worked out many ways of adapting to their difficult situation, these different modes of adaptation are not necessarily mutually consistent, and none of them is fully satisfactory. Individual members of the Paṟaiyar community in Chingleput show a profound ambivalence toward their status in the community and toward their own nature as persons. This ambivalence is manifested in their songs, which also seem to provide them with a medium for the development of a coherent sense of self.

The work of Robert Coles (1967) could provide a model for further understanding the art of untouchables in India.

3. Daniel (1984) provides a full description of how in a Tamil village people's bodies are at one with the bodies of their houses (conceived as themselves living organisms), with the soil on which they live, and with the substances such as semen that flow from within one person to within another. Soil, food, house materials, semen, words, and all other such substances that flow among persons and of which persons are composed contain *kuṇams*, the moral and spiritual qualities of persons, so that as these substances are exchanged and intermingled, so are the essential attributes of identity and personhood. Trawick (1978) similarly describes processes by which, in the Tamil world, substances are transformed from tangible material quantities to feelings and finally to spirits, and how the spirits and feelings of a man and a woman are mingled in the mingling of sexual fluids.

4. Mauss (1938) demonstrates, by exemplifying, how deeply ingrained in the thought of Western social scientists is this view of the self as sacred and inviolable. One dissenting view is offered by Peirce (cited in Singer 1980), who, like Bakhtin, considered the self to be the same internally as the world of many selves that it belonged to, so that Peirce was able to say, "The most solitary meditation is dialogue."

5. We were not entirely unjustified in thinking that the songs might contain "errors," since the singers themselves would sometimes decide that a particular song had been botched and would sing it over again, as though to correct it. Where I and my assistant overstepped our bounds was in independently deciding that some performances had not been what the singer intended. Even the best of musicologists and folklorists (Lord 1960; Emeneau 1958; Feld 1982) admit to being guided by their own aesthetic feeling in choosing which people's songs to study and which songs to select as exemplary of a genre. Even in the process of listening to a song, if the singer can see our faces, we exert a selective influence upon what is sung.

6. In the best-known studies (Dumont 1970; Inden and Nicholas 1977), hierarchy is represented as a value in opposition to equality as another value—one or the other value being dominant according to context (political versus religious contexts, contexts of intimacy versus contexts of community, and so on). In Dumont's view, hierarchy (as a religious value) "encompasses" equality (as a political principle) in South Asia.

Classic studies of purity and pollution and the concern with boundary maintenance in certain sectors of South Asian society include Harper (1964), Khare (1976), and Dumont (1970). All of these studies link "purity" as a value very closely with "hierarchy" as a value. Both individuals and castes are bounded entities that are ranked according to how "pure" they are. Recently, Appadurai (1986) and others have questioned the extent to which hierarchy is (as Dumont claims) the dominant mode of social thought in South Asia. As an alternative to Dumont's view, Marriott and Inden (1977), Inden and Nicholas (1977), and Daniel (1984) offer general discussions of the "dividuality" and fluidity of persons in South Asian cultures. The term "dividual" was coined by McKim Marriott to indicate the idea that, for South Asians, the self is essentially nondiscrete and unbounded.

7. Spirit possession is common throughout South Asia and often represents a dramatization, within the body of a single person, of family conflicts or sexual conflicts (see, for example, Claus 1975 and Trawick 1982). Possessing spirits, whether demons or deities, have distinct personalities, histories, and desires, which must be accommodated and harmonized with the needs and desires of the possessed personality if trouble is to be avoided. Possession is not always pathological. Heads of families may communicate with the spirits of deceased ancestors in dreams and may be treated as embodiments of these ancestors' personalities and desires when major family decisions must be made. One of the parallels between songs and possessing spirits in Tamil Nadu is that both songs and spirits enable the possessed or singing person to give articulate voice to her most deep-seated feelings, even though these feelings may not be socially approved. For both spirits and songs are specially framed so that the person through whose mouth they emerge may deny responsibility for them, even in the process of creating them. Consider in this light Muttammāḷ's song about adultery and abortion.

8. The influence of Martin Buber, whom Bakhtin called "the greatest philosopher of the twentieth century" (Frank 1986), is evident here. "I am particularly indebted to him," Frank reports Bakhtin to have said, "in particular, for the idea of dialogue. Of course, this is obvious to anyone who reads Buber." In his most famous book, *I and Thou*, Buber spoke for a heartfelt recognition of the subjectivity of the other. Bakhtin's view that an author should give the voices of his or her characters their freedom has special relevance not only to South Asianists but to ethnographers in general, for in ethnography, the notion that voices other than that of the author have autonomous wills is not at all mystical. As Clifford (1986) pointed out, the "voices" in our published "fictions" are in fact the voices of real and living people, transformed though these voices may be in our work. If we can learn to loosen our hold over our informants' voices somewhat, allow the confusions that they engender in us to remain, let them pluralize us as they themselves have been pluralized, then we can come closer to our goal of putting the "authentic reality" of others into writing.

CHAPTER 4. ON THE EDGE OF THE WILD

Note to epigraph: "'Now, We Have a Democratically Elected Totalitarian Government'—Arundhati Roy," *Dawn,* May 23, 2014.

1. Trouillot (1995, 2003) pointed out that people of the North Atlantic created a "slot" into which "savages" were placed. A whole discourse was created by North Atlantic scholars to describe such savages. In this way there came to be two worlds, a savage one

and a civilized one. Trouillot singled out Lévi-Strauss for helping to create this dichotomy, although Lévi-Strauss took pains to say that all human beings share the same mind. But postcolonial, high-caste people in India try their hardest to show how English they are, and how white they are, and in precolonial times in India, the caste system still held sway.

2. Thurston and Rangachari (1907, 388–406). Of the Nilgiri Iruḷars, Thurston wrote: "The Irulas are the darkest-skinned of the Nilgiri tribes. . . . The name Irula, in fact, means darkness or blackness (irul), whether in reference to the dark jungles in which the Irulas, who have not become domesticated by working as contractors or coolies on planters' estates, dwell, or to the darkness of their skin, is doubtful."

"Some of them are splendid cattle-men, that is, in looking after the cattle possessed by some enterprising planter . . ."

"When not engaged at work on estates or in the forest, the Irulas cultivate, for their own consumption, ragi (*Eleusine Coracana*), samai (*Panicum miliare*), tenai (*Setaria italica*), tovarai (*Cajanus indicus*), maize, plantains, etc. They also cultivate limes, oranges, jack fruit (*Artocarpus integrifolia*), etc."

"At Kallampalla temple is a thatched building, containing a stone called Mariamma, the well-known goddess of small-pox, worshipped in this capacity by the Irulas. A sheep is led to this temple, and those who offer the sacrifice sprinkle water over it, and cut its throat. The pujari sits by, but takes no part in the ceremony. The body is cut up, and distributed among the Irulas present, including the pujari."

"The following account of an Irula temple festival is given by Harkness. [183] 'The hair of the men, as well as of the women and children, was bound up in a fantastic manner with wreaths of plaited straw. Their necks, ears, and ankles were decorated with ornaments formed of the same material, and they carried little dried gourds, in which nuts or small stones had been inserted. They rattled them as they moved, and, with the rustling of their rural ornaments, gave a sort of rhythm to their motion. The dance was performed in front of a little thatched shed, which, we learnt, was their temple. When it was concluded, they commenced a sacrifice to their deity, or rather deities, of a he-goat and three cocks. This was done by cutting the throats of the victims, and throwing them down at the feet of the idol, the whole assembly at the same time prostrating themselves . . .'"

"'The Irulas,' a recent writer observes, generally possess a small plot of ground near their villages, which they assiduously cultivate with grain, although they depend more upon the wages earned by working on estates. Some of them are splendid cattle-men, that is, in looking after the cattle possessed by some enterprising planter, who would add the sale of dairy produce to the nowadays pitiable profit of coffee planting. The Irula women are as useful as tweeding, and all estate work. In fact, planters find both men and women far more industrious and reliable than the Tamil coolies.'"

"'By the sale of the produce of the forests,'" Harkness writes, "'such as honey and beeswax, or the fruit of their gardens, the Irulas are enabled to buy grain for their immediate sustenance, and for seed. . . . When the corn is ripe, if at any distance from the village, the family to whom the patch or field belongs will remove to it, and, constructing temporary dwellings, remain there so long as the grain lasts. Each morning they pluck as much as they think they may require for the use of that day, kindle a fire upon the nearest large stone or fragment of rock, and, when it is well heated, brush away the embers, and scatter the grain upon it, which, soon becoming parched and dry, is readily reduced to meal, which is made into cakes. The stone is now heated a second time, and the cakes are put on it to bake. Or, where they have met with a stone which has a little concavity, they will, after heating it, fill the hollow with water, and, with the meal, form a sort of porridge. In this way the whole family, their friends, and neighbours, will live till the grain has been consumed. The whole period is one of merry-making. They celebrate Mahri [Māri?] for whom they performed animal sacrifices, for whom they performed animal sacrifices, , and invite all who may be passing by to join in the festivities. These families will, in return, be invited to live on the fields of their neighbours. Many of them live for the remainder of the year on a kind of yam, which grows wild, and is called Erula root. To the use of this they accustom their children from infancy.'"

Thurston continues, "Some Irulas now work for the Forest Department, which allows them to live on the borders of the forest, granting them sites free, and other concessions. Among the minor forest produce, which they collect, are myrabolams, bees-wax, honey, vembadam bark (*Ventilago Madraspatana*), avaram bark (*Cassia auriculata*), deer's horns, tamarinds, gum, soapnuts, and sheekoy (*Acacia concinna*)."

". . . The collection of honey is a dangerous occupation. A man, with a torch in his hand, and a number of bamboo tubes suspended from his shoulders, descends by means of ropes or creepers to the vicinity of the comb. The sight of the torch drives away the bees, and he proceeds to fill the bamboos with the comb, and then ascends to the top of the rock. The Irulas will not (so they say) eat the flesh of buffaloes or cattle, but will eat sheep and goat, field-rats, fowls, deer, pig (which they shoot), hares (which they snare with skilfully made nets), jungle-fowl, pigeons, and quail (which they knock over with stones)."

"They informed Mr. Harkness that, 'they have no marriage contract, the sexes cohabiting almost indiscriminately; the option of remaining in union, or of separating, resting principally with the female . . .'"

"The marriage ceremony, as described to me, is a very simple affair. A feast is held, at which a sheep is killed, and the guests make a present of a few annas to the bridegroom, who ties up the money in a cloth, and, going to the bride's hut, conducts her to her future home. Widows are permitted to marry again."

"It is recorded by Harkness that 'during the winter, or while they are wandering about the forests in search of food, driven by hunger, the families or parties separate from one another. On these occasions the women and young children are often left alone, and the mother, having no longer any nourishment for her infant, anticipates its final misery by burying it alive.'"

Of the Iruḷars of Chingleput, Thurston writes, "The Irulas, or Villiyans (bowmen), who have settled in the town of Chingleput, about fifty miles distant from Madras, have attained to a higher degree of civilisation than the jungle Irulas of the Nilgiris and are defined, in the Census Report, 1901, as a semi-Brahmanised forest tribe, who speak a corrupt Tamil."

"Roots, wild fruits, and honey constitute their dietary, and cooked rice is always rejected, even when gratuitously offered. They have no clear ideas about God, though they offer rice (wild variety) to the goddess Kanniamma. The legend runs that a Rishi, Mala Rishi by name, seeing that these people were much bothered by wild beasts, took pity on them, and for a time lived with them. He mixed freely with their women, and as the result, several children were born, who were also molested by wild animals. To free them from these, the Rishi advised them to do puja (worship) to Kanniamma."

"Their chief source of livelihood is husking paddy (rice), but they also gather sticks for sale as firewood in return for pice, rice, and sour fermented rice gruel, which is kept by the higher classes for cattle. While husking rice, they eat the bran, and, if not carefully watched, will steal as much of the rice as they can manage to secrete about themselves. As an addition to their plain dietary they catch field (Jerboa) rats, which they dig out with long sticks, after they have been asphyxiated with smoke blown into their tunnels through a small hole in an earthen pot filled with dried leaves, which are set on fire. When the nest is dug out, they find material for a meat and vegetable curry in the dead rats, with the hoarded store of rice or other grain. They feast on the bodies of winged white-ants (Termites), which they search with torch-lights at the time of the seasonal epidemic appearance."

"Some Irulas are herbalists, and are believed to have the powers of curing certain diseases, snake-poisoning, and the bites of rats and insects. . . . They have no fixed place of abode, which they often change. Some live in low, palmyra-thatched huts of small dimensions; others under a tree, in an open place, in ruined buildings, or the street pials (verandah) of houses."

3. Edugreen, "The History of Forests in India," http://edugreen.teri.res.in/explore/forestry/history.htm (accessed November 19, 2014).

4. The story of Kanyammā is based on fieldwork done in Pukkatturai, near the town of Chingleput, in 1980. The grant for this project was from the American Institute of Indian Studies. This chapter is a revised and updated version of Trawick (2002).

5. Between 1980 and 1984, the head of the family, Raghava Reddiar, a good man, died of throat cancer, a terribly painful disease. The man who had been my host died of heart disease in 1998. The women now live in the city of Chingleput. One of the children, after he had grown and become independent, died in a car accident. The rest of the children are grown and married, all the boys and some of the girls are professionally employed in Chennai. The first of the grandchildren, now an adult woman, is also married. All of the children have been educated past high school.

CHAPTER 5. THE LIFE OF SEVI

1. Because Sevi in the introduction to her performance refers to Siṅgammā as "a child from the house of Kuṟavars," I have chosen to follow her lead in this chapter and to refer to the nomadic scavengers in Tamil Nadu as Kuṟavars. The situation is complicated

by the fact that there exists in southern Tamil Nadu another caste called Kuṟavars who are not nomadic and who are distinct from the nomadic Kuṟavars discussed in this chapter. The content of Sevi's song clearly shows that the Kuṟavars she refers to are not the settled laborers but the nomadic scavengers more commonly called Narikkuṟavars.

Of Dalits' first writing of their lives in North India, Pandey (2013, location 3791) says, "the 'community' is the omnipresent; hence, the subject who writes and the object of reflection are not easily separated. On occasion, an apparently unconscious slide from first- to third-person narration, and the other way around, signals the particularity of that experience—possibly suggesting also that the first-person voice cannot bear the weight of the life being relived."

2. There is an unresolved debate concerning the degree to which South Indian people of untouchable castes accept the principle of caste hierarchy. Berreman (1971), Mencher (1974), and Gough (1973) argue that untouchables subscribe to an essentially egalitarian ideology. Moffatt (1979) argues that untouchables do not question the principle of social hierarchy; what they do sometimes question is their own place within the existing order. In this volume I have tried to show that the verbal art of Tamil untouchables does covertly challenge some of the principles of caste hierarchy. A theme running through very many of their songs is the injustice of their fate. It is not implied that exclusion from the good things of life is all right for others but not for them. It is implied that the act of exclusion on the basis of pollution is itself an absolute wrong.

Nevertheless, it would be false to deny that untouchables believe in the reality of ritual pollution. And the fact that they have "their own untouchables" irrefutably bespeaks their acceptance, at least in some contexts and for some purposes, of "the system." I think the simple truth is that they are not firmly on one side or the other. They accept or deny hierarchy according to the situation they find themselves in. Many of the songs of untouchables show strong ambivalence both toward their own status as persons in the community and toward the social order itself, which has afflicted them with that status.

3. My comparison of Sevi's life story and the life story of the spirit in whom she is interested is not without reason or precedent. Many observers have noted that in South Asia the personalities and life histories of deities and their worshippers tend to be intimately intertwined (Claus 1975; Kakar 1981; McDaniel 1989; Nuckolls 1987; Obeyesekere 1981; Roy 1972; Trawick 1980, 1990a). In Tamil Nadu it is common for individuals to consciously identify with and emulate particular deities, even when they don't formally worship those deities. Female identity in particular is tied up with the personalities of deities.

4. Literature describing relations between speech style and speaker personality (either as expressed by the speaker, or as interpreted by listeners) is massive (for example, Bakhtin 1984; Friedrich 1979a; Goffman 1981; Tannen 1984), although, of course, it would be a mistake to attempt to establish simple one-to-one linkages between particular stylistic features and particular personality traits. Stylistic indices of a speaker's self-image are evident even on a commonsense level and have been of interest especially to feminist sociolinguists in recent years. In the United States and elsewhere, females as well as members of other subordinate groups are often punished beginning in childhood

for demonstrating high degrees of verbal proficiency. In the United States, for instance, articulate and verbally powerful females are castigated and stigmatized as chatterboxes, back talkers, and nags. Consequently they learn to keep their mouths shut. Females in American schools, though they are consistently better performers than males in written tests of verbal ability, learn not to exercise this ability in face-to-face encounters, but rather to remain mute, to be "dumb." Silence and inarticulacy (in the presence of male peers, parents, teachers, etc.) become their hallmarks. When they do speak, their speech is broken: that is, hesitant, audible only with difficulty, childlike, heavily qualified, and easily controverted and interrupted. The speaker must assume that she will not have her listener's attention for very long, therefore she learns to keep her messages not only "soft" but also simple and short. She then becomes defined as incapable of producing a sustained and coherent monologue, and it is concluded that the reason for her verbal incoherence is her inability to maintain an orderly train of thought (cf. Michaels and Cazden 1986). Because her communications necessarily are in pieces, she is viewed as scatterbrained. Inarticulacy finally becomes a symptom of femaleness, as well as an expression of it. Women are flawed, therefore their speech must also be flawed, otherwise they are not true women (Lakoff 1975).

In the United States, moreover, since females are regarded as more emotional than males, females often "intentionally" adopt what could aptly be called broken speech (creaky voice, sobbing laughter, hesitancy and unevenness of breath, falsetto syllables, frequent self-interruption and self-correction, departure from established grammatical conventions and habitual speech patterns) to signal that they are overwhelmed by emotion, hence "out of control," hence both feminine and sincere. The incorporation of such "weeping features" into speech or song is a powerful and direct way of portraying feelings of grief, personal loss, and incompletion; indeed this set of features, together with the affective associations just named, may constitute a kind of sociolinguistic universal (Urban 1989).

In villages of Tamil Nadu, speech style is an important index both of gender and of caste status. In villages of Tamil Nadu, speech style is an important index both of gender and of caste status. Untouchables risk severe punishment if they adopt the habits, including speech habits, of higher castes. Criticism and complaint, if expressed at all, must be expressed by them in roundabout ways and with extreme circumspection. *Centamir*, "high" or literate Tamil, is the language of privilege, of purity, and of truth. Only the literate (viz., high-caste males, with few exceptions until very recently) are afforded the opportunities to master and wield it. *Koccai tamiṛ*, "low" or street Tamil, is thought to be crude, offensive, and incapable of expressing "high thoughts." This is the language attributed to low-caste people.

Even certain high-caste women who live with literate, scholarly men and know by heart thousands of lines of "high Tamil" poetry (which they teach their children) may in ordinary conversation disclaim any knowledge of "beautiful words" and deliberately choose to speak "low" or "vulgar" Tamil as a way of challenging men's right to dictate the way women should speak (Trawick 1990b). Like American blacks, low-status Tamils escape becoming linguistic cripples because most of their verbal interactions are with each other rather than with executors of the rules of the dominant culture. In their own world, they develop high proficiency at verbal art, encouraging, critiquing, and applauding each other's efforts from childhood on (cf. Heath 1983). And, for reasons that are partly aesthetic and partly political, they elaborate among themselves an esoteric language that remains partly or wholly opaque to "outsiders" (cf. Labov 1972; Kochman 1981). Sevi, like others of her status, may be a victim of what McDermott (1985) calls "systematic inarticulacy." She is defined by people in authority over her as inarticulate, and she is forced by them to be this way, at least in her direct communications with them. And yet, I try to argue here, her very mistakes are eloquent.

5. The term *urimai* means "kinship," "kindness," and "friendship." To an American, these three concepts are all different from each other. But to Sevi, they are all the same. More formally, in Tamil legalese, *urimai* means "ownership."

6. A note on genre. People in Tamil Nadu commonly sing songs addressed to gods. There are probably thousands of these. Their performance is not necessarily limited to a particular context, although the songs are most likely to be performed on the occasion of festivals to the gods in question. I have often heard young people singing songs to particular gods not so much because they were devotees of those gods as because they liked the songs. A god may even increase in popularity because of the release of some particularly attractive song addressed to him. (I am thinking here of the cinema song "Ayyappan.") I have not done any kind of extensive study of contemporary Tamil songs addressed to gods, and if such a study has been done by someone else, I am unaware of it. The "god songs" (*teyvappāḍḍu, kaḍavuḷ pāḍḍu*) with which I am familiar generally stress the god's positive, auspicious attributes. Like the Siṅgammā song, many of them seem pervaded with longing.

7. Exclusion from caste and family is the ultimate remaindering. "Of all kinds of punishment the hardest and most unbearable for a Hindu is that which cuts him off and expels him from his caste. . . . This expulsion from caste, which follows either an infringement of caste usages or some public offense calculated if left unpunished to bring dishonor on the whole community, is a kind of social excommunication, which deprives the unhappy person who suffers it of all intercourse with his fellow creatures. It leaves him, as it were, dead to the world" (DuBois 1906, 38). Some things have not changed.

8. This remainder, a leftover piece of lore from a time long past, is the Atharva Veda. It is cited by Kristeva (1982, 76) in her argument suggesting that Indian consciousness defines the self in terms of place, and that such a self lives in a world of incomplete separations, of remainders (while a self defined in terms of language lives in a world of discrete categories and absolute divisions).

9. Daniel (1984) writes about the necessity of leftovers, of there being always something extra in a transaction and always something left out in a creation. Narayan (1943) also writes of the necessity of imperfection.

10. Stylistic devices such as enjambment are inherently polysemous, just as words are. They can and do mean many things. Often in poetry and song, such devices are used because of their ambiguity, because the artist desires to say more than one thing, to say contradictory things, to exercise his or her skill in the dreamlike act of condensing several

messages into a single image, or simply to avoid committing herself to, and reaping the punishment for, a particular statement which she nonetheless wishes to communicate. It is well documented that people in oppressed positions often express their opinions and desires indirectly and ambiguously (spirit possession is the classic example).

"Partial isomorphisms," or similarities, between formal properties of a given discourse and properties of the topic of that discourse, are a common feature of poetic speech (Jakobson 1960; Friedrich 1979b), and indeed of casual conversation in general. Tannen (1984) has cogently argued that such iconicity—which runs the range from onomatopoeia to complex parallelisms between syntax and history, verbal morphology, and physical anatomy—may even be a necessary tool in the establishment of coherence in discourse. My suggestion that there may be an iconic relation between Sevi's grammatically fragmented speech style and the brokenness of the life she describes should therefore not raise any eyebrows. The discovery of poetic iconicity is always "after the fact," and the creation of such iconicity is in most cases not the result of conscious design. Therefore, it is generally futile to try to prove that a speaker intended a particular figure of speech to function as such.

Given a text such as Sevi's, it would therefore be foolish to attempt to demonstrate beyond doubt that for some particular form some particular meaning is intended. Doubtless for any such text more than one meaning is intended by the artist, and others still may be read into it by the audience and developed further when members of the audience perform the text before others. In such a situation, the best one can do is seek to establish the plausibility of a particular interpretation by answering questions such as these: Is this a meaning that a person such as the artist might want to convey? Is the form of the message consistent with the meaning we are attributing to it? Is the meaning we are attributing to this message congruent with other meanings that have been conveyed by the speaker herself in other messages, or by other speakers in similar situations? Is the meaning we are attributing to this message congruent with the apparent overall meaning(s) of the text at hand? In other words, does it fit? Does it make sense? Or not?

The subject of Sevi's song is a nomadic woman who is murdered and becomes a disembodied, wandering spirit. When Sevi uses enjambment in her song, she puts the name of this spirit at the end of the line, drawing out the final syllable and taking a deep breath before beginning the next line. The listener is made to wait, to find out what happens next to the subject, Siṅgammā. I interpret Sevi's use of enjambment in this song as essentially iconic: the partial and temporary disconnectedness of the name mirrors the partial and temporary disconnectedness of the person to whom the name belongs. A simple, but powerful, poetic figure—the hanging voice as a sign of the homeless soul. Elsewhere, of course, similar devices might be used in different ways to different effects.

11. Cf. Blackburn (1988) on the emotional depth of death stories in Tamil. Blackburn argues that in the performance tradition he studied, Tamil people are inclined to identify and sympathize especially strongly with story heroes and heroines who die tragic deaths, and are likely to become possessed by the spirits of the protagonists when death stories are told; whereas stories of auspicious events evoke less powerful feelings.

CHAPTER 6. THE SONG OF SIṄGAMMĀ

This chapter and Chapter 5 are updated and revised versions of Trawick 1991. Research for these chapters was carried out under a Humanities Fellowship from the Rockefeller Foundation.

1. Of the Kuṟavañji drama of the eighteenth century, Peterson (2008) writes: "The Kuravanci is an opera-like drama, with a dramatic plot unfolding in a sequence of songs intended to be enacted through dance. The stereotyped plot unfolds in three segments: "Seeing the god of the local temple or the king riding in procession with his retinue, a high-born lady falls hopelessly in love with him. In the second segment, a kuṟavañji or kuṟatti, a wandering female of the Kuṟavar hill tribe and eponymous principal character of the play, appears and offers to help the lovelorn woman. After praising the god and the temple in the lady's town, the kuṟatti names the hills with which her family is associated and the many places to which she has traveled. She describes the hill landscape and the kuṟavar ways of life, and uses kuṟavar divinatory techniques to foretell the heroine's union with the hero. The lady handsomely rewards the kuṟatti with gold and jewels. The third segment begins with a detailed description of the kuṟatti's husband, the birdcatcher Siṅgan, trapping birds in the rice fields owned by the temple. While hunting, the birdcatcher suddenly realizes that his wife is missing. Maddened by desire, he leaves the birds, sets out to search for her, and finally meets her on the streets of the town. In the lively dialogue that follows, the fortune-teller wittily parries her jealous husband's questions about her activities, and the couple is reunited. The play ends with verses in praise of the god and temple."

2. There are many temples to Draupadi in Tamil Nadu and in Sri Lanka. The Draupadi temple in Mēlūr is just one. But Veḷḷaiccāmi in Mēlūr does not mention Draupadi in his song about Siṅgammā. And M. D. Muthukumaraswamy in his detailed article about the Draupadi Kuṟavañji Kūttu in the town of Kulamanthai does not mention Siṅgammā. It appears that the Kuṟavañji character is too generic for Siṅgammā to be included by name in the festivals or plays where the Kuṟavañji is featured.

Now there are three characters here to be considered: Draupadi of the Mahābhārata, the Kuṟavañji of drama, and Siṅgammā of Mēlūr. The distance separating Mēlūr and Kulamanthai is more than three hundred kilometers by road and five to six hours traveling time by bus. This may be why the events of one town are not known to the other. But the three characters are closely connected.

One feature shared by the Kuṟavañji drama and Veḷḷaiccāmi's recounting of the Siṅgammā story is the naming and description of places through which Siṅgammā and the Kuṟavañji have traveled. A second thing in common is the ultimate triumph of each over her husbands or brothers. Another thing in common is the resplendent beauty of each, gained by the Kuṟavañji's cleverness as a fortune-teller, by Draupadi by birth, and by Siṅgammā by song and chant. The great difference between the Kuṟavañji Kūttu, the stories of Draupadi, and the songs of Siṅgammā is that the Kuṟavañji Kūttu is a romantic comedy whereas the Siṅgammā story in all its versions is tragic. So is the Draupadi story.

Siṅgammā had five brothers, whom, upon her apotheosis, she firmly blamed for the sexual dishonor she endured and for her ghastly bloody death afterward. At best, her brothers did nothing to protect her. She was their unmarried younger sister. It was her brothers' responsibility to protect her. But they were in the Mēlūr marketplace at the same time she was; at least one of them saw her and ignored her, and they mutely stood by while higher-caste men raped her. Sevi suggests in her song that maybe Siṅgammā sold herself in the market for money. A modern sensibility might ask, so what? Her brothers murdered her on the pretext that she had dishonored them. Then they dismembered her body and buried the pieces under their dwelling place. Were they not hiding her body out of their own sense of shame, out of their realization that they had done something unforgivable? Something terribly wrong? A third sensibility would remind us that Siṅgammā accepted her brothers' decision to kill her. Therefore did she not collude in her own murder? But by the time Veḷḷaiccāmi performs her story, all doubts about the innocence of Siṅgammā are gone. She was not only young and innocent, but incomparably beautiful.

Draupadi, heroine of the Mahābhārata, is another angry goddess. Perhaps she, too, hundreds of years ago, was a real human being, harboring human ambiguities, provoking human doubts. It is said in the Mahābhārata that her scent could be smelled for miles around, her thighs were shapely, her breasts swelling, her waist slender, her eyes like lotus flowers, her hair like a dark cloud around her face, her skin tender and of a matchless color, her appearance young. Was she perhaps too desirable? But if so, was that her fault? These are questions that women may ask of other women. Draupadi was born by accident, as the secondary consequence of a fire sacrifice meant to produce a perfect son. She was the fire, the sacrifice, the impossible beauty, and the deadly mistake all in one. Then, because of another mistake, Draupadi was married to five men. After a ceremony and a contest among prospective suitors, Draupadi chose the archer Arjun to be her husband. Arjun went home to his mother to tell her he had won a great prize. His mother, not asking what the prize was, told Arjun to share the prize equally with his brothers. Polyandry is not an accepted form of marriage among most caste Hindus. But Arjun obeyed his mother unquestioningly, even though his mother had not known the wrong she was asking. Draupadi served each husband perfectly.

Here one may question the meaning of dharma. Dharma means doing what you are supposed to do, doing the right thing. And certainly it is hard to know what the right thing is. But dharma does not mean fairness to all. Each category of creature, each particular being, has a dharma he or she or it is meant to perform. And dharma is not fair. At the same time, dharma is the law that all must follow, the law of the universe.

Marriage to five brothers was a great wrong done to Draupadi. The oldest of the brothers was a compulsive gambler and he gambled his wife Draupadi into the hands of his worst enemy. Draupadi was subjected to sexual dishonor by this enemy. Her husbands did nothing to protect her. It took intervention by the god Krishna to save her from public disrobing. Draupadi swore that she would wash her hair only with the blood of the two enemies who sought to shame her. Ultimately, she did just this.

But what really happened to the real woman whom no man or god could protect?

Forcible public nudity is still a punishment in India against women, notably lower-caste ones who are considered to have stepped out of place. The disrobing of Draupadi remains the most popular event in religious plays about her. Actors and audience are so moved by this event that they go into trance at the performance of it.

Muthukumaraswamy writes, "Possession or trance is a regular feature of Therukoothu (street theater) performances. Both the actors and members of the audience slip into trance during ritually charged performances such as 'Disrobing of Draupadi.'" It may be that the very ambiguity, the very uncertainty of the goddess they worship, drives the worshippers mad.

Hiltebeitel writes (2001, 242–45) of the irony of Draupadi's situation and of her words when she finds herself trapped and tells the man who comes to take her away as a slave: "How do you speak so, an usher? What Rajaputra would wager his wife? The king was befooled and crazed by the dice. Was there nothing else for him to stake?" And Hiltebeitel adds, "In these questions, she sounds angry, incredulous, and then sarcastic." Draupadi's husband, the king of dharma, has sold himself into slavery. What sane king would do that? And then, having become a slave, he has sold his wife into slavery. A slave owns nothing. How can he sell his wife as though he owns her? This is against the law. How can the king of the law act thus illegally?

3. According to the report of the Kaḷḷars who maintain the Siṅgammā shrine in Mēlūr, most of those who become possessed by the spirit of Siṅgammā are young women of the Paṟaiyar community, like Sevi herself. When they become possessed they dress in Narikkuṟavar clothes, chant in the Narikuṟavar tongue, and demand Narikuṟavar food (such as jackal meat) as an offering. The people of Mēlūr, the exorcist Veḷḷaiccāmi, and the Narikuṟavars who pass through Mēlūr on their rounds all differ in their opinions concerning the precise community of nomads from which Siṅgammā arose, and who the historic Siṅgammā was is a matter that may never be determined. In any case, the cult of Siṅgammā is not under the control of any of the nomadic scavengers, who know about this cult but are remarkably uninterested in it. Rather, the Siṅgammā cult seems to be built upon the image of nomadic scavengers that people of other castes, especially Paṟaiyars, have developed. Cf. Moffatt (1979) and McGilvray (1983) on the relationship between Kuṟavars and Paṟaiyars in Tamil and Sri Lankan society.

Glossary
of Tamil Words and Phrases

ammā—அம்மா—mother

ammāḍi—அம்மாடி—dear mother

ammāvē romba karutuṇḍuḍḍāru—அம்மாவே ரொம்ப கருதுண்டுட்டார—"He was thinking much about mother"

āṇavam—ஆணவம்—pride

Aṇṇi—அண்ணி—wife's older sister

anta iḍattilē pātikka tānē ceyyutu—அந்த இடத்திலே பாதிக்க தானே செய்யுது—"When he spoke, a woman's heart, in that place it causes it to be truly affected"

anta iḍattilē urimai tānē irukkum—அந்த இடத்திலே உரிமை தானே இருக்கும்—"In that place is true kindness"

appā—அப்பா—father

appā mēlē urimai paḍḍu—அப்பா மேலே உரிமை பட்டு—feeling kindness toward father

aṛukiṟa—அழுகிற—crying

āthivāsis—ஆதிவாசி indigenous people, original people

āttā—ஆத்தா—mother

avaḷ aṛaku kāḍḍa—அவள் அழகு காட்ட—to show her beauty

āvēcam—ஆவேசம்—demonic possession

ayiṟa pāḍḍu—ஆயிர பாட்டு—crying song

ayyā—அய்யா—sir

Bāmini—பாமினி—name of a goddess

Bampaiyan vīḍu namāḷukku romba urimaiyānavakuḷḷo—பம்பையன் வீடு நம்மாளுக்கு ரொம்ப உரிமையானவகுள்ளோ—"(The people of) Bambaiyan's house are very kind to us"

Bavāni—பவானி—Bhavani, an eight-armed goddess, with a weapon in each hand, who killed the king of demons

cēttuppiḍḍāka—சேத்துப்பிட்டாக—they had him admitted (to the hospital)

cettuppōccē—செத்து போச்சே—died, dead and gone

cittāḍai—சித்தாடை—small dress for a little girl

cittappā vīḍu—சித்தப்பா வீடு—the house of father's younger brother

cuṇḍal—சுண்டல்—a South Indian bean dish

-dā payyā—அடா பையா—"Hey, boy!"
-ḍī—டீ—suffix meaning "girl"
eccilai—எச்சிலை—spittle leaf
eṅgaḷ—எங்கள்—our (exclusive)
ennē petta ammāvē—என்னே பெத்த அம்மாவே—"o mother who bore me"
ennē vaḷatta pāvingaḷē—என்னே வளத்த பாவங்களே—"o pitiful people who raised me"
ennē vaḷatta tāṟē/tāyē—என்னை வளத்த தாழே / தாயே—"o mother who raised me"
enthaccātikkāravuka vīḍḍulēyum—எந்தச்சாதிக்காரவுக—in a house belonging to people of no caste
ēṟi—ஏறி—lake
ēṟināl—ஏறினால்—if one mounted
ēṟṟappāḍḍu—ஏற்றப்பாட்டு—lifting song, work song
eṛuti poḍḍu vaccu—எழுதி பொட்டு வச்சு—made (him) write it (put his signature on it)
eṛutikkuḍuttiḍḍāka—எழுதிக்குடுத்திட்டாக—they wrote and gave (they signed something over to someone else)
intha kaiyi cōrammāyiruccu—இந்த கையி சோரமாயிருச்சு—"This hand is ruined."
Iruḷar இருளர்—name of a tribe, "Dark People"
Jadaragni—ஜதராக்னி—name of the husband of Rēṇukā Paramēswari
jāti—சாதி / ஜாதி—caste
jātilēyum taḷḷuvaḍi—ஜாதிலேயும தள்ளுவடி—made to leave the caste
joḍu—ஜொடு—a couple, a matched pair
Kāci Vicālāḍci—காசி விசாலாட்சி—the wide-eyed goddess of Benares
kāḍḍukkāraṅgaḷ—காட்டுக்காரங்கள்—people of the forest/wasteland
kāḍu—காடு—forest, wasteland, uncultivated land
kai rēkai—கை ரேகை—signature, handwriting
Kāliammā—காலியம்மா—goddess of time, destruction, and death
Kallānthili—கல்லாந்திலி—name of a town
Kaḷḷar—கள்ளர்—name of a caste, "Thieves"
Kāmāḍci—காமாட்சி / காமாக்ஷி—goddess with loving eyes
Kamalā—கமலா—name of a woman
Kāñci Kāmāḍci—காஞ்சி காமாட்சி—goddess with loving eyes who lives in Conjeevaram
kaṇṇāḍi—கண்ணாடி—mirror
Kanyammā—கன்யம்மா—name of a goddess, "Virgin Mother," "Virgin Girl"
kārakkāy—காரக்காய்—a kind of wild fruit
kārappū—காரப்பூ—a kind of wild flower
Karumāriamman—கருமாரியம்மன்—"Black Māriamman"
karutāmē irunthirukkirāru—கருதாமே இருந்தக்கிறாரு—"he must not have been thinking"
kātal pāḍḍu—காதல் பாட்டு—love song
Katpakambāḷ—கற்பகம்பாள்—name of the goddess of the wish-fulfilling tree
Katpakavalli—கற்பகவல்லி—name of the young goddess of the wish-fulfilling tree

kāttām macci—காத்தாம் மச்ச—"wind-like cousin," or "cousin made of wind."
koḍi—கொடி—vine
kōlam—கோலம்—ornamental design in front of a doorstep
Komanampaḍḍi—கொமனம்பட்டி—a village near Mēlūr
kummippāḍḍu—கும்மிப்பாட்டு- hand-clapping song
kula teyvam—குல தெய்வம்—family god
kulaicukum—குலைசுகும்- dismember
kunnēṟi—குன்னேறி—"climbing the hills"
Kuppusāmy—குப்புசாமி—a man's name
Kuṟatti—குறத்தி—another name for a female member of the Hunter tribe
Kuṟavañji—குறவஞ்சி—female member of the Kuṟavar Hunter tribe
Kuṟavar—குறவர்—name of a tribe, "Hunters"
kuṟi—குறி—sign, mark, target
kuruvi—குருவி—small bird
Kuruvikkāraṅgaḷ—குருவிக்காரங்க—people who catch small birds
Lakshmi—லக்ஷ்மி லட்சுமி—goddess of wealth
Liṅgāvaḍi—லிங்காவடி—name of a village near Mēlūr
mā—மா—mother, woman
maḍal—மடல்—letter or message
Madurai Mīnāḍci—மதுரை மீனாட்சி—goddess with fish-shaped eyes who lives in Madurai
makiṛ—மகிழ்—a kind of small flower
makiṛam—மகிழம்—a kind of small, pretty flower
makuḍam—மகுடம் > மகிழம்பூ—a kind of small pretty flower
Malayāḷi—மலையாளி—a woman from Kerala, woman from the mountains
Mallikā—மல்லிகா—Jasmine, also a girl's name
māmā—மாமா—uncle
māṅgalayam—மாங்கல்யம்—a pendant signifying marriage, less formally called tāli
maṅgam cambā—மங்கம சம்பா—a kind of sweet or red paddy
Manthaiveḷi—மந்தைவெளி—village commons, pasture ground
māṟi—மாறி—changed
Māriamman—மாரியம்மன்—name of the goddess of rain and smallpox
marutākkōḍḍaiyilē—மருதாக்கொடையிலே—in the fortress of Madurai
Mēlūr—மேலூர்—name of a town near Madurai
Mīnakshi—மீனாக்ஷி—goddess with fish-shaped eyes
moḍcam—மோட்சம்—freedom
mōḍu—மோடு > vīḍu—வீடு—house
moksha—மோக்ஷா—மோட்சம்—freedom
mūccu—மூச்சு—breath
Muntakkanniyamman—முண்டக்கண்ணியம்மன—name of the aged goddess
Murugan—முருகன்—name of the god of war and beauty
muttam—முத்தம்—kiss

Muttammāḷ—முத்தம்மாள்—woman's name
muttu—முத்து—pearl
nāḍḍu vaidyam—நாட்டு வைத்தியம்—country medicine
naliñcu pōna pāvi—நலிஞ்சு போன பாவி—"poor sinner who has wasted away"
naliñcu pōna taṅgāḷ—நலிஞ்சு போன தங்காள—"younger sister who has wasted away"
nallappāmbu—நல்லப்பாம்பு—cobra
nambikkai—நம்பிக்கை—belief
nāṅgaḷ—நாங்கள்—we (exclusive)
nannānē—நன்னானே—word in a song
Narikuṟavaṅgaḷ—நரிக்குறவங்க—name of a tribe, "Jackal Hunters"
nī nān—நீ, நான்—"you, I."
Nīlammā—நீலம்மா—"blue woman," a woman's name
nīlappāḍḍu—நீலப்பாட்டு—"blue song," sad song, crying song
nīyā nānā—நீயா நானா—"Is it you or is it me?"
noṇḍi aṇṇan—நொண்டி அண்ணன்—lame older brother
Ōm nama sivāya—ஓம் நம சிவாய—an invocation of Siva
Ōm parāsakti—ஓம் பராசக்தி—an invocation of Śakti
oppāri—ஒப்பாரி—lament
ōr āṇ, oru peṇ—ஓர் ஆண் ஒரு பெண்—one man, one woman
oru rāvutta vīḍu—ஒரு ராவுத்த வீடு—a Muslim house
oru tuśḍakkāravuka vīḍḍulē—ஒரு துஸ்டக்காரவுக வீட்டுலே—in a polluted person's house
orukuṟava vīḍḍuppiḷḷai—ஒரு குறவ வீட்டு பிள்ளை—child of a Kuṟavar house
paḍai—படை—make, prepare, cook
Pāḷayam—பாளையம்—a place called war camp
pañcam—பஞ்சம்—famine
paṅgāḷi vīḍu—பங்காளி வீடு—the house of father's brothers
Paṟaiyar—பறையர்—name of a caste, "Drummers"; also a derogatory term for anyone of low caste
Parasurāman—பரசுராமன்—name of the eldest son of Rēṇukā Paramēswari
paricu aḷḷi pōḍuvāṅga—பரிசு அள்ளி போடுவாங்க—"they serve nice gifts"
patti—பத்தி—womanly virtue
pattivam illai—பத்திவம் (பத்தியம்) இல்லை—no title (to the property)
pattivam/pattiyam—பத்திவம / பத்தியம்—title, ownership
pāva kāraṇam patittirāḷ—பாவக்காரணம பதித்திராள்—she empowers the cause of sin
pāvi—பாவி—sinner, person to be pitied
Periyapāḷayam—பெரியபாளையம்—a place called big war camp
periyappā vīḍu—பெரியப்பா வீடு—the house of father's older brother
peruccāḷi—பெருச்சாளி—bandicoot, big rat
peruccāḷi pōḍuvāṅga—பெருச்சாளி போடுவாங்க—they feed (us) big rats
piḍiyāḷ—பிடியாள்—a person to hold
piḷḷai—பிள்ளை—child

Piḷḷaiyār—பிள்ளையார்—Ganesh, the elephant-headed god

pittunatē pārappā—பித்துனதே பாரப்பா—"See the madness, boy!"

poḍḍiyilē—போட்டியிலே < பெட்டியிலே—on a bed (lit. "in or on a box")

poḍḍu—பொட்டு—auspicious red dot on a woman's forehead, signifying that she is married

Poṅgal—பொங்கல்—festival of the sun where poṅgal (milk rice) is served

poṇṇē—பொண்ணே—"Hey, woman!"

pū nākam—பூ நாகம்—a snake or worm that lives in a flower; also, according to Tamil Lexicon, "very poisonous"

puli kuḍḍi—புலிக்குட்டி—baby tiger

pūvōḍakkāri—பூவோடக்காரி—women or girl, still wearing flowers, whose husband has not died

Rājā Rājēswari—ராஜா ராஜேஸ்வரி—name of a goddess

rāvuttar vīḍu—ராவுத்தர் வீடு—Muslim house

Reḍḍiyār—ரெட்டியார்—member of a land-owning caste

Rēṇukā Paramēswari—ரேணுகா பரமேஸ்வரி—name of the mythic woman who became Māriamman

romba nāḍōḍiṇḍu vaccukkōṅgo—ரொம்ப நாடொடிண்டு வச்சுக்கொங்கொ—They kept her in a very uncivilized way

śakti—சக்தி—spiritual power

Sevi—செவி—a woman's name

Sevukapperumān—செவுகப்பெருமான—name of a family god

sevvaraḷi—செவ்வரளி—beautiful but poisonous red oleander

siṅgam—சிங்கம்—lion

Siṅgammā—சிங்கம்மா—name of a woman of the Kuṟavar tribe

Siṅgampudukāri—சிங்கம்புதுகாரி—name of a family goddess

Siṅgan—சிங்கன்—Kuṟavar man's name

Siṅgi—சிங்கி—Kuṟavar woman's name

sīruḍu nāḷil—சீருடு நாளில்—on the day of giving gifts

Sītalā—சீதளா—"the cool one," goddess of smallpox in Bengal

tālilēyum . . . jātilēyum taḷḷuvaḍi—தாலிலேயும . . . ஜாதிலேயும தள்ளுவடி—excluded from the tāli . . . from the jāti

taṅgāḷē—தங்காளே—"o, little sister"

tāṛai—தாழை < தாழம்—pandanus

tāṛam—தாழம்—pandanus tree, pandanus flower

Tāṛanūr—தாழனூர்—town named after the pandanus flower

tārēnyā—தாரேன்யா—"I will give, sir"

tāṛttappaḍḍavarkaḷ—தாழ்த்தப்பட்டவர்கள்—"people who have been put down"

tāy moṛi—தாய் மொழி—mother tongue

teyvappāḍḍu, kaḍavuḷ pāḍḍu—தெய்வப்பாட்டு, கடவுள் பாட்டு—songs of gods, songs of God

tillālē—தில்லாலே—word in a song

tīṇḍā—தீண்டா—untouchable
tīṇḍu—தீண்டு—defile by touch, poison as with a snake's bite
Tiruvērkāḍu—திருவேற்காடு—place name
tōṛi—தோழி—girl's companion
toyappu—தொயப்பு—agreement
toy appukku vanthiruvāṅga—தொயப்புக்கு வந்திருவாங்க—"They will come to an agreement"
uḍankolailē aḍiccu—உடங்கொலைலே அடிச்சு—"Beating one's own (wife) with rage"
uḷḷūrccilē tānppā—உள்ளூர்சில தான்பா—"Right in the middle of town, boy!"
uṇmaikaḷai colliḍuccu—உண்மைகளை சொல்லிடுச்சு—she told truths
unnum koñcam oḍḍi pōnga—உன்னும கொஞ்சம் ஒட்டி பொங்க—"Move a little farther away"
urimai—உரிமை—kindness, kinship, family
urimai illai—உரிமை இல்லை—without kindness
urimaiyāvē nenacciraccu—உரிமையாவே நெனச்சிரச்சு—thought (of him) with kindness
uyir—உயிர்—life
vakaiyarā—வகையரா—lineage
Valaccappaḍḍi—வலச்சப்பட்டி—a village near Mēlūr
vaḷarttē(n)—வளர்த்தே(ன்)—"I grew"/"You grew" (transitive)
vāṛai—வாழை—banana, plantain
vārattilē—வாரத்திலே—on the border(s)
vāṛkkai—வாழ்க்கை—life
Vattippaḍḍi—வத்திபட்டி—name of a village near Mēlūr
veḍi—வெடி—explosion, firework
veḍikkai—வெடிக்கை—bursting, laughter
veḍikkai teriyilē—வெடிக்கை தெரியில்லை—"I don't see the fireworks" or "I don't see the joke"
vēlai—வேலை—work
Veḷḷaiccāmi—வெள்ளைச்சாமி—a man's name
veḷḷaikkaraṅga—வெள்ளைக்காரங்கள்—white people
Vicālāḍci—விசாலாட்சி விசாலாக்ஷி—goddess with wide eyes
vīḍu—வீடு—house
Villiyar—வில்லியர்—name of a tribe, "Bow People"
vīra peṇmaṇi—வீர பெண்மணி—"heroic jewel of a woman"
viriyan pāmbu—விரியன் பாம்பு—Russell's viper
virodha bhakti—விரோதப்பற்று—devotion through enmity, angry devotion
Yama—யமா—god of death
yānai kuḍḍi—யானைக்குட்டி—baby elephant

References

Abu-Lughod, Lila. 1987. *Veiled Sentiments: Honor and Poetry in a Bedouin Society*. Berkeley: University of California Press.

Adiga, Aravind. 2008. *The White Tiger*. New York: Free Press.

Adigal, Ilango. 1965. *Shilappadikaram*. Translated by Alain Danielou. New York: New Directions.

Allocco, Amy L. 2013. "From Survival to Respect: The Narrative Performances and Ritual Authority of a Female Hindu Healer." *Journal of Feminist Studies in Religion* 29 (1): 101–17.

Ambedkar, B. R. 1936. *Annihilation of Caste*. Annotated critical edition. London: Verso Books, 2014.

Angelou, Maya. 1967. *I Know Why the Caged Bird Sings*. New York: Random House.

Anthony, David W. 2007. *The Horse, the Wheel, and Language: How Bronze Age Riders from the Eurasian Steppes Shaped the Modern World*. Princeton, N.J.: Princeton University Press.

Appadurai, Arjun. 1971. "Bureaucratic Corruption in India and the Hindu Tradition of Gift-giving." Manuscript.

———. 1986. "Is Homo Hierarchicus?" *American Ethnologist* 13:745–61.

Arnold, David. 1993. *Colonizing the Body*. Berkeley: University of California Press.

Babb, Lawrence. 1970. "Marriage and Malevolence: The Uses of Sexual Opposition in a Hindu Pantheon." *Ethnology* 9 (2): 137–48.

——— .1978. *The Divine Hierarchy: Popular Hinduism in Central India*. New York: Columbia University Press, 1975.

Bakhtin, Mikhail N. 1968. *Rabelais and His World*. Translated by Helene Iswolsky. Cambridge, Mass.: MIT Press.

———. 1978. *Readings in Russian Poetics: Formalist and Structural Views*. Edited by Ladislav Matejka and Krystyna Pomorska. Ann Arbor: Michigan Slavic Contributions.

———. 1981. "Discourse in the Novel." In *The Dialogic Imagination*, edited by Michael Holquist and Caryl Emerson, 259–422. Austin: University of Texas Press.

———. 1984. *Problems of Dostoevsky's Poetics*. Edited and translated by Caryl Emerson. Minneapolis: University of Minnesota Press.

Bateson, Gregory. 1968. "Conscious Purpose *vs*. Nature." In *The Dialectics of Liberation*, edited by David Cooper, 34–39. New York: Penguin Books. (Reprinted in Gregory

Bateson, ed., *Steps to an Ecology of Mind*, 426–39. New York: Ballantine Books, 1972.)

Beck, Brenda E. F. 1969. "Color and Heat in South Indian Ritual." *Man*, n.s., 4 (4): 553–72.

———. 1982. *The Three Twins: The Telling of a South Indian Folk Epic*. Bloomington: Indiana University Press.

Berreman, Gerald. 1960. "Caste in India and the United States." *American Journal of Sociology* 66 (2): 120–27.

———. 1971. "The Brahmanical View of Caste." *Contributions to Indian Sociology*, n.s., 5:16–23.

Bird-David, Nurit. 1999. "'Animism' Revisited: Personhood, Environment, and Relational Epistemology." *Current Anthropology* 40 (S1): S67–S91.

Biswas, Soutik. 2012. "How India Treats Its Women." BBC News, December 29. http://www.bbc.com/news/world-asia-india-20863860?print=true.

Blackburn, Stuart H. 1988. *Singing of Birth and Death: Texts in Performance*. Philadelphia: University of Pennsylvania Press.

Boas, Franz. 1927. *Primitive Art*. London: Cambridge University Press.

Bourguignon, Erik. 1976. *Possession*. San Francisco: Chandler and Sharp.

Brent, Joseph. 1998. *Charles Sanders Peirce: A Life*. Bloomington: Indiana University Press.

Briggs, Charles. 1992. "'Since I Am a Woman, I Will Chastise My Relatives': Gender, Reported Speech, and the (Re)production of Social Relations in Warao Ritual Wailing." *American Ethnologist* 19:337–61.

———. 1993. "Personal Sentiments and Polyphonic Voices in Warao Women's Ritual Wailing: Music and Poetics in a Critical and Collective Discourse." *American Anthropologist* 95:929–57.

British Museum. 2015. "Indus Seal." http://www.britishmuseum.org/explore/highlights/highlight_objects/asia/s/indus_seal.aspx.

Brueck, Laura R. 2014. *Writing Resistance: The Rhetorical Imagination of Hindi Dalit Literature*. New York: Columbia University Press.

Bryant, Edwin. 2001. *The Quest for the Origins of Vedic Culture*. New York: Oxford University Press.

Burke, Edmund. (1757) 1990. *A Philosophical Enquiry into the Origin of Our Ideas of the Sublime and Beautiful*. Edited and with an introduction by Adam Phillip. Oxford University Press.

Campbell, Charlie. 2014. "India's 'Untouchables' Are Still Being Forced to Collect Human Waste by Hand." *Time Magazine*, August 25. http://time.com/3172895/dalits-sewage-untouchables-hrs-human-waste-india-caste/.

Carstairs, G. Morris. 1967. *The Twice-Born*. Bloomington: Indiana University Press.

"Caste-Related Violence in India." *Wikipedia*. http://en.m.wikipedia.org/wiki/Caste-related_violence_in_India.

Chandran, Leena. 2014. "Hidden in Plain Sight." *Manorama Online*, September 17.

http://english.manoramaonline.com/news/features/gandhi-is-more-than-just-a-family-heirloom-arundhati-roy.html.

Clark-Decès, Isabelle. 2005. *No One Cries for the Dead: Tamil Dirges, Rowdy Songs, and Graveyard Petitions.* Berkeley: University of California Press.

———. 2014. *The Right Spouse: Preferential Marriages in Tamil Nadu.* Stanford, Calif.: Stanford University Press.

Claus, Peter. 1975. "The Siri Myth and Ritual: A Mass Possession Cult of South India." *Ethnology* 14 (1): 47–58.

Clifford, James. 1986. "Introduction: Partial Truths." In *Writing Culture: The Poetics and Politics of Ethnography*, edited by James Clifford and George Marcus, 1–26. Berkeley: University of California Press.

Cohen, Lawrence. 2012. "Notes on Love in a Banaras Garden." Presented at the annual meeting of the American Anthropological Association. Unpublished manuscript, files of the author.

Cohn, Bernard. 1954. "The Camars of Senapur: A Study of the Changing Status of a Depressed Caste." PhD dissertation, University of Chicago.

Coles, Robert. 1967. *Children of Crisis: A Study of Courage and Fear.* Boston: Little, Brown.

Coote, Mary P. 1977. "Women's Songs in Serbo-Croatian." *Journal of American Folklore* 90:331–38.

Crapanzano, Vincent. 1977. Introduction to *Case Studies in Spirit Possession*, edited by Vincent Crapanzano and Vivian Garrison, 1–40. New York: John Wiley.

Cruikshank, Walter. 1965. *Medical Microbiology.* Baltimore: Wilkins and Williams.

Daniel, E. Valentine. 1984. *Fluid Signs: Being a Person the Tamil Way.* Berkeley: University of California Press.

Daniel, Sherry. 1980. "Marriage in Tamil Culture: The Problem of Conflicting 'Models.'" In *The Powers of Tamil Women*, edited by Susan S. Wadley. Syracuse: Maxwell School of Citizenship and Public Affairs, Syracuse University.

Davis, Marvin. 1976. "A Philosophy of Hindu Rank from Rural West Bengal." *Journal of Asian Studies* 36:5–24.

De Beauvoir, Simone. (1949) 2011. *The Second Sex.* New York: Vintage Books.

Derrida, Jacques. 1974. *Of Grammatology.* Translated by Gayatri Spivak. Baltimore: Johns Hopkins University Press.

Dirks, Nicholas. 2001. *Castes of Mind: Colonialism and the Making of Modern India.* Princeton: Princeton University Press.

Dixon, C. W. 1962. *Smallpox.* London: J. and A. Churchill.

Doniger, Wendy, ed. 1981. *The Rig Veda: An Anthology.* London: Penguin Books.

———. 2009. *The Hindus: An Alternative History.* London: Penguin Books.

Doolittle, W. Ford. 2000. "Uprooting the Tree of Life." *Scientific American* 90–95, February 1.

Douglas, Mary. 1969. *Purity and Danger.* London: Routledge and Kegan Paul.

Downey, Gregory, and Daniel H. Lende. 2012. "Neuroanthropology and the Encultured

Brain." In *The Encultured Brain: An Introduction to Neuroanthroplogy*, Chapter 2. Cambridge, Mass.: MIT Press.

DuBois, Abbé J. A. 1906. *Hindu Manners, Customs, and Ceremonies*. Translated from the French by Henry K. Beauchamp. Oxford: Clarendon Press.

Dué, Casey. 2003. "Ancient Greek Oral Genres." *Oral Tradition* 18 (1): 62–64.

Dumont, Louis. 1957. *Hierarchy and Marriage Alliance in South Indian Kinship*. Occasional Papers of the Royal Anthropological Institute, No. 12. London: Royal Anthropological Institute.

———. 1959. "Possession and Priesthood." *Contributions to Indian Sociology* 3: 55–74.

———. 1970. *Homo Hierarchicus*. Revised edition. Chicago: University of Chicago Press.

Emeneau, Murray. 1958. "Oral Poets of South India: The Toda." *Journal of American Folklore* 71:312–24.

———, ed. 1970. *Toda Songs*. Oxford: Clarendon Press.

Encyclopaedia Britannica. 2014. "Indus Civilization." http://www.britannica.com/EBchecked/topic/286837/Indus-civilization.

Evidence Team. n.d. Minority Voices Newsroom. "Atrocities against Dalit Women and Access to Justice." http://www.minorityvoices.org/force_download.php?file=data/files/final/news_1389/ACCESSTOJUSTICEfinalreport.pdf.

Fanon, Franz. 1963. *The Wretched of the Earth*. New York: Grove Press.

Feld, Steven. 1982. *Sound and Sentiment: Birds, Weeping, Poetics and Song in Kaluli Expression*. Philadelphia: University of Pennsylvania Press.

Feld, Steven, and Aaron A. Fox. 1994. "Music and Language." *Annual Review of Anthropology* 23:25–53.

Flueckiger, Joyce. 1996. *Gender and Genre in the Folklore of Middle India*. Ithaca: Cornell University Press.

Fontanella-Khan, Amana. 2014. "India's Feudal Rapists." *New York Times*, June 4. http://www.nytimes.com/2014/06/05/opinion/indias-feudal-rapists.html.

Frank, Jerome. 1961. *Persuasion and Healing*. Baltimore: Johns Hopkins University Press.

Frank, Joseph. 1986. "The Voices of Mikhail Bakhtin." *New York Review of Books* 33 (16): 56–60.

Freeman, James. 1979. *Untouchable: An Indian Life History*. Stanford, Calif: Stanford University Press.

Friedrich, Paul. 1979a. "Poetic Language and the Imagination: A Reformulation of the Sapir Whorf Hypothesis." In *Language, Context, and the Imagination: Essays by Paul Friedrich*, selected and introduced by Anwar S. Dil, 441–512. Stanford, Calif.: Stanford University Press.

———. 1979b. "Speech as a Personality Symbol: The Case of Achilles." In *Language, Context and the Imagination*, 402–440. Stanford, Calif.: Stanford University Press.

———. 1989. "Language, Ideology, and Political Economy." *American Anthropologist* 91:295–312.

Gadamer, Hans-Georg. 1976. *Philosophical Hermeneutics*. Berkeley: University of California Press.

Gaikwad, Rahi. 2012. "Dalit Women at the Receiving End." *The Hindu*, September 25. http://www.thehindu.com/news/national/dalit-women-at-the-receiving-end/article 3934877.ece.

Geertz, Clifford. 1960. *The Religion of Java.* New York: Free Press

———. 1983. *Local Knowledge: Further Essays in Interpretive Anthropology*. New York: Basic Books.

Gimbutas, Marija. 1965. *Bronze Age Cultures in Central and Eastern Europe*. The Hague: Mouton.

Goffman, Erving. 1981. "The Lecture." In *Forms of Talk*, 160–96. Philadelphia: University of Pennsylvania Press.

Gold, Ann Grodzins, and Bhoju Ram Gujar. 2002. *In the Time of Trees and Sorrows: Nature, Power, and Memory in Rajasthan.* Durham, N.C.: Duke University Press.

Gorringe, Hugo. 2015. "Beyond 'Dull and Sterile Routines'?: Dalits Organizing for Social Change in Tamil Nadu; The Tamil Context." Abstract. *Cultural Dynamics* 22 (2): 105–119.

Gough, Kathleen. 1955. "Female Initiation Rites on the Malabar Coast." *Journal of the Royal Anthropological Institute of Great Britain and Ireland* 85: 45–80.

———. 1973. "Harijans in Thanjavur." In *Imperialism and Revolution in South Asia*, edited by K. Gough and H. P. Sharma. New York: Monthly Review Press.

Guha, Ranajit. 1997. *Dominance without Hegemony: History and Power in Colonial India*. Cambridge. Mass.: Harvard University Press.

Gumperz, John J. 1982. *Discourse Strategies*. Cambridge: Cambridge University Press.

Hallowell, Irving. 1941."The Social Function of Anxiety in a Primitive Society." *American Sociological Review* 7: 869–81.

Hanchett, Suzanne. 1975. "Hindu Potlatches: Ceremonial Reciprocity and Prestige in Karnataka." In *Competition and Modernization in South Asia*, edited by Helen E. Ullrich, 27–59. New Delhi: Abhinav Publishers.

Hardgrave, Robert. 1969a. *The Nadars of Tamilnad: The Political Culture of a Community In Change*. Berkeley: University of California Press.

Hardgrave, Robert. 1969b. "The New Mythology of a Caste in Change." *Journal of Tamil Studies* 1:61–87.

Harper, Edward. 1964. "Ritual Pollution as an Integrator of Caste and Religion." *Journal of Asian Studies* 2:151–97.

Hart, George. 1975. *The Poems of Ancient Tamil and Their Sanskrit Counterparts*. Berkeley: University of California Press.

Heath, Shirley Brice. 1983. *Ways with Words: Language, Life, and Work in Communities and Classrooms.* New York: Cambridge University Press.

Henderson, Donald A. 1976. "The Eradication of Smallpox." *Scientific American* 245, October 1, 25–33.

Hiltebeitel, Alf. 2001. *Rethinking the Mahabharata: A Reader's Guide to the Education of the Dharma King.* Chicago: University of Chicago Press.

The Hindu. 2013. "Atrocities against Dalit Women Occur More In South: Study." http://

www.thehindu.com/todays-paper/tp-national/tp-tamilnadu/atrocities-against-dalit-women-occur-more-in-south-study/article5220031.ece.

The Hindu. 2013. "Love in the Time of Caste." http://www.thehindu.com/features/the-yin-thing/love-in-the-time-of-caste/article4960041.ece

The Hindu. 2014. "Poverty, Child, Maternal Deaths High in India: UN Report." http://www.thehindu.com/news/national/poverty-child-maternal-deaths-high-in-india-un-report/article6188227.ece.

Hocart, A. M. 1927. *Kingship*. London: Oxford University Press

Holton, Gerald. 1988. *Thematic Origins of Scientific Thought: Kepler to Einstein*. Cambridge, Mass.: Harvard University Press.

Holwell, J. Z. 1767. "An Account of the Manner of Inoculating for the Smallpox in the East Indies." London: College of Physicians. (Reprinted in Dharampal, *Indian Science and Technology in the Eighteenth Century: Some Contemporary European Accounts*, Delhi: Impex India, 1971).

Hopkins, Kathryn. 2008. "Human Development: Child Mortality Stays High Despite India's Boom." *Guardian*, July 27, 2008. http://www.guardian.co.uk/world/2008/jul/28/india.internationalaidanddevelopment.

Human Rights Watch. 1999. "The Context of Caste Violence." *India: Human Rights Watch*. http://hrw.org/reports/1999/india/India994–04.htm.

———. 2008. "'Legacy of Communal Violence." *India: Human Rights Watch*, January 31. www.hrw.org/legacy/englishwr2k8/docs/2008/01/31/india17605.htm.

Hymes, Dell. 1971. Preface to *Creolization and Pidginization of Language*, 3–11. Cambridge: Cambridge University Press.

Inden, Ronald, and Ralph Nicholas. 1977. *Kinship in Bengali Culture*. Chicago: University of Chicago Press.

Ingold, Timothy. 2000. *The Perception of the Environment*. London: Routledge.

———. 2011a. *The Perception of the Environment: Essays on Livelihood, Dwelling and Skill*. London: Routledge.

———. 2011b. *Being Alive: Essays on Movement, Knowledge and Description*. London: Taylor and Francis.

International Dalit Solidarity Network. n.d. *Violence against Dalit Women*. "Briefing Note Prepared for the 11th Session of the Human Rights Council." International Dalit Solidarity Network – Cordaid – Justice & Peace Netherlands – National Campaign on Dalit Human Rights – Feminist Dalit Organisation Nepal. http://idsn.org/fileadmin/user_folder/pdf/New_files/Key_Issues/Dalit_Women/HRC-11_briefing_note_-_Violence_against_Dalit_Women.pdf.

Irudayam, Aloysius S. J., Jayshree P. Mangubhai, and Joel G. Lee, eds. 2006. *Dalit Women Speak Out: Caste, Class and Gender Violence in India*. New Delhi: National Campaign on Dalit Human Rights. Overview Report of Study in Andhra Pradesh, Tamil Nadu/Pondicherry, and Uttar Pradesh.

"Irula People." *Wikipedia*. en.wikipedia.org/wiki/Irulas.

"Irular." 2006. *Focus on People*. www.focusonpeople.org/irular.htm.

Jagannath, G. 2013. "80% Dalit Women Face Violence in Inter-Caste Marriage." *Deccan Chronicle*. March 4. http://archives.deccanchronicle.com/130304/news-current-affairs/article/80-dalit-women-face-violence-inter-caste-marriage.

Jakobson, Roman. 1960. "Closing Statement: Linguistics and Poetics." In *Style in Language*, edited by Thomas Sebeok, 350–77. Cambridge, Mass.: MIT Press.

Janacek, L. 1989. *Janacek's Uncollected Essays on Music.* Translated and edited by Mirka Zemanová. London: Marion Boyars.

Jassal, Smita Tewari. 2012. *Unearthing Gender: Folksongs of North India.* Durham, N.C.: Duke University Press.

Jayanth, Malarvizhi. 2011. "Krishnaveni's Story." PSW Weblog, July 28. https://keepingcount.wordpress.com/2011/07/.

Jayasuriya, J. H. F. 1967. *The Challenge of Tuberculosis.* Colombo, Sri Lanka: Wesley Press.

Jeffrey, Craig. 2010. *Timepass: Youth, Class and the Politics of Waiting in India.* Stanford, Calif.: Stanford University Press.

Joshi, Barbara R., ed. 1986. *Untouchable! Voices of the Dalit Liberation Movement.* London: Zed Books.

Kakar, Sudhir. 1978. *The Inner World: A Psychoanalytic Study of Childhood and Society in India.* New Delhi: Oxford University Press.

Kandasamy, Meena. 2014. *The Gypsy Goddess.* Atlantic Books.

———. 2014. *Meena Kandasamy's Poems.* http:/meenakandasamy.wordpress.com/2008/06/22/index-of-poems/.

Keller, Evelyn Fox. 2010. *The Mirage of a Space Between Nature and Nurture.* Durham, N.C.: Duke University Press.

Keyes, Charles F., and E. Valentine Daniel, eds. 1983. *Karma: An Anthropological Inquiry.* Berkeley: University of California Press.

Khare, R. S. 1976. *The Hindu Hearth and Home.* Durham, N.C.: Carolina Academic Press.

Kiev, Ari. 1968. *Curanderismo: Mexican-American Folk Psychiatry.* New York: Free Press.

Knipe, David. 1991. *Hinduism: Experiments in the Sacred.* Waveland Press.

Kochman, Thomas. 1981. *Black and White Styles in Conflict.* Chicago: University of Chicago Press.

Kohn, Eduardo. 2013. *How Forests Think: Toward an Anthropology Beyond the Human.* Berkeley: University of California Press.

Kolappan, B. 2013. "The Great Famine of Madras and the Men Who Made It." *The Hindu*, August 22. http://www.thehindu.com/news/cities/chennai/the-great-famine-of-madras-and-the-men-who-made-it/article5045883.ece.

Kolenda, Pauline. 1964. "Religious Anxiety and Hindu Fate." In *Religion in South Asia*, edited by E. B. Harper, 71–82. Seattle: University of Washington Press.

———. 1968. "The Functional Relations of a Bhangi Cult." *Indian Anthropologist* 11:21–35.

Krishnan, Murali. Delhi. 2014. "Gang Rape Exposes India's Violent Caste System." *Deutsche Welle*, June 2. http://www.dw.de/gang-rape-exposes-indias-violent-caste-system/a-17676877.

Kristeva, Julia. 1982. *Powers of Horror: An Essay on Abjection*. Translated by Leon Roudiez. New York: Columbia University Press.

Labov, William. 1966. *The Social Stratification of English in New York City*. Cambridge: Cambridge University Press.

———. 1972. *Language in the Inner City: Studies in the Black English Vernacular*. Philadelphia: University of Pennsylvania Press.

———. 2013. *The Language of Life and Death: the Transformation of Experience in Oral Narrative*. Cambridge: Cambridge University Press.

———. 2014. *Dialect Diversity in America: The Politics of Language Change*. Charlottesville: University of Virginia Press.

Lakoff, George, and Mark Johnson. 2008. *Metaphors We Live By*. Chicago: University of Chicago Press.

Lakoff, Robin. 1975. *Language and Woman's Place*. New York: Harper and Row.

———. 2000. *The Language War*. Berkeley: University of California Press.

Landy, David. 1977. "Conceptions of Healing Statuses and Roles." In *Culture, Disease, and Healing*, edited by David Landy. New York: Macmillan.

Langer, Susanne. 1957. *Philosophy in a New Key*. Cambridge, Mass.: Harvard University Press.

Lawler, Andrew. 2008. "Indus Collapse: The End or the Beginning of an Asian Culture?" *Science* 320 (5881): 1281–83.

Leach, Edmund R. 1965. *Political Systems of Highland Burma*. Boston: Beacon Press.

Leslie, Charles. 1976. "The Ambiguities of Medical Revivalism in Modern India." In *Asian Medical Systems*, edited by Charles Leslie, 356–67. Berkeley: University of California Press.

Lévi-Strauss, Claude. 1963. "The Sorcerer and His Magic." In *Structural Anthropology*, translated by C. Jacobson and B. G. Schoepf, 1:167–85. New York: Basic Books.

———. 1966. *The Savage Mind*. London: George Weidenfeld and Nicolson.

———. 1969. *Mythologiques*. Volume 1, *The Raw and the Cooked*. Chicago: University of Chicago Press.

———. 1978. *Myth and Meaning*. Toronto: University of Toronto Press.

———. "Race, History and Culture." *Ethics* (March 1996).

Lewis, I. M. 1971. *Ecstatic Religion*. Middlesex: Penguin Books.

Lord, Albert B. 1960. *The Singer of Tales*. Cambridge, Mass.: Harvard University Press.

———. 1990. *Epic Singers and Oral Tradition*. Ithaca: Cornell University Press.

Mangubhai, Jayshree. 2006. *Dalit Women Speak Out: Caste Class and Gender Violence in India Overview*. New Delhi: National Campaign on Dalit Human Rights. http://www.academia.edu/4045320/.

Marks, Jonathan. 2013. The Nature/Culture of Genetic Facts. *Annual Review of Anthropology* 42: 247–67.

Marriott, McKim. 1955. "The Feast of Love." In *Krishna: Myths, Rites, and Attitudes*, edited by M. Singer, 200–231. Chicago: University of Chicago Press.

Marriott, McKim, and Ronald Inden. 1974. "Caste Systems." *Encyclopedia Britannica* 3:982–91.

———. 1977. "Toward an Ethnosociology of South Asian Caste Systems." In *The New Wind: Changing Identities in South Asia*, edited by Kenneth David. The Hague: Mouton.

Mauss, Marcel. 1925. *The Gift: Forms and Functions of Exchange in Archaic Societies.* Translated by Ian Cummison. New York: W. W. Norton.

———. 1938. "Une catégorie de l'esprit humain: La notion de personne, celle de 'moi.'" *Journal of the Royal Anthropological Institute* 68.

Mauss, Marcel, and Henri Hubert. 1898. *Sacrifice: Its Nature and Function.* Translated by W. D. Halls. Chicago: University of Chicago Press.

Mayell, Hillary. 2003. India's "Untouchables" Face Violence, Discrimination. *National Geographic News*, June 2. http://news.nationalgeographic.com/news/2003/06/0602_030602_untouchables.html.

McDaniel, June. 1989. *The Madness of the Saints: Ecstatic Religion in Bengal.* Chicago: University of Chicago Press.

McDermott, Ray. 1985. Lecture delivered to N.E.H. Summer Institute on Humanistic Approaches to the Study of Linguistics. Georgetown University, Washington, D.C.

McGilvray, Dennis B. 1983. "Paṟaiyar Drummers of Sri Lanka: Consensus and Constraint in an Untouchable Caste." *American Ethnologist* 10 (1): 97–115.

Mencher, Joan. 1974. "The Caste System Upside Down, or the Not-So-Mysterious East." *Current Anthropology* 15:469–93.

Merleau-Ponty, Maurice. 1962. *Phenomenology of Perception.* London: Routledge.

Michaels, Sarah, and Courtney Cazden. 1986. "Teacher-Child Collaboration as Oral Preparation for Literacy." In *Acquisition of Literacy: Ethnographic Perspectives.* Norwood, N.J.: Ablex.

Miller, Barbara. 1981. *The Endangered Sex: Neglect of Female Children in Rural North India.* Ithaca: Cornell University Press.

Mines, Diane P. 2005. *Fierce Gods: Inequality, Ritual, and the Politics of Dignity in a South Indian Village.* Bloomington: Indiana University Press.

Minsky, Marvin. 1985. *The Society of the Mind.* New York: Simon and Schuster.

Moffatt, Michael. 1979. *An Untouchable Community in South India: Structure and Consensus.* Princeton, N.J.: Princeton University Press.

Mukherji, Anahita. 2014. "Degrees of Bias." *Times of India*, September 14. http://timesofindia.indiatimes.com/Home/STOI/Deep-Focus/Degrees-of-bias/articleshow/42417903.cms.

Muthukumaraswamy, M. D. 2006. "Fieldwork Report: Discourse of the Blurred Genre: Case of Draupadi Kuravanchi Koothu." *Indian Folklore Research Journal* 3(6): 38–65.

Nabokov, Isabelle. 2000. *Religion Against the Self: An Ethnography of Tamil Rituals.* New York: Oxford University Press.

Nagarajan, Vijaya. 2007. "Threshold Designs, Forehead Dots, and Menstruation Rituals:

Exploring Time and Space in Tamil Kolams." In *Women's Lives, Women's Rituals in the Hindu Tradition*, edited by Tracy Pinchman, 85–105. New York: Oxford University Press.

Narasimhan, Haripriya. 2011. "Adjusting Distances: Menstrual Pollution among Tamil Brahmins." *Contributions to Indian Sociology* 45: 243–68.

Narayan, R.K. 1943. *Malgudi Days*. London: Penguin.

Narula, Smrita. 1999. "Broken People: Caste Violence Against India's 'Untouchables.'" *Human Rights Watch*, April 1. http://www.refworld.org/docid/3ae6a83f0.html.

The News Minute. 2015. "How Does India's Caste System Work in the 21st Century? Quora User Hits the Bull's Eye." Thenewsminute.com, November 13.

Nicholas, Ralph. 1981. "The Goddess Sitala and Epidemic Smallpox in Bengal." *Journal of Asian Studies* 41 (1): 21–44.

———. 1982. "The Village Mother in Bengal." In *Mother Worship: Theme and Variations*, edited by James Preston, 192–209. Chapel Hill: University of North Carolina Press.

Nicholas, Ralph, and Aditi Nath Sarkar. 1976. "The Fever Demon and the Census Commissioner: Sitala Mythology in Eighteenth and Nineteenth Century Bengal." In *Bengal: Studies in Literature, Society, and History*, edited by Marvin Davis, 3–68. South Asia Series No. 27. East Lansing: Michigan State University, Asian Studies Center Occasional Papers.

"'Now, We Have a Democratically Elected Totalitarian Government'—Arundhati Roy." 2014. Dawn.com, May 23. http://www.dawn.com/news/1108001.

Nuckolls, Charles. 1987. "Culture and Causal Thinking: Prediction and Diagnosis in Jalari Culture." PhD dissertation, University of Chicago.

———. 1989. "Being and Becoming a Traditional Curer in Coastal Andhra Pradesh (India)." Manuscript.

Obeyesekere, Gananath. 1981. *Medusa's Hair*. Chicago: University of Chicago Press.

Office of the High Commissioner of Human Rights. 2013. "The Situation of Rural Dalit Women: Submission to Discussion on CEDAW General Comment on Rural Women; Article 14 by Navsarjan Trust (India), FEDO (Nepal) and the International Dalit Solidarity Network—September 2013." http://www.ohchr.org/Documents/HRBodies/CEDAW/RuralWomen/FEDONavsarjanTrustIDS.pdf.

O'Flaherty, Wendy Doniger. 1976. *The Origins of Evil in Hindu Mythology*. Berkeley: University of California Press.

———. 1980a. *Women, Androgynes and Other Mythical Beasts*. Chicago: University of Chicago Press.

———. 1980b. Introduction to *Karma and Rebirth in Classical Indian Traditions*, edited by Wendy Doniger O'Flaherty, ix–xxv. Berkeley: University of California Press.

Omvedt, Gail. 2015. *The Dravidian Movement*. http://www.ambedkar.org/gail/Dravidian movement.htm.

Pandey, Gyanendra. 2013. *A History of Prejudice: Race, Caste, and Difference in India and the United States*. Cambridge: Cambridge University Press.

Pandian, Anand. 2012. Comments on "Love and War: Papers in Honor of Margaret

Trawick's Ethnographic Practice." Presented at the annual meeting of the American Anthropological Association. Unpublished manuscript, files of the author.

Pandian, Anand, and M. P. Mariappan. 2014. *Ayya's Accounts: A Ledger of Hope in Modern India.* Bloomington: Indiana University Press.

Parry, Jonathan. 1982. "Sacrificial Death and the Necrophagous Ascetic." In *Death and the Regeneration of Life*, edited by Maurice Bloch and Jonathan Parry, 74–118. Cambridge: Cambridge University Press.

Peirce, Charles Sanders. (1892) 1940. "The Law of Mind." In *The Philosophy of Peirce: Selected Writings*, edited by Justus Buchler, 339–53. London: Kegan Paul, Trubner.

———. (1897) 1940. "Logic as Semiotic: The Theory of Signs." In *The Philosophy of Peirce: Selected Writings*, edited by Justus Buchler, 98–119.London: Kegan Paul, Trubner.

Peterson, Indira Viswanathan. 2008. "The Drama of the Kuṟavañci Fortune-Teller." In *Tamil Geographies: Cultural Constructions of Place and Space in South India*, edited by Martha Ann Selby and Indira Viswanathan Peterson. Albany: State University of New York Press.

Pope, Kevin O., and John E. Terrell. 2008. "Environmental Setting of Human Migrations in the Circum-Pacific Region." *Journal of Biogeography* 35 (1): 1–21.

Radin, Paul. 1927. *Primitive Man as Philosopher*. New York: D. Appleton Co.

Ram, Kalpana. 2013. *Fertile Disorder: Spirit Possession and Its Provocation of the Modern.* Honolulu: University of Hawai'i Press.

Ramanujan, A. K. 1967. *The Interior Landscape: Love Poems from a Classical Tamil Anthology*. New York: New York Review of Books/Poets.

———. 1986. "Who Needs Folklore?" In *Another Harmony: New Essays on the Folklore of India*, edited by Stuart Blackburn and A. K. Ramanujan. Berkeley: University of California Press. (Reprinted in Vinay Dharwadker, ed., *The Collected Essays of A. K. Ramanujan*, Oxford University Press, 1999, 532–52).

———. 1990. "Is There an Indian Way of Thinking?" In *India through Hindu Categories*, edited by McKim Marriott. Newbury Park, Calif.: Sage Publications.

———. 1991. *Folktales from India: Oral Tales from Twenty Indian Languages*. New York: Pantheon Books.

Rao, A. Ramachandra. 1972. *Smallpox*. Bombay: Kothari Book Depot.

Ravikumar. 2009. *Venomous Touch: Notes on Caste, Culture and Politics*. Translated from Tamil to English by R. Azhugarasan. Kolkata: Mandira for Stree.

Ravikumar and R. Azhagarasan, eds. 2012. *The Oxford India Anthology of Tamil Dalit Writing*. New Delhi: Oxford University Press.

Redfield, Robert. 1957. *The Little Community: Viewpoints for the Study of the Human Whole*. Chicago: University of Chicago Press.

Redfield, Robert, and Milton Singer. 1954. Seminar entitled "Comparison of Cultures: The Indian Village." Manuscript.

Rediff.com. 2013. "India Remembers Delhi Braveheart." Rediff.com, December 16. http://www.rediff.com/news/slide-show/slide-show-1-in-photos-india-remembers-delhi-braveheart/20131216.htm.

Rhodes, Andrew J., and E. E. Van Rooyen. 1958. *A Textbook of Virology*. 3d edition. Baltimore: Wilkins and Williams.

Rich, Arnold R. 1951. *The Pathogenesis of Tuberculosis*. 2d edition. Springfield, Ill.: Charles.

Rivers, Thomas M. 1948. *Viral and Rickettsial Infections of Man*. New York: J. B. Lippincott.

Rosaldo, Renato I. 1984. "Grief and a Headhunter's Rage: On the Cultural Force of Emotions." In *Text, Play and Story: The Construction and Reconstruction of Self and Society*, edited by Stuart Plattner and Edward Bruner, 178–95. 1983 Proceedings of the American Ethnological Society. Washington, D.C.: American Ethnological Society.

Rouch, Jean. 1973. *Les maitres fous*. Film.

Roy, Arundhati. 2014. Introduction to B. R. Ambedkar, *Annihilation of Caste*: Annotated critical edition. London: Verso Books.

Roy, Manusha. 1972. *Bengali Women*. Chicago: University of Chicago Press.

Rudolph, Lloyd, and Suzanne Rudolph. 1967. *The Modernity of Tradition*. Chicago: University of Chicago Press.

Sahlins, Marshall. 2013. *What Kinship Is—And Is Not*. Chicago: University of Chicago Press.

Scheub, Harold. 1977. "The Technique of Expansible Image in Xhosa *Ntsomi* Performances." In *Forms of Folklore in Africa*, edited by Bernth Lindfors, 37–63. Austin: University of Texas Press.

Schneider, David. 1980. *American Kinship: A Cultural Account*. Chicago: University of Chicago Press.

Scuto, Dr. Giuseppe. 2008. "Caste Violence in Contemporary India." http://www.dalits.nl/pdf/CasteViolenceInContemporaryIndia.pdf.

Selby, Martha Ann. 2011. *Tamil Love Poetry: The Five Hundred Short Poems of the Aiṅkuṟunūru*. New York: Columbia University Press.

Sen, Amartya. 1981. *Poverty and Famine: An Essay on Environment and Deprivation*. London: Oxford University Press.

Seremetakis, Nadia. 1991. *The Last Word: Women, Death, and Divination in Inner Mani*. Chicago: University of Chicago Press.

Seung, Sebastian. 2012. *Connectome: How the Brain's Wiring Makes Us Who We Are*. Boston: Houghton Mifflin Harcourt.

Shah, Ghanshyam, et al. 2006. *Untouchability in Rural India*. New Delhi: Sage Publications.

Shaji, K. A ,V. Senthil Kumaran, and S. Karthick S. 2012. "Inter-Caste Marriage Sparks Riot in Tamil Nadu District, 148 Dalit Houses Torched." *Times of India*, November 9. http://timesofindia.indiatimes.com/india/Inter-caste-marriage-sparks-riot-in-Tamil-Nadu-district-148-dalit-houses-torched/articleshow/17151170.cms.

Shulman, David. 1992. *The Hungry God: Hindu Tales of Filicide and Devotion*. Chicago: University of Chicago Press.

Singer, Milton. 1972. "Industrial Leadership, the Hindu Ethic, and the Spirit of Socialism." In *When a Great Tradition Modernizes*. New York: Praeger.

———. 1980. "Signs of the Self: An Exploration in Semiotic Anthropology." *American Anthropologist* 82:485–507.

Soundararajan, Thenmozhi. 2014. "India's Caste Culture Is a Rape Culture." *Daily Beast*, June 9. http://www.thedailybeast.com/witw/articles/2014/06/09/india-s-caste-culture-is-a-rape-culture.html.

Srinivas, M. N. 1966. *Social Change in Modern India*. Berkeley: University of California Press.

———. 1976. *The Remembered Village*. Oxford: Oxford University Press.

Srinivasan, Mahesh, Yarrow Dunham, Catherine M. Hicks, and David Barner. 2015. "Do Attitudes toward Societal Structure Predict Beliefs about Free Will and Achievement? Evidence from the Indian Caste System." *Developmental Science*, March 5, 1–17.

Stein, Burton. 1960. "The Economic Function of a Medieval South Indian Temple." *Journal of Asian Studies* 19:163–76.

Stocking, George W., Jr., ed. 1974. *A Franz Boas Reader: The Shaping of American Anthropology, 1883–1911*. New York: Basic Books. (Reprinted in 1982 and 1989 by University of Chicago Press.)

Subramanian, R. 2012. "Inter-Caste Marriage Triggers Violence in Tamil Nadu District." *India Today*, November 26. http://indiatoday.intoday.in/story/inter-caste-marriage-violence-tamil-nadu-vanniers-dalits/1/234837.html.

Suryawanshi, Sudhir. 2015. "Five Lakh Hindu-OBC People to Embrace Buddhism by 2016." Mumbai: DNA India, January 3. http://www.dnaindia.com/mumbai/report-five-lakh-hindu-obc-people-to-embrace-buddhism-by-2016–2049100.

Tamil Nadu Women's Forum. 2007. "Unheard Voices: Dalit Women." *Third World Resurgence* No. 200, April. http://www.twnside..org.sg/title2/women/2007/TWR200p44.doc.

Tannen, Deborah. 1982. "The Oral/Literate Continuum in Discourse." In *Spoken and Written Language*. Norwood, N.J.: Ablex.

———. 1984. *Conversational Style: Analyzing Talk Among Friends*. Norwood, N.J.: Ablex.

———. 1987. *That's Not What I Meant*. New York: Ballantine.

———. 1990. *You Just Don't Understand*. New York: Ballantine.

———. 1998. *The Argument Culture*. New York: Random House.

Thurston, Edgar. 1909. *Castes and Tribes of Southern India*. Vol. 2, C TO J. Madras: Government Press.

Thurston, Edgar, and K. Rangachari. 1907. *Castes and Tribes of Southern India*. Volume 2 of 7, 388–406. Government of British India. Madras: Government Press.

Times of India. 2007. "Can't Change Caste, SC to College Student." *Times of India*, December 1. http://timesofIndia.Indiatimes.com/India/cant-change-caste-sc-to-college-student/articleshow/2586617.cms?referral=pm.

Times of India. 2015. "As Sewer Deaths Continue in Tamil Nadu, Plea Seeks Relief." *Times of India*, February 7. http://timesofindia.indiatimes.com/city/chennai/As-sewer-deaths-continue-in-Tamil-Nadu-plea-seeks-relief/articleshow/46150652.cms.

Trawick (Egnor), Margaret. 1970. "The Lingayats of Mysore: A Study in the Acquisition of Power and Prestige." BA honors thesis, Harvard University.

———. 1978. "The Sacred Spell and Other Conceptions of Life in Tamil Culture." PhD dissertation, University of Chicago.

———. 1980. "On the Meaning of Sakti to Women in Tamil Nadu." In *The Powers of Tamil Women*, edited by Susan S. Wadley, 134. Maxwell Center, South Asia Series. Syracuse: Syracuse University Press.

———. 1983a. "The Changed Mother, or What the Smallpox Goddess Did When There Was No More Smallpox." *Contributions to Asian Studies* 18: 24–45.

———. 1983b. "Death and Nurturance in Indian Systems of Healing." *Social Science and Medicine* 17 (14): 935–45.

———. 1986. "Internal Iconicity in Paṟaiyar Crying Songs." In *Another Harmony: New Essays on the Folklore of India*, edited by Stuart Blackburn and A. K. Ramanujan, 294–344. Berkeley: University of California Press.

———. 1988a. "Spirits and Voices in Tamil Songs." *American Ethnologist* 15 (2): 193–215.

———. 1988b. "Ambiguity in the Oral Exegesis of a Sacred Text." *Cultural Anthropology* 3 (3): 316–51.

———. 1990a. "Untouchability and the Fear of Death in a Tamil Song." In *Emotion and Discourse in Anthropology*, edited by Catherine Lutz and Lila Abu-Lughod, 186–206. Cambridge: Cambridge University Press.

———. 1990b. *Notes on Love in a Tamil Family*. Berkeley: University of California Press.

———. 1991. "Wandering Lost: A Landless Laborer's Sense of Place and Self." In *Gender, Genre and Power in South Asian Expressive Traditions*, edited by Arjun Appadurai, Frank Korom, and Margaret Mills, 224–66. Philadelphia: University of Pennsylvania Press.

———. 1995. "The Story of the Jackal-Hunter Girl." In *Culture/Contexture: Explorations in Anthropology and Literary Studies*, edited by E. V. Daniel and Jeffrey Peck, 58–83. Berkeley: University of California Press.

———. 2003. "Lamenting the Loss of the Forest: Songs of an 'Assimilated' Tribe." In *Society: Tribal Studies, Volume 5. Concept of Tribal Society*, edited by Deepak Kumar Behera and Georg Pfeffer, 160–85. New Delhi: Concept.

———. 2007. *Enemy Lines: Warfare, Childhood and Play in Batticaloa*. Berkeley: University of California Press.

Trouillot, Michel-Rolph. 1995. *Silencing the Past: Power and the Production of History*. Boston: Beacon Press.

———. 2003. *Global Transformations: Anthropology and the Modern World*. New York: Palgrave Macmillan.

Turner, Victor. 1969. *The Ritual Process: Structure and Anti-structure*. Chicago: Aldine.

Twain, Mark (Samuel Clemens). 1884. *The Adventures of Huckleberry Finn*.

Urban, Greg. 1988. "Ritual Wailing in Amerindian Brazil." *American Anthropologist*, n.s., 90 (2): 385–400.

Venkatanarayanan, S. 2014. "Casteist Pheromone in Elementary Schools of Tamil Nadu." *Economic and Political Weekly* 49 (26–27), June 28.

Vidan, Aida. 2003. *Embroidered with Gold, Strung with Pearls: The Traditional Ballads of Bosnian Women*. Cambridge, Mass.: Harvard University Press.

Visvanathan, S. 2005. "Disempowering Dalits." *Frontline* 22 (10), May 7. http://www.frontline.in/static/html/fl2210/stories/20050520002603900.htm.

Viswanath, Rupa. 2014. *The Pariah Problem: Caste, Religion, and the Social in Modern India*. New York: Columbia University Press.

Volosinov, V. N. 1978. "Reported Speech." In *Readings in Russian Poetics: Formalist and Structuralist Views*, edited by L. Matejka and K. Pomorska, 149–75. Ann Arbor: Michigan Slavic Publications.

Wadley, Susan S. 1980. "Sitala: The Cool One." *Asian Folklore Studies* 39 (1): 33–62.

Wells, Spencer. 2002. *The Journey of Man: A Genetic Odyssey*. Princeton, N.J.: Princeton University Press.

Whitehead, Henry. 1921. *Village Gods of South India*. London: Oxford University Press.

Wickett, Elizabeth. 2010. *For the Living and the Dead: The Funerary Laments of Upper Egypt, Ancient and Modern*. London: I. B. Tauris.

Wilce, James M. 2009. *Crying Shame: Metaculture, Modernity, and the Exaggerated Death of Lament*. Malden, Mass.: Wiley Blackwell.

Woese, Carl. 1998. "The Universal Ancestor." *Proceedings of the National Academy of Sciences* 95 (12): 6854–59.

Wolanksy, Emanuel. 1980. "Microbacteria." In Bernhard D. Davis, Renato Dulbaco, Harman N. Eisen, and Harold S. Ginsberg, *Microbiology*, 3d edition. New York: Harper and Row.

Worsley, Peter. 1968. *The Trumpet Shall Sound: A Study of Cargo Cults in Melanesia*. New York: Schocken Books.

Yalman, Nur. 1963. "On the Purity of Women in the Castes of Ceylon and Malabar." *Journal of the Royal Anthropological Institute of Great Britain and Ireland* 93 (1): 25–58.

Zola, Émile. 1880. *Nana*. Paris: Les Rougon-Macquart.

Index

Acknowledgments

I am grateful to all the people who helped me with this book. First come those who sang for me and talked with me in Tamil Nadu toward the writing of this book: Lakshmi, Sarasvati, Vasantā, Pushpam, Kamalā, Nīlammā, Muttammāḷ, Kanyammā, Sevi, Veḷḷaiccāmi, Rāghupathi, Gnāna Sundari, Jagathambā, and many others whose names I do not know. Lakshmi was the guardian, cook, caregiver, and companion of me and my little son Daniel for years until we lost her. Kuppusāmy found Sevi, and many other people in Liṅgāvaḍi who told their stories for me. Without Kuppusāmy's help, I would never have found the song and story of Siṅgammā. J. Bernard Bate found Veḷḷaiccāmi and recorded his chant for me. Ann Grodzins Gold persistently urged me to publish these chapters in book form. Martha Ann Selby and Diane Mines went through first drafts of this book, provided commentary and criticism, and convinced me it was worthwhile to carry on. Diane Mines will carry on where I must leave, writing the stories of wandering, homelessness, place, environment, and wilderness in Tamil Nadu. Indira Viswanathan Peterson shared my interest in the Kuṟavars and wrote about Tamil plays of the eighteenth century involving Kuṟavars as star characters. Martha Selby showed me passages about Kuṟavars in Sangam literature, offered other information that has helped me write this book, corrected errors, and provided commentary on an early draft. M. D. Muthukumaraswamy helped me with transliteration and kindly put up with my unorthodox transliterating technique. Judith Kinnear, former vice-chancellor of Massey University, provided me with a grant to assist in the writing of this book. My output is long overdue, Professor Kinnear, and I thank you for your patience. People who helped me to write this book include Lila Abu-Lughod, Arjun Appadurai, Frank Korom, David Ludden, Catherine Lutz, Margaret Mills, and Rajam Ramamurthy. I thank them for their helpful comments on earlier versions of this book. Others who helped me, sometimes without even knowing it, include Brad Weiss, Lawrence Cohen, David Shulman, Don Handelman, McKim Marriott, Paul

Friedrich, Raveen S. Nathan, Ramanitharan Kandiah, Samantha Cotta, Emily Gallardo, Mabel Johnson-Gallardo, Sandy Varao, the late Cora Dubois, the late S. R. Sivaram, the late S. R. Themozhiyar, the late A. K. Ramanujan, the late Alfred B. Lord, the late Vesta Margaret Irwin Trawick, and last but not least, my kind and loving husband, Ronald Roy Johnsen.